Spices and Seasonings

Food Science and Technology

Y. H. Hui, Series Editor

F. Schenck and R. Hebeda, Starch Hydrolysis Products
J. H. Prentice, Dairy Rheology
D. R. Tainter and A. T. Grenis, Spices and Seasonings

Spices and Seasonings

A Food Technology Handbook

Donna R. Tainter
Anthony T. Grenis

Donna R. Tainter   Anthony T. Grenis
Tone Brothers, Inc.   Chicago Spice Co.
P.O. Box AA   1270 Mark Street
Des Moines, IA 50301   Elk Grove Village, IL 60007

Library of Congress Cataloging-in-Publication Data

Tainter, Donna R.
    Spices and seasonings : a food technology handbook / by Donna R.
Tainter and Anthony T. Grenis.
        p.   cm. — (Food science and technology)
    Includes bibliographical references and index.
    ISBN 1-56081-572-8
    1. Spices. 2. Condiments. I. Grenis, Anthony T. II. Title.
III. Series: Food science and technology (VCH Publishers)
TP420.T35   1993
664'.53—dc20   93-7798
                                                                         CIP

This book is printed on acid-free paper. ∞

Printed in the United States of America
ISBN: 1-56081-572-8 VCH Publishers, Inc.
ISBN: 3-527-89572-8 VCH Verlagsgesellschaft

Printing history:
10 9 8 7 6 5 4 3 2 1

VCH Publishers, Inc.   VCH Verlagsgesellschaft mbH   VCH Publishers (UK) Ltd.
220 East 23rd Street   P.O. Box 10 11 61   8 Wellington Court
New York, N.Y. 10010-4606   69451 Weinheim   Cambridge CB1 1HZ
                              Federal Republic of Germany   United Kingdom

Preface

There are only a few books available on spices and almost none on seasonings. Most spice books were written before 1980.

Our aim in writing this book was to include information which is not readily available from other sources. The first four chapters on spice importation, processing, quality control, and the spices themselves were written to give practical information to the spice processor and purchasing agent as well as basic information for the food technologist writing specifications. Most other reference books available give a wealth of information, but do little for helping to sort out what is important and what is not. All too often, spice specifications contain obsolete and contradictory information that would make it impossible for a spice processor to meet. Our book tries to define important parameters and give realistic specifications. We know of no other book which addresses these issues, especially how spices are imported and processed. Our goal was to provide practical information to the spice processor, the purchasing agent who buys either raw or processed spices, the food technologist who formulates with spices, and the quality assurance food technologist who deals with incoming spices and specifications.

Chapter 6 addresses recent research in the spice and extractives area, including antioxidant and antimicrobial properties of spices. There are numerous references cited if the reader wants additional information. Most of this research has not been reviewed in previous books.

We tried to present only the commonly used spices in the trade. Although onion and garlic are used for flavoring as spices are, these were not included since they are vegetables, and not spices. For more information on these items, please contact the American Dehydrated Onion and Garlic Association, 650 California Street, Suite #800, San Francisco, California, 94108.

The section on seasonings is unique. It includes how to formulate seasonings for a variety of food items and includes sample formulations. The final chapter discusses the technology of duplicating seasoning blends and other useful, practical information when duplicating and developing seasoning blends. We know of no other book which addresses this area so completely.

We hope you find *Spices and Seasonings* a practical manual with quality information included that Food Technologists and Purchasing Agents can use.

Donna R. Tainter
Des Moines, IA

March 1993

Anthony T. Grenis
Elk Grove Village, IL

Contents

4. The Spices   31

Spices and Seasonings

1

United States Regulations as They Apply to Spices

1.1 Introduction

Although the practicing food technologist in the United States should have a firm understanding of the laws and regulations that apply to the food industry, it is important to review some of these issues as they apply directly to spices. Since most spices are grown outside of the United States, the application of these laws to imported foods is different. Whereas the Food and Drug Administration (FDA) has the authority to inspect all food processing plants in the United States to ensure compliance, it has no such authority outside the country. In order to ensure compliance with the Food, Drug, and Cosmetic Act, the FDA inspects the materials as they arrive in this country.

Spices are grown and harvested in many varied areas of the world as described in Chapter 4. Many of these areas are third world nations where the same ideas of food sanitation do not exist. Many spices are not raised as field crops but are often harvested directly from the jungles or hills where they are found growing naturally. Many times a family will pick up extra money by "harvesting" these spices and taking them into town to sell to a broker who will put together many such small lots before moving it to another larger broker. This method of harvesting will present some interesting problems when discussing sampling in Chapter 3.

While it is common for spices to be harvested in small quantities, it is also common for the harvesting, drying, and storage practices to be quite different from those that we would expect to see. While the spice is drying, it may not be protected from pests such as insects, rodents, birds and even larger animals. The damage they can cause and the extraneous material they can leave behind may all end up in a bag destined to be exported to the United States. In addition, damage and additional foreign material, such as insect or rodent contamination, can be picked up during storage and transportation. It is not unusual for spices to be stored outside or under nothing more than a metal roof in an attempt to keep the product dry.

1.2 Importation Procedures

The following is meant to highlight the steps that a product must follow to be legally imported into the country.

When a spice is imported into the United States, the importer must notify U.S. Customs. U.S. Customs has its own set of requirements that will be covered later. One of the U.S. Customs duties is to notify the FDA of the importation of regulated foods or cosmetics. The FDA starts its inspection procedures by examining the import notice to decide if it wants or needs to sample the lot. Not all lots of spices are physically inspected by the FDA due to the availability of funds and personnel. If it decides that it does not need to sample the lot, the FDA issues a "May Proceed Notice" which it issues to Customs and to the importer. The "May Proceed Notice" indicates that the goods are released but does not preclude the FDA from taking further action should it find need to.

The FDA may decide that it wishes to sample the lot because of the nature of the product, the FDA's current priorities, or the FDA's past history with similar products. If it decides to sample, the FDA issues a "Notice of Sampling" to Customs and to the importer. The FDA will collect its sample and requires the lot to be held intact until it is released. The lot may be moved from the dock to a warehouse or other location with the permission of U.S. Customs.

The sample is sent to a FDA laboratory for testing. Should testing show the lot to be in compliance with the regulations, the FDA will issue a "Release Notice" to Customs and to the importer. Once again, this releases the product from FDA control but does not limit further action by the FDA.

Should the FDA laboratory turn up results that indicate the product is not in compliance with the regulations, the FDA will issue a "Notice of Detention and Hearing" to Customs and the importer. This notice will clearly state the deviations that were found and gives the importer 10 working days to produce evidence that the product does indeed conform or to show how the importer may make the product conform. This is the importer's only opportunity to defend the legality of the product. Should the importer not respond, the FDA will issue a "Notice of Refusal of Admission" to Customs and the importer. The "Notice of Refusal of Admission" means the product must be destroyed or exported under Customs supervision.

In most cases, the importer will respond to the "Notice of Detention and Hearing" and the FDA will conduct a hearing where evidence concerning the shipment will be discussed. This evidence may consist of results from a certified laboratory showing the product is indeed within the regulations or a request from the importer for permission to attempt to recondition the product to bring it into compliance. The request to recondition a product is called an "Application for Authorization to

Recondition" and specifically lists the steps that will be used to try to bring the product into compliance. These reconditioning steps will be covered in greater detail in Chapter 2.

If the importer presents evidence that the product does indeed comply, the FDA will conduct another inspection and sampling of the lot. If the FDA finds the lot to be in compliance, the FDA will issue a "Release Notice" to Customs and to the importer. Should the FDA still find the product out of compliance, the importer may file an "Application for Authorization to Recondition" or the FDA will issue a "Notice of Refusal of Admission" as above.

If the FDA grants the request to attempt reconditioning, the FDA will require that the product be held intact until the importer receives a formal release from the FDA. After the reconditioning has been tried, the FDA is notified and conducts a follow-up inspection and sampling of the product. If the product passes, the FDA will issue a "Release Notice" to Customs and to the importer. The FDA will also notify Customs of the FDA's charges for supervision of the reconditioning which Customs will collect from the importer.

If the follow-up sampling after reconditioning still indicates the product to be out of compliance, the FDA may allow a second attempt at reconditioning if it can be shown that the second attempt stands a reasonable chance of bringing the product into compliance. The FDA is reluctant to allow the same procedures to be followed a second time. If the second request for reconditioning is denied or not made, the FDA will issue a "Notice of Refusal of Admission" to Customs and the importer and notify Customs of its charges for the supervision of reconditioning attempt or attempts. The FDA then waits for confirmation of the destruction or exportation of the lot from Customs.

1.3 FDA Defect Action Levels (DALs)

The FDA's largest concern with spices is cleanliness. Although the FDA is also concerned about pesticides, microbiological problems, and even aflatoxins, its most obvious concern is the presence of insects and rodent contamination and foreign material. Being agricultural commodities, it is impossible to harvest most food items without any insect or rodent contamination. However, it is possible to control the amount of such contamination. The FDA has determined the levels of contaminants that the FDA believes can be achieved by proper agricultural and storage practices and has defined these levels as the Defect Action Levels (DALs). These DALs define the level of foreign materials below which the FDA will generally not take regulatory action against the products. These DALs establish a maximum limit of contamination. Products exceeding these limits will be challenged by the FDA. Products below these limits are generally assumed to be satisfactory. An interesting note here is that even though a spice might be below the DAL limits, the FDA can still take action against that spice if the FDA can show the product to be in violation of other sections of the Food, Drug, and Cosmetic Act. In particular, a spice may still be challenged by the FDA even if the product is in compliance with the DALs if the product is stored in an insect and rodent infested warehouse. In this case, the spice has been stored under unsanitary conditions where it may have been contaminated, which is in violation of the Food, Drug, and Cosmetic Act. It is important to remember that just because a spice is in compliance with the DALs, it doesn't mean the spice is safe from the FDA.

The current DALs as well as the ASTA Cleanliness Specifications are shown with each spice in Chapter 4. Although the limits for the ASTA (American Spice Trade Association) Cleanliness Specifications are the same or more stringent as the FDA DALs, the methods of sampling and analysis are slightly different. The ASTA sampling and analytical methods will be covered in greater detail in Section 1.6 since these results are the ones most likely to be seen if raw spices are purchased in the United States.

1.4 Customs Requirements

Although U.S. Customs handles much of the physical control of spice imports, they have limited responsibilities beyond that. U.S. Customs does collect any import duties that have been applied to the spices, but most spices arrive duty-free in the United States. Occasionally, certain spice exporting countries are penalized for political actions and all or selected products from these countries are charged with duties that the importer must pay. These duties can affect the market price for these spices since these duties must be passed on to the consumer.

U.S. Customs does have one additional requirement of its own. According to U.S. Customs regulations, all imported products must bear labeling indicating the country of origin when sold at the consumer level unless the product has been substantially transformed in the United States. Cleaning, grinding, and microbiological reduction treatments are not substantial processes and, at retail, containers of spices are to be labeled by country of origin. Spices used as ingredients in other food products have been substantially transformed and this country of origin requirement does not apply. According to U.S. Customs, since a spice processor cannot always determine where his spices are going to be used, the processor should always carry forward the country of origin labeling on his products. However, in the spice trade, the country of origin labeling is rarely followed. Two practical issues stand in the way. The first is that, in many cases, there are not sufficient differences in the product from different countries to be able to tell by appearance or by analysis what country a particular spice came from. The result in the trade is that these spices are often purchased based only on cost considerations and it becomes a difficult task to track each separate lot through processing to ensure the correct label is applied to each container. The second practical issue resulting from this inability to distinguish countries of origin by appearance or analysis is that spices are often traded between countries. It is quite possible for a spice from Greece to have been grown in Turkey, or a spice from France to have been grown in Egypt. Although the desired source may grow the spice in question, they often supplement their supplies by buying from other sources. Although not found on a regular basis, finding a few original

Turkish labels on bags stenciled "Greek Oregano" is a sure clue that this practice does occur. It must be noted, however, that it is a legal requirement to include country of origin labeling on retail products.

1.5 U.S. Department of Agriculture Regulations

The United States Department of Agriculture (USDA) also inspects shipments of spices from time to time to prevent the importation of noxious weeds and insect pests. In particular, the USDA closely watches for the Khapra beetle, a pest that could be particularly devastating to grain crops in the United States. This beetle is found in India and its surrounding countries. The USDA keeps a close eye on imports of spices in burlap bags from these areas. The USDA even inspects spice processors receiving spices from these countries to ensure that this pest cannot get a foothold in this country. The USDA inspection of spices is basically limited to the pests they are trying to exclude from the country.

1.6 American Spice Trade Association

An important element in the spice business in the United States is the American Spice Trade Association (ASTA). ASTA was formed with the initial intent of developing some standardization in the way spices were traded in the United States. Before this, each broker or seller would write his own contract, with terms varying from contract to contract. A group interested in developing some uniformity within the trade met and the result was the American Spice Trade Association. This group is currently international in scope and has been helpful in cleaning up many of the abuses that were prevalent in the spice industry years ago. Although originally established by the brokers and sellers, ASTA has developed into an organization where the needs of the sellers, the processors, and end users are represented. Many of the analytical methods discussed in Chapter 3 were originally developed to monitor the possible adulteration of spices.

1.6.1 Industry Cleanliness Standards

In 1968, the New York Regional Office of the FDA met with ASTA members and offered an interesting proposition to ASTA concerning an industry-sponsored self-monitoring of the cleanliness of imported spices. At the time, approximately 75% of all spices were being imported through the Port of New York. The spice imports were increasing at a 5% annual rate and the FDA was using half of its available manpower inspecting spices. The object of this meeting was to set up an industry-maintained program that would shift some of the responsibilities of ensuring the cleanliness of imported spices from the FDA to the industry members. The program offered by the FDA (but which has never become official) was that the FDA would allow industry members the option of FDA conditional release if the industry members would guarantee that shipments found to be adulterated would be returned to the country of origin or reconditioned before being allowed to enter the trade. This adulteration would be detected by sampling and analysis by an "ASTA Approved Laboratory."

Although the FDA offer has never been formalized, the ASTA cleanliness program offers buyers and users of spices the best opportunity to ensure the cleanliness of the spices they buy. Although the current ASTA program does contain a number of loopholes, the ASTA members recognize they exist and are working to close them.

As a quick review of the industry plan, the ASTA program requires the importer to have the imported lot sampled and tested by an independent laboratory. The testing in this program is done much the same way as the FDA would do it itself. Lots passing the ASTA testing procedure theoretically conform to the FDA DALs. Lots failing the ASTA procedure are also eligible for reconditioning much the same way the FDA would allow. The industry sampling covers all lots of imported spices traded by ASTA members within the United States, whereas the FDA sampling does not. This dual inspection system is often confusing to many people, especially the shippers who find that the FDA has issued a "May Proceed" notice only to find the material has been found not in compliance with the American Spice Trade Association cleanliness specifications. The end result of this ASTA cleanliness program is a certificate from the independent lab stating that the lot is or is not in compliance with the ASTA Cleanliness Specifications.

Although the industry program is not perfect, the system does have the advantage that every lot is examined by an independent laboratory. It is suggested that this program is of sufficient value that a spice user is well advised to see that his spice supplies are purchased through this program.

1.6.2 ASTA Contracts

Before the mechanics of the sampling program are discussed in Chapter 3, it is probably important to discuss ASTA's standardized contracts. As originally stated, ASTA was established to bring some uniformity into the trading of spices. This was accomplished by the development of a set of standardized contracts that clearly establish the terms that these spices are bought and sold under. ASTA has four standard contract forms that are used to cover nearly all the spices bought by spice processors. ASTA has also observed the need for a contract to be used by the processor for use with transactions with the end users of the spices. This contract is under development now and should be ready for the trade shortly.

Although the ASTA contracts are primarily designed for use by the grower/importer/broker and the further processor of the spices, it is possible for anyone from processor to end user to buy their spices in the "raw" state and avoid the costs associated with the processors. For the time being, it is worthwhile remembering that as far as the quality of the product, there are two basic guarantees in each type of contract.

The first guarantee is that goods sold under these contracts meet all requirements of the Food, Drug, and Cosmetic Act. In essence, this is the only guarantee that one would theoretically need before the product can be used. It must be remembered that some of these lots have never been seen by the broker/importer selling the lot and that the lot may not have been inspected by the FDA. The authors have seen many lots of spices arrive under this contractual guarantee containing insects, live rodents, visible mold, and even germinating seeds. It would be very foolish to rely on this guarantee without inspecting the product. This guarantee, however, is the one that will be the backbone for most quality claims.

The second guarantee under ASTA spice contracts is that the lot passes the ASTA Cleanliness Specifications. There are a number of problems with the guarantee:

1. ASTA currently has very little control over the quality of work performed by the ASTA approved laboratories. The approved labs are checked for the capability to perform the tests (that they have the facilities, equipment, and manpower to perform the testing) but there is no program in place to control the quality of the analysis. Since these commercial labs are in business to make money, they are going to do the kind of job that will bring them repeat business. If this means a quick once-over, then that is what they will do. There appears to be a two tier system. There are labs that look out for the interests of the importers and labs that look out for the interests of the buyer. The importers know which are which. This is not to say that the importer will not use a "buyers" lab if they know they have a clean lot they are dealing with. Having the right "certificate" can facilitate deals with processors who are serious about the cleanliness of the spices they buy.
2. The ASTA contract only requires that the goods have an ASTA Cleanliness Certificate, but does not say anything about the age of the certificate. A certificate 2 years old is as good as one issued yesterday. Any lot of spice sitting in an insect infested warehouse is surely going to become contaminated in that time.
3. Sending a certificate to a buyer for a lot other than the one contracted for and shipped is a common trick that is still used. Sometimes the product can arrive at the buyer's dock significantly before the cleanliness certificate arrives at the accounting department (the cleanliness certificate is generally sent with the invoice). This separation of documents from the shipment allows such substitutions to go unnoticed.

Until recently, the most common abuse of the ASTA cleanliness program was resampling until a "clean analysis" was found. Some lots may be sampled and analyzed for cleanliness a half dozen times or more before a passing ASTA Cleanliness Certificate was obtained. This was a great program for the seller, since it just about ensured that a given lot of spice could "pass." However, for the buyer, it just meant once more that anything goes and an ASTA Cleanliness Certificate was really no assurance that the lot passed any cleanliness guarantee at all. In 1987, ASTA established a program called the Commodity Tracking Program that was meant to help alleviate this resampling problem. ASTA's program meant that lots could only be tested one time through a tracking procedure they established. This has significantly helped to clean up this abuse.

There are ways buyers can use the current system to ensure the goods they buy do indeed conform to the ASTA Cleanliness Specifications. Initially, the buyer must determine which of the approved labs are most likely to give an honest appraisal of the condition of the samples received. This is not the easiest task, but by asking around, it should be possible to identify the buyer's lab and the seller's labs. Once a laboratory has been decided on, all contracts can be written specifying that the ASTA cleanliness certificate must come only from this lab. An additional stipulation to the contract is also very practical. Requiring that the ASTA certificate be dated not older than 3 or 4 weeks is a reasonable compromise between asking for a new certificate, which is apt to cost significantly more, and allowing the product to become infested by sitting in a poorly run warehouse.

As an additional protective measure, ensure that the cleanliness certificate arrives prior to the arrival of the product and compare the markings on the bags as received with the recorded markings on the certificate. If they don't match up, more investigation should be done.

It must be noted that ASTA is also aware of the problem of shopping for a lab to give clean certificates and is reviewing its system of approving labs. The industry may someday see an approval system that checks on the labs' performance as well as its capabilities.

Suggested Reading List

1. American Spice Trade Association, *Clean Spices, A Handbook for ASTA Members.* Englewood Cliffs, New Jersey.

2. American Spice Trade Association, *Cleanliness Specifications for Unprocessed Spices, Seeds, and Herbs Revised–May, 1991.* Englewood Cliffs, New Jersey, 1991.

3. *Importing Foods Into the United States.* HHS Publication No. (FDA) 84-2141, Department of Health and Human Services, Public Health Service, Food and Drug Administration.

2

Spice Processing

2.1 Introduction

Although this chapter is not designed to be a complete primer on the subject of the cleaning and grinding of spices, it is very helpful to understand the principles involved when preparing spice specifications. An understanding of what can and cannot be done by a spice processor will reduce misunderstandings when developing spice specifications.

In the United States, spices can enter the food supply as raw uncleaned spice, raw cleaned spice, ground uncleaned spice, or ground cleaned spice. Spices can also be postprocessed to reduce microbial counts. All too often spice buyers look only at pricing issues and forget that these spices are used as food items. There is a large market for spices that have not seen any cleaning procedures other than that obtained during harvesting. A spice processor that has adequate spice cleaning facilities can quite easily show a collection of trash that has been pulled out of lots of "cleaned" spices. Besides the common stones, rodent droppings, and insects, the authors have seen nails, baling wire, nuts and bolts, cigarette packages, dead rodents, fist-sized rocks, charcoal, wood, and numerous other items pulled out of spice lots that theoretically comply with FDA regulations. It is still too easy for a spice supplier to just transfer a spice from the original bale or bag to his box and claim that the spice has been cleaned. Finding the one large stone or piece of glass is an impossibility for the user's quality control departments. It is much better to know that the processor has the appropriate cleaning and grinding equipment and knows how to use them.

2.2 Spice Cleaning

All spice cleaning equipment takes advantage of a physical difference between the spice and the foreign material being removed. Most often these physical differences revolve around shape and density. The closer in shape and density the foreign material is to the spice in question, the more difficult it is to remove. Before moving on to the types of equipment that are used, it must be stated that these cleaning operations do cost money. There is the cost of the cleaning equipment, the labor, and most importantly the loss of product that inherently comes with the cleaning operation. It is nearly impossible to perform a cleaning operation at reasonable production rates that results in a pile of foreign material completely free of spice and a pile of spice completely free of foreign material. To be sure that most of the foreign material is being removed, some spice must also be removed. The opposite of this is also true: at reasonable production rates, it is impossible to guarantee the absence of any foreign material in a lot of cleaned spice. A specification needs to be written for how much foreign matter is allowed in the cleaned spice. This specification has to be checked from time to time to ensure that the equipment is working properly. Here, some very simple checks can work well. One simple check is to drop about a pound of black pepper into a beaker and use a stream of water to flush the pepper berries out, leaving any rocks or heavier foreign material in the bottom of the beaker. If anything is found, the system needs some adjustment. Some sort of laboratory examination of the product is needed to really determine if the cleaning equipment is working correctly.

2.2.1 Magnets

Every spice cleaning system should include magnets in as many locations as possible. Magnets should not be thought of as protection only for the end users but also for the processor since magnetic material needs to be removed so it won't damage the milling equipment. Although there are a wide variety of magnet styles, there is no one magnet that is perfect for all systems. The placement and maintenance of the magnets is also important. No magnet will pull a small piece of metal through a solid flowing stream of dense spice. To be effective, the magnetic surface must come in very close proximity to the metal and be designed such that the flow of spice over the magnet cannot brush the metal piece back off the magnet and into the product. In addition, the magnet must be cleaned frequently since even well-designed magnets can only hold so much metal before the flow of spices will knock the metal back into the product.

Typical magnets come in bar and plate forms. To be effective, the spice should flow in a loose stream over the magnet. Systems that bounce the spice particles over more than one magnet are the most effective.

Cleaning of the magnets is very important. An effective cleaning procedure will include documentation of cleaning frequency, as well as records showing the type and amount of material collected.

2.2.2 Sifters

The most basic cleaning operation is the utilization of sifters. By running the spice over a set of screens, one can remove particles both larger and smaller than the spice that is being cleaned. Although the principle sounds easy enough, it is generally very difficult in operation. Remembering that spices are often not uniform round spheres, but uneven oval seeds or random pieces of leaves, the problem becomes much more difficult. Sifters are generally not often used for cleaning, but for sizing. If the farmer doing the harvesting does any cleaning at all, it is generally not much more than a simple sifting operation to remove large debris.

2.2.3 Air Tables

Probably the most versatile piece of cleaning equipment for spices is the air table or gravity separator. This piece of equipment is usually the one piece that a processor obtains first and uses most often. At first look, an air table seems to defy nature. The heavy material comes off the high end of the table and the light material comes off the low end of the table. A look at the following diagrams will show how this is accomplished. In Figure 2.1, there is a wire mesh screen with a stream of air blowing up through it, suspending the spice particles just over the top of the screen. Naturally, the lighter pieces are suspended higher than the heavier pieces. The lighter pieces are represented by "L's" and the heavier pieces are represented by "H's." The very lightest pieces are actually blown out of the system by the air stream. In Figure 2.2, the screen is tilted and all the spice particles have moved to the bottom end of the screen. In Figure 2.3, a rotational vibration has been imparted to the screen. This rotational vibration is adjusted so as to just touch the heavier particles and tap them. The screen is built such that these taps tend to push the heavier particles up the screen where another rotation of the screen taps the heavier particles again and again. This repetitive tapping "walks" these heavier particles up the screen as shown in Figure 2.4. Since the screen does not "tap" the lighter particles, they continue to migrate towards the lower end and cause a separation. In practice, the tilt of the screen, the rotational vibration of the screen, and the airflow

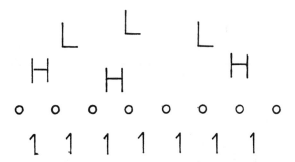

Figure 2.1   Wire screen with air flow through bottom suspending light (L) and heavy (H) particles above screen.

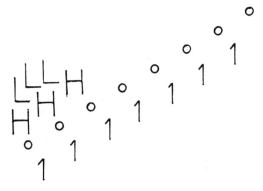

Figure 2.2   Tilted screen showing all particles settling towards bottom of screen.

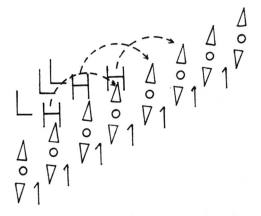

Figure 2.3   Tilted screen with vertical vibrational motion "tapping" lower, heavier particles.

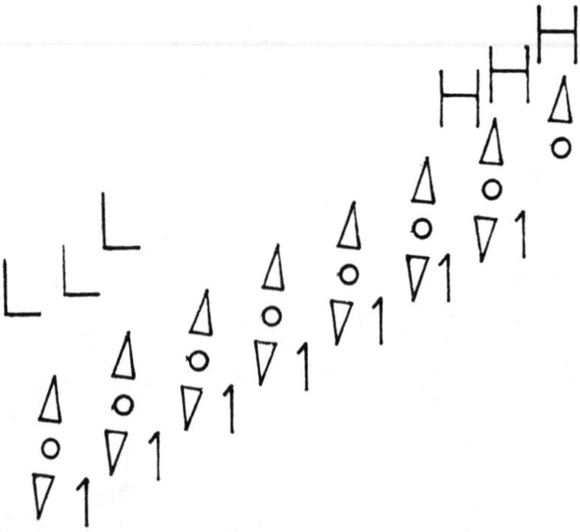

Figure 2.4   Result of "tapping" of heavier particles, moving them up the screen.

through the screen are adjusted so that the cleaned spice migrates to the middle of the screen, the heavy filth migrates to the top of the screen, and the light filth migrates to the bottom of the screen. Often the very center is collected as clean spice, the very top discarded as heavies and the very bottom discarded as lights while the area between the heavies and the cleaned spice are recycled for another pass. The area between the lights and cleaned spice are also generally recycled through the system again. This recycling allows a relatively narrow range of cleaned spice to be pulled from the center and sends the marginal material back to be recleaned.

Although the air table is a very versatile piece of equipment, it does have its limitations. An air table can separate particles of the same size and of different densities. It can separate particles of the same density and different sizes. But, it may or may not be able to separate particles of different sizes *and* different densities if the airstream floats a large surface area particle of relatively heavier weight at the same height as a small surface area particle of lighter weight. Since the air table separation is accomplished by how far the airstream suspends the particles above the screen, it is understandable how particles of varying sizes and weights might be suspended at the same height over the screen.

2.2.4 Destoners

Destoners work on the same principle as the air tables but are generally much smaller in size. Where an air table is able to separate the product stream into as many divisions as is desired, a destoner is generally set up to remove only the heavier stones and rock. Destoners usually have a much smaller screen surface than an air table and are set up to only remove the heaviest pieces. Once again, by varying the air flow, the incline of the screen, the vibration of the screen, and the type of screen, it is possible to make the stones "walk" up the screen and thus affect a separation from the lighter material. Destoners are often used by themselves or with the "heavies" off the airtable to reclaim more good product from the "heavies" stream.

2.2.5 Air Separators

Although air separators can be designed in many ways, the basic principle is the same in all. The principle can be represented by a narrow stream of spice falling through a horizontal air stream. In general, the heavier particles will fall straight down through the air stream, while the lighter particles are blown to the side, causing a separation. Air separators are built in a number of styles, sometimes using a vertical flow of air, but the principle is the same.

2.2.6 Indent Separators

The indent separator tries to make use of the difference in shape between the spice and the foreign material. The spice is fed into one end of a revolving drum. The outside of this drum is lined with uniformly shaped cavities that the particles can fit into. The cavities are sized so that the desired shape of the spice particle will fit well. The centrifugal force from the rotating drum will hold the right shaped particles in the cavities longer than it will hold particles that will not fit well in the cavities. The rotational force lifts the correctly shaped particles and when they do eventually fall out of the cavities, they are collected in a trough and moved out of the machine. The particles of the wrong shape eventually fall out the far side of the revolving drum.

By varying the shape of the cavities (indents) and the rotation of the drum, very effective separations can be made based on size or shape. Indent separators are quite effective in removing stems from herbs and oblong seeds.

2.2.7 Spiral Separators

Spiral separators work well separating round seeds from nonround foreign material. A spiral separator is a "U" shaped trough that is curved into a downward spiral much like a child's curved slide at a park. By feeding spices into the top of the separator, the round particles gain speed as they roll down the chute. As the round particles pick up speed, centrifugal force drives the round particles up the side of the chute. The nonround particles do not roll and cannot gain the same momentum and end up sliding down the center of the chute. A splitter at the bottom of the chute separates the round particles that have "climbed" the side of the chute from the non round particles that slide down the center of the chute. The principle is much the same as cars coming off a banked turn on a race course. The faster cars move to the top of the bank while the slower cars can take a course closer to the bottom.

Spiral separators are amazingly simple devices since there is no need for motors or blowers. Gravity drives the entire operation.

2.3 Spice Reconditioning

Spice reconditioning was discussed in Chapter 1 as a method to remove contaminants and bring spices into conformance with both Federal law and ASTA Cleanliness Specifications. Reconditioning involves nothing more than cleaning steps outlined above. The FDA wants to know how the spice is planned to be reconditioned prior to performing the work. They may want to supervise the operation to ensure adequate removal of the contaminant. Under ASTA procedures, supervision is not necessary, but the lot must be resampled and tested by the independent laboratory. If the lot is passed by the laboratory, ASTA's tracking program will tell if the lot was in fact reconditioned; a fact that the buyer may well want to know.

If faced with an imported lot that needs to be reconditioned or just recleaned, there are companies that specialize in these operations and have a good understanding of FDA requirements. They will be able to offer excellent advise as to how to proceed.

The importer of the goods is usually responsible for the entire cost of reconditioning. In many cases it is difficult to get the overseas shipper to pay these costs. For someone wishing to import their own spices, and save a few pennies, it is worthwhile remembering the types of problems that may arise.

2.4 Spice Grinding

The basics of spice grinding are very simple. There are a variety of mills used to grind spices and they are generally designed to cut, crush, or shatter the spice particles.

First of all, the process of grinding ruptures a number of the glands in the spice that contain the volatile oil and frees this oil for reaction or evaporation. It is this rupturing of the oil glands that presents the biggest problem in grinding. Along with the volatile oil being more exposed, grinding also generates some heat which will tend to vaporize this oil leading to a reduction in flavor strength. Any spice that you can smell during grinding is experiencing some degree of flavor loss. While no grinding system can ensure no flavor loss, it is in the grinder's best interest to keep the temperatures as low as possible to minimize the loss of volatile oil.

Most spice mills are designed to pass the spice through very quickly and minimize the heat buildup. The choice of mill that the processor will use for a particular spice is often determined by the temperature rise during processing. Various mills can be configured in various manners by changing internal screens, speed, and internal clearances to control the heat buildup. Grinding the spice to a finer particle size will increase the temperature. Producing a larger particle will generally result in a lower temperature. This choice of mills and processing procedures is what controls the through put of the spice. It is in the processor's best interest to grind the spice at as high a rate as possible while trying to maintain an adequate quality.

A few processors utilize liquid nitrogen to keep the temperature very low and minimize oil losses. Although cryogenic grinding is not wide spread, there is value in its use. By freezing the spice and solidifying the volatile and fixed oils, these spices grind and sift a lot easier. Since the spice is frozen, it shatters when subjected to a milling operation. By maintaining very cold temperatures, cryogenic grinding can retain more of the flavor components which are normally lost during regular ambient grinding. Cryogenic spices contain more volatile components as well as more of the lower molecular weight volatile components, resulting in more flavor and a different balance of flavor, more true to the natural, unground spice. In addition, other differences include a higher moisture content in ground spices since there is no heat involved to evaporate some of the moisture. Cryogenic grinding will also minimize oxidative deterioration of the flavors due to the nitrogen blanket during grinding. For the food technologist, cryogenic spices can have advantages. First of all, a spice ground cryogenically may have a different flavor profile. The top notes may be an advantage in the right product, giving a fuller flavored product. Since the product has more flavor, less spice can be used to achieve the same flavor level.

Milling operations often include a sifting operation. The mills may have internal screens that in part dictate the final particle size, or the sifting operation may be a separate operation where the oversized particles are returned to the mill for further processing. In either case, the setup of the mill or sifters determine the particle size of the finished spice.

It is important to look at the particle size control of the ground spice since nearly all spice specifications contain a granulation parameter. Many granulation specifications have been developed without regard to the processes used to produce ground spices. All too often it appears that a granulation specification is developed by taking a sample of the ground spice and running it through a set of laboratory screens to develop a "particle size survey" (x amount on a U.S. Standard 30 mesh screen, y amount on U.S. Standard 40 mesh screen, etc.). With this survey in hand, the food technologist develops a range around each screen used that theoretically ensures every lot of spice will look similar as far as granulation is concerned. The fallacy here is that not all lots of spice produced on the same mill will have the same distribution of particle sizes. And certainly, different mills used by different processors are going to give different distributions. If the intent is to develop a specification that only one spice processor can meet, this type of granulation specification is going to do it. It is in the user companies' best interest to develop specifications as broad as possible in order to allow as much competition for suppliers and therefore reduce the user's cost. For those cases where a very strict granulation specification is necessary for some reason, possibly for spices that can be visually seen in the finished product, then it is certainly correct to be very specific.

As an aid in writing reasonable granulation specifications, it is worthwhile to review how spice processors control the particle size of their spices. Most spice mills will produce a wide variety of particle sizes for any given setup of equipment and choice of spice. For the most part, a distribution of particle sizes is not unlike a normal distribution as represented by a bell shaped curve. There will be some quite large particles as well as some very small particles. For the most part, this bell curve is quite broad and it is very difficult to tighten this curve to any significant degree. A sifting operation changes the shape of the distribution significantly by cutting off very abruptly the coarse or fine end of the range. By developing a granulation specification by the survey method described earlier, the exact shape of this bell curve may inadvertently be described, thus making it very difficult for any spice processor to produce the exact same product on a continuous basis.

One needs to take a close look at the parameters of importance that need to be controlled when developing a granulation specification. In most cases, the spice particles should be small enough that they are not visually obvious or felt by the mouth when consumed. Large pieces of ground allspice in a wiener would be undesirable because they would stand out visually and they would feel like sand in the mouth when consumed. Here particles smaller than a U.S. Standard (U.S.S.) 30 mesh are probably sufficient. Specifying particles that are significantly finer may be detrimental since it takes more grinding and correspondingly higher temperatures and volatile oil losses. Specifying how much of the allspice must pass a U.S.S. 40, 50, or 60 mesh screen is of no importance if it can't be seen or detected in the finished product anyway. It is worthwhile to discuss with the spice processor what is their standard granulation specifications so something that is even just a little finer than a standard product is not specified. It is interesting to note that cinnamon is generally ground fairly fine, a U.S.S. 60 or 80 mesh, because it feels very gritty on the tongue at coarser sizes. This is one spice where cryogenic grinding does offer advantages since the product usually is ground very finely; the liquid nitrogen keeps it cold and prevents excessive oil loss.

Granulations are usually described using screen sizes. Most laboratories have access to a set of laboratory screens that are numbered by U.S.S. screen sizes. In general, the size of the screen can be thought of as the number of openings in the screen per inch. In general, a U.S.S. #4 mesh screen has 4 openings to the inch. A U.S.S. #8 mesh screen has 8 openings to the inch. Thus the larger the number, the smaller the particle.

To complicate the matter further, there are a number of systems of numbering screen sizes and a U.S.S. #8 mesh is not necessarily the same size as a Tyler #8. A comparison of these screen systems is shown in Table 2.1. Descriptions of a 28 mesh, 30 mesh, and 32 mesh black pepper may all have the same particle size, depending what screen numbering system is being used. Therefore, when discussing granulation specifications, it is very important to specify the screen numbering system. It appears that most industry specifications are written based on U.S.S. screen sizes.

There are special cases where the particle size must be controlled to a relatively narrow range. The common industry practice here is to use a −/+ designation. Thus a −30+80 mesh black pepper (often referred to as dustless since the fines have been removed) is one that passes a 30 mesh screen and is retained on an 80 mesh screen. In general, a spice with this particle range is produced by sifting off the coarser and the finer particles. Although spices sifted in this way have a quite uniform, distinct particle size, it must be remembered that the fine product being produced is probably a by-product that the processor has to sell at a lower price. An example of the black pepper demonstrates the case quite well. Using a 30 mesh

Table 2.1 Comparison of Various Screen Size Measurement Systems. This information shows the closest match of screen sizes for various measurement systems. The actual aperture for each match is not necessarily identical and some tolerance is needed to build into specifications.

U.S.S. Screen	Tyler Screen	Mill Screen	Stainless-steel Screen
4	4	4	
6	6	6	
8	8	9	
10	9	10	
12	10	12	14
14	12	14	16
16	14	16	18
18	16	18	22
20	20	22	24
25	24	26	28
30	28	30	32
35	32	36	38
40	35	40	48
45	42	45	56
50	48	55	66
60	60		74
80	80		94

black pepper (everything passing a 30 mesh screen without the fines being removed) as the starting point, a $-30+80$ black pepper will be discussed. A second processing step is added to remove the fines or the 80 mesh material. The extra processing dictates a higher cost. In addition, there is not a strong demand for the 80 mesh fines so it usually sells at a lower price. This lower price for the fines separated out of the 30 mesh material boosts the price of the $-30+80$ black pepper to a greater degree.

As can be seen in Table 2.1, actual production screens are not identical in size to U.S.S. laboratory screens. To prevent problems translating from one measurement system to the other, specifications are often written giving some tolerances. For example, a product ground as a U.S.S. 30 mesh product is often specified as 100% to pass a U.S.S. #25 and a minimum of 95% to pass a U.S.S. #30 screen. This builds in the tolerances for screen variation as well as some wear and tear in production screens. Using the 100% through a U.S.S. #25 screen specification also ensures that no very large particles are present in the finished product, which could be present if there is a problem with the mill screens during grinding.

2.5 Postprocessing Treatments

The postprocessing treatments referred to in this section are those that are used to control or reduce microbiological populations found in spices as they are harvested. For example, it is not unusual to find lots of black pepper with total plate counts in the range of 4–10 million colonies per gram. For some applications this is not a problem, but for others where there is not a significant heat processing step in the finished food item, these high microbiological loads can lead to a drastically reduced shelf life. Although these treatments are being referred to as postprocessing treatments, they can actually be applied to the whole spice or the ground spice. In general, these treatments are commonly applied to the spice in their finished form and in their finished packaging.

A common industry practice is to refer to these treatments as sterilization or "bacteria treatment." Neither of these terms are accurate. The treated spice is not commercially sterile nor has it been treated with bacteria.

2.5.1 Ethylene Oxide

Ethylene oxide (often abbreviated as ETO) has been used on spices to reduce microbiological populations for many years. It has been proven to be a very effective process to significantly reduce the microbiological populations of spices. Ethylene oxide is not an easy material to handle, especially with the advent of the Occupational Health and Safety Act (OHSA), the Environmental Protection Agency (EPA), and California's Proposition 65 regulations. Ethylene oxide is generally considered to be a carcinogen, especially via inhalation. There do appear to be some questions as to its carcinogenicity when ingested on a spice.

Ethylene oxide is currently approved for use on spices (21 CFR 193.200) to control microbiological populations and insect infestations with a residue of not more than 50 ppm in the spice after treatment. Ethylene oxide appears to be effective at killing insects in all stages. A number of spices (in particular, coriander and fennel) will harbor insect eggs that appear to be laid in or on the spice as it ripens in the fields. Treating these spices with ethylene oxide will kill the eggs and effectively prevent these pests from hatching when conditions are favorable.

To treat the spice, it is sealed in a chamber, the air evacuated and either pure ethylene oxide or a mixture of ethylene oxide and other gases are released into the chamber. After a determined dwell time, the chamber is again evacuated to remove the remaining ethylene oxide. To bring the residual ethylene oxide to acceptable limits, additional evacuations may be performed. Blends of spices can be treated with ethylene oxide as long as no salt is present. Salt will react with ethylene oxide to form chlorohydrins which are toxic.

By proper selection of time, temperature, and concentration of ethylene oxide, it is possible to achieve significant reductions in microbiological populations. A very typical specification for an ethylene oxide treated spice would be a plate count of 50,000 colonies per gram maximum, yeasts and molds of 500 colonies per gram maximum and coliforms of 10 colonies per gram maximum. Industry practice does vary as far as the guarantees that are made. Some processors will routinely guarantee a maximum plate count of 10,000 or even 5,000 colonies per gram as a maximum. The characteristics of the particular spice will dictate what levels can be reached. For example, an ethylene oxide treated coarse ground black pepper will have much lower counts than a fine ground black pepper since there is much better gas penetration into the fairly open coarse black pepper. In addition, if the spice has lower initial counts, the total plate count after treatment with ethylene oxide can be lower than if the spice started with very high microbiological counts.

Some spices, such as cloves, do not typically have high microbiological counts, possibly due to the antimicrobial nature of its volatile oil constituents (see Chapter 6). Special ETO treatment in these cases may not offer significant advantages.

The type of container used to hold the spice during ethylene oxide treatments is important to discuss. If the spice is treated in the original burlap bags, the gas penetration is excellent and the microbiological kill is good. If the same spice is packed in a heavy polyethylene bag, heat sealed, and placed in a corrugated box that could withstand the vacuum pulled in the treatment process, there would be essentially no kill since the ethylene oxide would not have free access to the spice. Some custom ethylene oxide processors will guarantee finished microbiological levels and others will only guarantee that an established process has been used. If your processor will only guarantee that a specified process has been used, it is important that you not pack your spice in a package that will prevent good penetration.

Ethylene oxide is now under close scrutiny by the EPA. The EPA has requested data concerning the residues of ethylene oxide in treated spices. The actual registrants of ethylene oxide have declined to conduct the required testing since ethylene oxide use on spices makes up such a small portion of the total ethylene oxide used in the United States. The American Spice Trade Association has recognized the extreme importance of this treatment process to the spice trade and plans to invest 2– 2.5 million dollars for testing to satisfy the EPA's requirements. This testing could allow the continued use of this very effective treatment. Without it, the spice trade will have lost one of its most effective weapons against microbiological pests.

2.5.2 Propylene Oxide

Propylene oxide is a weak sibling compared to ethylene oxide. Propylene oxide is also approved as a microbiological treatment process for spices but is not nearly as effective as ethylene oxide. Although propylene oxide is not currently facing the same EPA problems as ethylene oxide, it is expected that if the EPA bans the use of ethylene oxide on spices, it seems reasonable that propylene oxide would eventually face the same fate. Many of the spice processors in California have switched to propylene oxide treatments for their paprikas and chili peppers because of the problems with ethylene oxide and its inclusion on the Proposition 65 list.

2.5.3 Irradiation

Irradiation of spices has been shown to be a very effective method of reducing microbiological populations.

Normal irradiation treatments provide nearly commercially sterile spices with no off flavors or hazardous residues. Although many spice users do specify irradiation of their spices because of the effectiveness of the treatment, many more food processors strictly forbid the use of irradiated spices. This happens because the food companies are concerned that a consumer activist group will find out they are using irradiated ingredients. Many recent studies have actually shown consumer acceptance of the process when it is explained to them. Consumer education is the most important factor in the widespread use of irradiation. Study after study has also demonstrated its effectiveness and safety. The main problem with these studies is that it is theoretically impossible to prove without any doubt the safety of something. It is easy to prove that something can cause harm, but looking for the one small hazard that the process might present is an impossible task. It is very easy to question these studies by simply pointing out that there is always the remote possibility that something has been overlooked. Many people familiar with the microbiological hazards that untreated spices can present would prefer to use irradiated spices rather than untreated ones.

It appears now that irradiation of chicken is nearing approval. The poultry processors may have a stronger story to tell: irradiation or salmonella. If the poultry industry is able to present its case to the buying public in a strong enough way that irradiation of poultry becomes an accepted practice, the spice industry should be able to ride on its coattails. Until then, irradiation of spices will probably not become an important factor in the spice industry.

One significant drawback to the irradiation of spices in the United States at this time is that irradiated spices must be labeled as having been irradiated. There is currently no test available to reliably tell if a spice has been treated. Therefore, the FDA has required labeling as a way to identify that the product has been irradiated. The FDA has approved irradiation of spices (21CFR 179.26) up to a dosage of 3 megarads and requires that all irradiated foods be labeled. However, an irradiated spice used as an ingredient in another food product that has not been irradiated is not required to bear the labeling.

The irradiation process is quite simple since the spices can be readily irradiated after processing with the spice packed in its final container. The packaged spice is exposed to the irradiation source for a predetermined amount of time, resulting in an essentially sterile finished spice.

The regulations allowing the use of irradiation on spices has been misread by the industry in the past. The regulations (21CFR 179.26) allow:

> For microbial disinfection of the following dry or dehydrated aromatic vegetable substances: culinary herbs, seeds, spices, teas, vegetable seasonings, and blends of the aromatic vegetable substances. Turmeric and paprika may also be irradiated when they are to be used as color additives. The blends may contain sodium chloride and minor amounts of dry food ingredients ordinarily used in such blends.

There are two very important points made in these regulations. Vegetable seasonings are not clearly defined. When a food processor used irradiated mushroom pieces, the FDA stepped in and said no. In general, it is the FDA's interpretation that vegetable pieces are vegetables and cannot be irradiated under this section. However, vegetable powders not represented in the finished product as the characterizing ingredient (such as onion powder in French onion soup) can be irradiated. Be sure to clear any questions with your legal department.

Point 2 to consider is that *minor* amounts of dry ingredients that are used in seasonings can be used. The authors have seen "seasoning" blends containing only minor amounts of authorized ingredients being irradiated. These may lead to FDA problems when they are detected.

2.5.4 Steam Sterilization

Although steam sterilization is not normally applied as a postprocessing treatment, it makes sense to describe it here with other "sterilization" processes. This technique is usually applied to the whole spice before grinding. In this process, the whole spice is subjected to high-temperature steam which surface "sterilizes" the spice. This is a somewhat difficult process to apply since moisture and heat is applied to the spice. It is important that the spice not be heated any longer than necessary to prevent significant loss of flavor components. In addition, the moisture added must be removed to prevent unwanted mold growth after treatment.

Steam sterilization is offered by a limited number of processors and apparently cannot be used on all spices (especially herbs) or ground spices. There is some hope that further advances in this process may allow its broader use.

Suggested Reading List

1. American Spice Trade Association, *Clean Spices, A Handbook for ASTA Members.* Englewood Cliffs, New Jersey.

2. American Spice Trade Association, *Cleanliness Specifications for Unprocessed Spices, Seeds, and Herbs, revised May, 1991.* Englewood Cliffs, New Jersey, 1991.

3. Kiss, M.I. "Irradiation of Spices and Herbs." *Food Technol. Aust.* 36:362, 1984.

4. Kiss, I. and Farkas, J., "Irradiation as a Method for Decontamination of Spices." *Foods Rev. Int.* 4:77, 1988.

5. Hsieh R.C. et al. Process for Sterilization of Spices and Leafy Herbs. U.S. Patent 4,844,933, 1989.

6. Hsieh R.C. et al. Apparatus for Sterilization of Spices and Leafy Herbs. U.S. Patent 4,967,651, 1990.

7. Pesek, C.A., Wilson, L.A., and Hammond, E.G., "Spice Quality: Effect of Cryogenic and Ambient Grinding on Volatiles." *J. Food Sci.* 50(3): 599–601, 1985.

8. Pruthi, J.S., *Spices and Condiments: Chemistry, Microbiology, Technology,* Advances in Food Research Supp. 4. Academic Press, Inc. New York, 1980.

9. Sharma, A., Padwal-Desai, S.R., and Nair, P.M., "Assessment of Microbiological Quality of Some Gamma Irradiated Indian Spices." J. Food Sci. 54:489, 1989.

10. Tjaberg, T.B., Underdal, B., and Lunde, G., "The Effect of Ionizing Radiation on the Microbiological Content and Volatile Constituents of Spices." *J. Appl. Bacteriol.* 35:473, 1972.

11. Vajdi, M. and Pereira, R.R. "Comparative Effects of Ethylene Oxide, Gamma Irradiation and Microwave Treatments on Selected Spices." *J. Food Sci.* 38:893, 1973.

12. Wesley, F., Bourke, B., and Darbbishire, O., "The Formation of Persistent Toxic Chlorohydrins in Foodstuffs by Fumigation with Ethylene Oxide and with Propylene Oxide." *J. Food Sci.* 30:1037, 1965.

CHAPTER

3

Quality Issues Dealing with Spices

3.1 Introduction

This chapter will deal with the quality issues of spices. The parameters of concern generally revolve around cleanliness, safety, or economic elements. The cleanliness elements are set forth in Federal law such as FDA DALs or in trade practices such as the ASTA Cleanliness Specifications. These were discussed in Chapter 1. Safety issues include microbiology and moisture levels. The economic issues have to do with the flavor level and granulation.

The spice industry has worked together to develop a set of standard methods of analysis that help define how these parameters are measured. The current set of industry adopted methods is available from the American Spice Trade Association, 580 Sylvan Avenue, P.O. Box 1267, Englewood Cliffs, New Jersey 07632 (Phone 201-568-2163).

The most important point to remember when working with these methods is that they are strictly empirical methods. This means that the trade defines "moisture" as the result of the specified testing procedure, not necessarily a strict measure of how much water is present in the product. The test methods, as accepted by the industry, need to be followed strictly to ensure that results are comparable from lab to lab. A modification to a test method that gives volatile oil readings higher or lower than the standard method are worthless, since the term "volatile oil," as used by the industry, is defined by the results of the established test.

This is not to say that a company cannot use a different testing method if it has some unique value for that company, but when talking to members of the trade, it is extremely important that one defines the test method being used. Comparing a Karl

Fisher moisture test method result against the ASTA moisture method will give different results. Only if the test method is described is the result understandable. For the most part, it is easiest and most accepted to use the methods as adopted by ASTA for establishing specifications.

The ASTA test methods are continually being refined to make the methods produce the most reliable and reproducible results.

3.2 Sampling

The biggest problem faced in the analysis of spices is collecting a sample representative of the lot as a whole. As discussed in Chapter 1, many lots of spices are a consolidation of small parcels from many small growers or harvesters. This means that a single large lot may face large variation in composition within the lot. Generally, the spice cleaning and grinding steps will eliminate some of this variation, but it will not remove all of it unless the product is blended. This variation is probably the cause of most of the problems between suppliers and users. Most spice processors will sample a given lot of spice many times while it is being processed and run a composite sample. This composite sample is a far better estimate of the overall lot quality than a single grab sample. As much time and effort needs to be put into the taking of the samples as put into the actual analytical work.

When testing a given lot for cleanliness, the ASTA Cleanliness Specifications require pulling samples from individual bags representing the square root of the total number of bags in the lot up to a maximum of 10 samples per lot. This is a good rule of thumb to follow when sampling any given lot of spice for any parameter. If these 10 samples are composited, the end result says nothing about the variation within lots, but does give a good idea of the overall lot average.

Some ASTA members are suggesting that the trade look at a three-class sampling program that would give a better idea of the composition of a given lot with less samples but more testing. Essentially this sampling program requires five individual samples from the lot to be analyzed for the parameter of concern. Based on the five individual results, statistics can be used to estimate the actual composition of the lot. This modification of the standard sampling plan has been slow to catch on, but some industry users have adopted similar plans, especially for microbiological examinations.

3.3 Sample Preparation

Nearly as important as sampling, the sample preparation is an important part of the testing procedure. Industry practice has established that all spice analysis should be conducted on spices that have been ground to pass a U.S.S. #20 mesh screen. Spices which are tested that are finer than this need no further preparation, but those spices purchased whole or coarsely ground will need further particle size reduction. It is important that this grinding takes place rapidly without any significant heat buildup. Laboratory mills that have a large mass of metal compared to the mass of spice being ground will help keep the temperatures of grinding down. Maintaining the mills in good working order with sharp knives and cutting surfaces is a must.

Remember that the entire sample must be ground to pass a U.S.S. #20 mesh screen. Material retained on a U.S.S. #20 mesh screen must be passed through the grinder again. While grinding some spices finer will give differing results, it is important to try to follow the standard method if one is looking for standardized results.

The storage of the sample is extremely important. Spice samples stored in poly-ethylene bags can lose an appreciable amount of volatile oil overnight. It is important that ground spice samples be stored in glass containers and preferably refrigerated.

3.4 Volatile Oil

The most commonly run test on spices is the volatile oil. The laboratory method consists of boiling the spice in water and collecting the condensed water and volatile oil. The amount of volatile oil is measured by volume and the results reported as "milliliter per 100 grams of spice." There are adaptations designed for certain spices. For example, the volatile oil of cassia has very nearly the same density as water and it is difficult to hold the oil in the trap. By adding a measured amount of xylene to the trap, it is easy to hold the oil. When the amount of oil is measured, the amount of xylene added is backed out of the calculation. For this method, it is very important to follow the test method word for word.

The volatile oil measurement is a fairly reliable indicator of flavor content for those spices where the principle flavoring components are in the oils. For example, red peppers have no volatile oil and the bite or heat comes from chemicals that are extracted into an oleoresin. Therefore, volatile oil is not done on red peppers.

The measurement of volatile oils in spices is also a good measure of the age and processing conditions the spice has seen. Ground spices will slowly lose their flavor and volatile oil after prolonged periods of storage. Spices that have seen high temperatures during grinding will also show losses of volatile oil.

3.5 Moisture

The measurement of moisture in spices presents some unusual problems. Moisture is usually measured in food products by measuring the weight loss of a sample stored under warm temperatures. The volatile oils typically found in spices are also lost during drying and this weight loss would also be measured as moisture. To resolve this problem, the trade has adopted a co-distillation method for most spices. In this test, the spice is covered with toluene and the toluene brought to its boiling temperature. The moisture in the spice co-distills with the toluene and as the toluene is condensed, the moisture separates from the toluene and is measured.

All spices can not be tested for moisture in the same way. Paprikas and other capsicum products tend to caramelize during the distillation with toluene and additional water is produced from this reaction. Thus, paprikas and capsicums are analyzed with the more traditional oven method.

Although it would seem that a Karl Fisher titration could be employed for spices, the cost and technical knowledge required has been a drawback to common acceptance. In addition, the small sample size usually used for Karl Fisher titrations may lead to erratic results.

The moisture level of spices is of practical importance as a control of microbiological growth. Although the measurement of water activity would be a much better indicator of potential for microbiological growth, the industry has established traditional moisture limits which have had the same effect. These limits for each spice are listed in Chapter 4. Moisture migration in large containers can be a significant problem, if stored in a warehouse with varying temperatures. For example, chili pepper exposed to falling temperatures can have moisture condense on the top of the bag, which could fall on top of the product and cause mold growth.

The moisture level of spices also affects the grinding characteristics of some spices. In particular, it is very difficult to produce a cracked bay leaf when the moisture level of the bay is very low. At low moistures, the leaves are very brittle and a large amount of fines are produced upon cracking. At higher moisture levels, the leaves are quite pliable and the excessive fines are not generated. When trying to grind bay into a fine mesh, the dryer leaves work better.

Extremely low moisture levels can also cause shelf-life problems. Very dry spices tend to lose flavor quicker than higher moisture spices after grinding. In paprika, it is very important to keep moisture levels reasonably high (9%–12%) to help retain extractable color. Color losses in very dry paprika can be excessive.

3.6 Total Ash and Acid Insoluble Ash

The total ash and acid insoluble ash content of spices is a measure of the amount of sand and grit in the spice. The total ash determination is performed by heating the sample until all the organic matter has been burned off. The acid insoluble ash is the material remaining after the total ash has been treated with hydrochloric acid. The acid insoluble ash is a fairly reliable indicator of the sand or grit content. It is important to remember that a perfectly clean spice does contain some inorganic minerals that are measured as acid insoluble ash. The levels shown in Chapter 4 are levels that can be attained by careful cleaning prior to grinding.

The total ash content is also a clue that some spices may have been limed. In this procedure, spices like ginger are treated with lime during the drying procedure to bleach the product. This added lime can show up as a higher total ash.

Paprikas and capsicum products are often treated with an anticaking agent such as silicon dioxide to help retain a free flowing product. These products will have a higher total ash and acid insoluble ash than products which are not treated.

3.7 Granulation

The particle size of spices is determined by sieving the material through a set of standard laboratory screens. Since many spices are quite oily, they tend to easily blind the screens and inhibit an accurate measurement of particle size distribution. To facilitate the laboratory screening process, the spice sample is treated with silicon dioxide. The test method dictates the sample size, the method of shaking, and the time of shaking. All of these parameters are important to ensure reproducible results. It is also important to ensure that the screens are clean and oil free. Regular rinsing of the screens with acetone is helpful.

3.8 Crude Fiber, Starch, and Nonvolatile Methylene Chloride Extract

The tests for crude fiber, starch, and nonvolatile methylene chloride extract are tools to detect adulteration of spices. Although not a common practice these days, these tests are useful for the detection of the addition of other nonspice organic matter. These tests are not regularly used.

The crude fiber test is essentially the same for determining crude fiber in other food products. High crude fiber results may occur if sawdust or other fibrous materials are added to a spice such as ginger.

The starch content of some spices can be a clue of adulteration with starchy materials such as flour. Some old, dry spices can take on a new appearance if vegetable oils are added. The nonvolatile methylene chloride (ether was the original solvent used for this test but has been abandoned due to flammability hazards) extract can help detect this addition.

3.9 Spice Specific Tests

There are a number of tests developed to measure the quality of individual spices. These tests measure an important property of a particular spice.

3.9.1 Piperine Level of White and Black Pepper

Piperine is the primary chemical responsible for the bite of white and black pepper. The accurate measurement of this chemical is important for controlling the important flavor contribution of these spices. For most applications, the piperine level of peppers is much more important than the volatile oil content which is the common test parameter specified in most specifications. Particularly in breaded and fried products, the bite of the pepper is much more important than the level of volatile oil. During the hot frying operation, much of the volatile oil is driven off.

The ASTA piperine method is a spectrophotometric procedure that is quite straightforward and easy to run.

3.9.2 Volatile Oil of Mustard Seed

The strong horseradish-type flavor from oriental mustard seed is quite different from the traditional volatile oils of other spices. The chemical responsible for the flavor is allyl isothiocyanate. In the mustard seed, this chemical is tied up and is only released after an enzyme reaction takes place. More information can be found in Chapter 4. It is impossible to determine the volatile oil of mustard via the standard steam distillation method. In this method, the allyl isothiocyanate is released by adding a source of the needed enzyme, distilling the allyl isothiocyanate, and trapping it in a solution of ammonium hydroxide. The allyl isothiocyanate is then measured by titration with silver nitrate.

3.9.3 Extractable Color of Turmeric

Turmeric is usually used for the bright yellow color it can provide to foods. The chemical, curcumin, is primarily responsible for the yellow color. It is quite easy to determine the curcumin content of turmeric by solvent extraction and measurement spectrophotometrically. Turmeric is usually sold based on the curcumin content.

3.9.4 Phenol Content of Nutmeg and Mace

Nutmeg and mace are grown in both the East and West Indies. Although the flavors are similar, they are different enough that they cannot generally be interchanged in a product. By measuring the phenol content of these two spices, it is quite easy to tell which origin one is dealing with. West Indian nutmeg and mace oils have a lower phenol content than East Indian nutmeg and mace oils.

3.9.5 Extractable Color of Paprika Products

The extractable color of paprikas and chili products is accomplished in much the same manner as turmeric. The color is extracted in acetone and measured spectrophotometrically. Paprikas are sold based on the amount of extractable color. The color is measured in color units or in ASTA units with 1 ASTA unit approximately equal to 40 color units.

3.9.6 Heat Level of Red Pepper

The heat level of red peppers is measured by one of two methods. The classic method is the Scoville test. In this procedure, the heat component (capsaicin) of the red pepper is extracted into an alcohol solution. Dilutions of this alcohol solution are made and given to a panel of five trained tasters. When three of the five panelists detect a threshold sensation of heat, the heat level is calculated from the dilution tasted. It is important that trained panelists be used since extra sensitive or high threshold individuals can severely affect the results. Although this test is the most widely used, it suffers from extreme variation from lab to lab. The interlab variation can be as high as + or − 50%. If a given lab can generate reproducible results on a given sample, reasonable control of heat can be maintained for a finished product. It is quite common for red pepper processors to compare test results with a users lab and use a factor to adjust the suppliers material to the users needs.

Another test method has also been accepted by ASTA. This method uses high-pressure liquid chromatography (HPLC). This test procedure measures the important capsaicinoids present and calculates the heat based on the amount of these found. The results are reported in terms of ASTA pungency units. The ASTA pungency units can be converted to Scoville units by multiplying the ASTA units by a factor of 15.

The HPLC method is significantly more reproducible than the Scoville method as long as the labs are using exactly the same method. The biggest problem here is that each lab seems to use their own modification. Even though the method is much more reliable, the $20,000 investment for equipment precludes many spice processors from running their own tests. Many processors will send their samples to a commercial laboratory for examination, but when paying for the testing on a per sample basis, there is always the tendency to do fewer samples than should really be done.

3.10 Microanalytical Determination of Filth

The microanalytical determination of filth is handled by performing a concentration of the light and heavy filth portions by floating away the bulk of the spice. The actual determination is accomplished by examining the light and heavy residue under a microscope and visually counting the insect fragments, rodent hairs, feather barbules, and other filth. A trained specialist is required to be able to identify the insect fragments from the other residue collected. Adequate training is available through commercial labs or the American Institute of Baking.

The counting of the plate under the microscope is a very time consuming proposition and questions regularly arise about the capability of the analyst. ASTA is reviewing a new methodology that could measure insect fragments via a colorimetric measurement of selected insect proteins. Although still in the experimental stage, this methodology would remove much of the subjective nature of this determination.

3.11 Microbiological Methods

ASTA has also published a manual of microbiological methods for spices. Copies of this manual are available from ASTA (address given in Section 3.1). The methods here are fairly straightforward and involve nothing significantly different than other food microbiological methods.

Suggested Reading List

1. American Spice Trade Association, *Official Analytical Methods of The American Spice Trade Association*, 3rd ed. Englewood Cliffs, New Jersey, 1985.

CHAPTER
4
The Spices

4.1 Allspice (*Pimenta dioica* L.)

4.1.1 Background Information

Allspice is a round berry about 1 cm in diameter. It is brown to reddish brown and is slightly rough to the touch due to the presence of many raised oil glands.[1] Allspice berries grow on a shiny leaved evergreen tree of the myrtle family indigenous to the Western Hemisphere. The spice itself is the dried, mature, unripe fruit of the tree. Early Spanish explorers discovered allspice and called it pimienta (pepper in Spanish) because of its resemblance to black peppercorns. This name evolved into pimento. About 80% of the allspice imported into the U.S. is grown in the Western Hemisphere, mainly in the Caribbean and Central America. The name allspice is derived from its sensory description: warm, sweet, and reminiscent of cloves, cinnamon, and nutmeg.

The Mayan Indians of Central America used allspice to embalm and preserve bodies. Allspice was much more popular in the early 20th century than it is today. During this time, Europeans used allspice for meat preservation and baking in large amounts. World War II caused a shortage of the spice in Europe and the popularity never regained what it once had been.[2]

4.1.2 Chemical and Physical Specifications

Allspice contains its essential oils in two separate parts of the plant. The oil can be distilled from the leaf of the tree—oil of pimento leaf, or from the berry itself—oil of pimento berry. The primary constituents of the allspice berry volatile, or essential oil, are eugenol (60%–75%), eugenol methyl ether, cineole, phellandrene, and caryophyllene.[3] Eugenol is also the main constituent of cloves, thus the flavor resemblance. The oil of pimento leaf has a different flavor profile, although once again the major component is eugenol. Veek and Russ (1973)[4] found 29 components of the leaf oil, although they could only identify 16 of them. The other compounds present vary in the leaf oil and are not present at the same level as the berry oil. Pimento berry oleoresin is also available for specialty applications. The volatile oil content of the oleoresin is 20%–30%.

The level of the volatile oil can vary; however, typical levels in good quality, fresh allspice are 3.3%–4.5%, most typically in the 3%–4% range. This level can vary between origins, weather, and harvest conditions, as well as due to drying and further processing. It has also been noted that the larger the berry size, the lower the volatile oil content.[5] Upon grinding, the volatile oil specification should probably be kept to about 2.5% due to volatilization during an ambient grinding process.

Another important chemical specification on the whole spice is moisture. ASTA has suggested moisture limits for whole spices. For allspice, this is 12.0%. Ash and acid insoluble ash levels in a cleaned, whole berry should be less than 5.0% and 1.0%, respectively. See Tables 4.1 and 4.2 for a summary of the typical chemical and physical specifications, including FDA DALs for whole and ground allspice. Nutritional composition for allspice can be found in Table 4.3.

Table 4.1   Whole Allspice: Chemical and Physical Specifications.

Specification	Suggested Limits
ASTA cleanliness specifications:	
Whole dead insects, by count	2
Mammalian excreta, by mg/lb	5
Other excreta, by mg/lb	5.0
Mold, % by weight	2.00
Insect defiled/infested, % by weight	1.00
Extraneous, % by weight	0.50
FDA DALs:	
Moldy berries by weight	Ave of 5%
Volatile oil[1]	3.0% min
Moisture[2]	12.0% max
Ash[1]	5.0% max
Acid insoluble ash[1]	1.0% max
Average bulk index (mg/100 g)	265

[1]   These are suggested limits that the authors put together from the data collected over the past 5 years. These numbers are equivalent to the level where most quality spice will fall into.
[2]   ASTA suggested maximum moisture level.

Table 4.2   Ground Allspice: Chemical and Physical Specifications.

Specification	Suggested Limits
FDA/DALs (6 subsamples):	
Insect fragments	Ave of 30 or more/10 grams
or	
Rodent hairs	Ave of 1 or more/10 grams
Volatile oil[1]	2.0% min
Moisture[1]	12.0% max
Total ash[1]	5.0% max
Acid insoluble ash[1]	1.0% max
Military specifications (EE-S-631J, 1981)	
Volatile oil (ml/100 g)	3.0 min
Moisture	10.0% max
Total ash	5.5% max
Acid insoluble ash	0.5% max
Granulation	95% min through a U.S.S. #25
Bulk index[2] (ml/100 g)	190

[1]   These are suggested limits that the authors put together from data collected in the past 5 years. These numbers are equivalent to the level where most quality spice will fall into.

[2]   Average bulk index. Granulation will effect number.

Table 4.3   Nutritional Composition of Allspice Per 100 Grams.

Composition	USDA Handbook 8-2[1] (Ground)	ASTA[2]
Water (grams)	8.46	9.0
Food energy (Kcal)	263	380
Protein (grams)	6.09	6.0
Fat (grams)	8.69	6.6
Carbohydrates (grams)	72.12	74.4
Ash (grams)	4.65	4.2
Calcium (grams)	.661	.800
Phosphorus (mg)	113	110
Sodium (mg)	77	80
Potassium (mg)	1,044	1,100
Iron (mg)	7.06	7.5
Thiamine (mg)	.101	.100
Riboflavin (mg)	.063	.060
Niacin (mg)	2.86	2.9
Ascorbic acid (mg)	39.2	39
Vitamin A activity (RE)	54	54

[1]   Composition of Foods: Spices and Herbs. USDA Agricultural Handbook 8-2. January 1977.

[2]   The Nutritional Composition of Spices, ASTA Research Committee, February, 1977.

4.1.3 Import Tonnage

Allspice was imported from 12 different countries into the United States in 1991. The total amount of allspice imported that year was 2.3 million pounds.[6] The monetary value this amount represents is over $1.8 million. This dollar breakdown is for the raw spice, before any additional cleaning or further processing takes place. A breakdown of the major exporting countries to the U.S. is as follows: Jamaica 38.5%, Honduras 19.5%, and Guatemala 17.5%. Mexico has been a significant source in past years, up to 21% in 1989; however, the volume imported into the United States in 1991 dropped to 55,000 pounds, or only 2.4% of the total U.S. imports.

4.1.4 Countries of Origin

4.1.4.1 Quality Differences

Jamaican allspice is considered the best quality. The volatile oil is higher than allspice from other sources. The size of the Jamaican berry is also somewhat smaller than its Mexican counterpart. Jamaican allspice is handpicked and stored in piles, undergoing a slight fermentation before drying in the sun. Generally, the allspice exported from some of the other Central American countries are more variable than those from Jamaica, probably due to the fact they are harvested from trees growing wild, as well as dried by individual collectors, rather than cultivated as they are in Jamaica.

4.1.4.2 Harvest Times

Jamaican allspice is harvested during August and September; Guatemalan and Honduran in July through October; and Mexican slightly earlier, in July and August.

4.1.5 Commercial Uses

Allspice is used in a variety of foods, mainly as a background flavor in combination with other sweet spices; e.g., in bakery items such as spice cakes and cookies. It is also used extensively in the processed meats industry, primarily in two forms: the essential oils (pimento leaf and pimento berry) and the oleoresin, to some extent, in products like bologna and wieners, as well as whole in pickling spices for corned beef, sauerbraten, and fish. Allspice is a major flavor contributor to Caribbean and Jamaican foods and spice blends.

4.2 Anise Seed (*Pimpinella anisum* L.)

4.2.1 Background Information

Anise seed is harvested from the fruit of an annual herb of the parsley family. Each fruit, mature at harvest, contains two carpels, each containing an anise seed. The seed is small and curved, about 0.5 cm long and grayish brown. It usually contains hair-like protrusions from each end of the seed. Star anise (*Illicium verum* Hook f.), although it has a similar flavor, is a different plant. It is the fruit of a small evergreen tree native to China. When ripe, the fruits open up and resemble a five pointed star, with one seed in each point. The volatile oil composition of anise seed and star anise are quite similar, thus the flavor resemblance.

Anise seed has a long history, being mentioned in the Bible in Matthew 23:23. From the King James Version: "for ye pay tithe of mint and anise and cummin." The Romans used the anise plant to ward off bad dreams by hanging one next to their beds, and the seed to flavor spice cakes to prevent indigestion.[7]

4.2.2 Chemical and Physical Specifications

The essential oil of anise is present at about the 1.5%–3.5% level, most often running at the high end. The primary constituent is anethole.[8] Other components in the volatile oil are anisaldehyde, anisketone, and methyl chavicol.[3] El-Wakeil et al.[9] found an increase in trans-anethole and a decrease in the other oil components of anise oil during extended storage. The flavor of anise is similar to licorice and the spice fennel, the latter also containing a high level of anethole. The essential oil of anise is commonly used, although an oleoresin is not.

Recommended moisture limits from ASTA is 10% in the whole spice. Ash and acid insoluble ash should be no greater than 6.0% and 1.0%, respectively. See Tables 4.4 and 4.5 for a summary of the suggested chemical and physical specifica-

Table 4.4   Whole Anise: Chemical and Physical Specifications.

Specification	Suggested Limits
ASTA cleanliness specifications:	
Whole dead insects, by count	4
Mammalian excreta, by mg/lb	3
Other excreta, by mg/lb	5.0
Mold, % by weight	1.00
Insect defiled/infested, % by weight	1.00
Extraneous, % by weight	1.00
FDA DALs (Condimental Seed): Adulteration with Mammalian excreta	Ave of 3 mg per lb
Volatile oil[1]	2.5% min
Moisture[2]	10.0% max
Ash[1]	6.0% max
Acid insoluble ash[1]	1.0% max
Average bulk index (mg/100 g)	230

[1]   These are suggested limits that the authors put together from the data collected over the past 5 years. These numbers are equivalent to the level where most quality spice will fall into.

[2]   ASTA suggested maximum moisture level.

Table 4.5   Ground Anise: Chemical and Physical Specifications.

Specification	Suggested Limits
FDA DALs	None
Volatile oil[1]	2.0% min
Moisture[1]	10.0% max
Total ash[1]	6.0% max
Acid insoluble ash[1]	1.0% max
Military specifications (EE-S-631J, 1981)	None
Bulk index[2] (ml/100 g)	175

[1]   These are suggested limits that the authors put together from data the authors collected in the past 5 years. These numbers are equivalent to the level where most quality spice will fall into.
[2]   Average bulk index. Granulation will effect number.

tions for the whole and ground spice, including the FDA DALs for the whole spice. Nutritional information can be found in Table 4.6.

One interesting item to note in this spice is that when the ground product is irradiated, a slightly putrid off odor and flavor results. The off flavor is enough that one spice company has stopped offering irradiated anise as a standard product. This contradicts most research that irradiation does not change the chemical properties of a spice when treated.[10–14] It is possible that it does, in limited cases, change the flavor balance of the essential oils. Further research in this area regarding this particular spice and the volatile oil profile before and after irradiation is needed.

Table 4.6   Nutritional Composition of Anise Seed Per 100 Grams.

Composition	USDA Handbook 8-2[1]
Water (grams)	9.54
Food energy (Kcal)	337
Protein (grams)	17.6
Fat (grams)	15.90
Carbohydrates (grams)	50.02
Ash (grams)	6.95
Calcium (grams)	.646
Phosphorus (mg)	440
Sodium (mg)	16
Potassium (mg)	1,441
Iron (mg)	36.96
Thiamine (mg)	—
Riboflavin (mg)	—
Niacin (mg)	—
Ascorbic acid (mg)	—
Vitamin A activity (RE)	—

[1]   Composition of Foods: Spices and Herbs. USDA Agricultural Handbook 8-2. January 1977. Supplement 1990.

4.2.3 Import Tonnage

Anise is imported mainly from Turkey into the United States. The total amount for the year 1991 was about 2.5 million pounds, broken down by country: 75.8% Turkey and 10.9% China. The monetary value for all imported anise for 1991 was about $2 million.[6]

4.2.4 Countries of Origin

4.2.4.1 Quality Differences

Anise is primarily imported from Turkey, although it is also imported from China, Egypt, India, and Spain, among others. From an industrial standpoint, the quality differences between anise seed from different origins are not significant and therefore specifications should not limit the spice to a specific country of origin.

4.2.4.2 Harvest Times

Turkish anise is harvested in August and September.

4.2.5 Commercial Uses

Anise is used in Italian sausage, pepperoni, pizza topping and other processed meat items. It is used in bakery products, and is an essential component of Italian anise cake and cookies. Oil of anise is used in the meat industry in Italian sausage and pizza toppings. Its primary use, however, is in licorice-flavored items such as candy and the liqueur anisette.

4.3 Basil (*Ocimum basilicum* L.)

4.3.1 Background Information

Basil is a leafy herb of the mint family that is grown primarily in Egypt and the United States. Some basil is also grown in and exported from France, although this is really a minor source at this point in time. Its relation to the mint family is seen, since basil possesses a minty flavor and odor. The herb is the leaves of a small bushy plant. The fresh leaves are about 5 cm long and 2 cm wide. When referred to as "whole basil," it usually means the broken pieces of leaves. The usage of basil in the United States has had phenomenal growth. In the last 25 years, import tonnage has increased over 100 fold, from about 40,000 lbs in 1964 to 4.7 million pounds in 1991.[6] In addition, domestic basil is now also a significant source.

The ancient Greeks avoided basil, stating that it "exists only to drive men insane" and "a she goat that browses on everything avoids basil alone."[15a] In India, however basil is sacred and is often buried with Hindus when they die. In Italy, suitors sometimes wear a leaf of basil in their hair to show their marital intentions.[7]

4.3.2 Chemical and Physical Specifications

Basil, as with most herbs, contains a very low percent of essential, or volatile oil, usually from 0.1% to 1.0%. Due to the low percent oil in the whole spice, the essential oil of basil is quite expensive. An oleoresin containing 2%–5% volatile oil is available, as well as an essential oil. Principal components of the volatile oil are methyl chavicol (estragole), linalool, and cineol.[8]

The ASTA suggested maximum moisture limit is 12%. Ash and acid insoluble ash levels are variable. Generally Egyptian basil has slightly higher levels than domestic. These values can range from 12% to 15% for ash and 1.0% to 2.5% for acid insoluble ash. See Tables 4.7 and 4.8 for a summary of the suggested chemical and physical specifications for basil, including the FDA DALs for leafy spices. Nutritional composition can be found in Table 4.9.

Paakkonen et al.[15b] has published sorption isotherms on Finnish basil. These researchers found that air dried basil did not have any significant changes in odor or flavor quality after 12 months storage.

4.3.3 Import Tonnage

The total tonnage of basil imported into the United States in 1991 was 4.7 million pounds, 15.4% from Mexico and 79.4% from Egypt. This represents $2.9 million.[6]

Table 4.7 Whole Basil: Chemical and Physical Specifications.

Specification	Suggested Limits
ASTA cleanliness specifications:	
Whole dead insects, by count	2
Mammalian excreta, by mg/lb	1
Other excreta, by mg/lb	2.0
Mold, % by weight	1.00
Insect defiled/infested, % by weight	1.00
Extraneous, % by weight	0.50
FDA DALs (Leafy Spices):	
Insect infested and/or moldy pieces by weight	Ave of 5%
Mammalian excreta, after processing, identified as to source when possible	Ave of 1 mg per lb
Volatile oil[1]	0.5% min
Moisture[2]	12.0% max
Ash[1]	15.0% max
Acid insoluble ash[1]	2.5% max
Average bulk index-imported (mg/100 g)	495
Military specifications (EE-S-631J, 1981)	<3% by weight of stems, excluding petioles

[1] These are suggested limits that the authors put together from the data collected over the past 5 years. These numbers are equivalent to the level where most quality spice will fall into.
[2] ASTA suggested maximum moisture level.

Table 4.8 Ground Basil: Chemical and Physical Specifications.

Specification	Suggested Limits
FDA DALs	None
Volatile oil[1]	0.5% min
Moisture[1]	12.0% max
Total ash[1]	15.0% max
Acid insoluble ash[1]	2.5% max
Military specifications (EE-S-631J, 1981)	
Volatile oil (ml/100 g)	trace
Moisture	11.0% max
Total ash	6.0% max
Acid insoluble ash	2.0% max
Granulation	95% min through a U.S.S. #35
Bulk index[2] (ml/100 g)	230

[1] These are suggested limits that the authors put together from the data collected in the past 5 years. These numbers are equivalent to the level where most quality spice will fall into.
[2] Average bulk index. Granulation will effect number.

Table 4.9 Nutritional Composition of Basil Leaves Per 100 Grams.

Composition	USDA Handbook 8-2[1] (Ground)	ASTA[2]
Water (grams)	6.43	6.0
Food energy (Kcal)	251	325
Protein (grams)	14.37	12.0
Fat (grams)	3.98	3.6
Carbohydrates (grams)	60.96	61.7
Ash (grams)	14.27	16.7
Calcium (grams)	2.11	2.1
Phosphorus (mg)	490	470
Sodium (mg)	34	40
Potassium (mg)	3,433	3,700
Iron (mg)	42	42.8
Thiamine (mg)	0.148	0.15
Riboflavin (mg)	0.316	0.32
Niacin (mg)	6.948	6.9
Ascorbic acid (mg)	61.22	61
Vitamin A activity (RE)	938	1,500

[1] Composition of Foods: Spices and Herbs. USDA Agricultural Handbook 8-2. January 1977.
[2] The Nutritional Composition of Spices, ASTA Research Committee, February, 1977.

4.3.4 Countries of Origin

4.3.4.1 Quality Differences

Basil is one of the spices which does have definite quality differences from one origin to another. Egyptian basil is generally darker gray in color and has more stems and other foreign material present than its domestic counterpart. It is mintier and harsher in flavor, but also more typical of basil. Basil grown in the United States is much more uniform in color and size. It is primarily grown in California. Domestic basil is available in various leaf sizes: fine cut (about $1/16$ in.), medium cut (about $1/8$ in.) and coarse cut (about $1/4$ in.). Domestic basil is also a physically and microbiologically cleaner product, one reason being that it is mechanically dried rather than air or sun dried, and then milled to the specific cut. You do pay for the higher quality, however. It is about 3 times the cost of Egyptian basil. If using a whole product for appearance, especially in cases where the bulk index is important, domestic is the product of choice since it is much more uniform in size and more attractive in appearance. If using basil in the ground form for flavor, it is much more economical and desirable to use the Egyptian product. Ground domestic basil is usually produced from basil stems. French basil is seldom used in the industrial market in the United States. French basil only accounted for about 2.7% of the imported basil in 1991. It is a higher priced product than Egyptian without being of significantly higher quality.

4.3.4.2 Harvest Times

Egyptian basil is harvested in June through September. Domestic basil has a long harvest season, from June to December. French basil is harvested in September and October.

4.3.5 Commercial Uses

Basil is used primarily in Italian dishes. It is a common flavor in tomato sauces, ricotta cheese mixes, and is the major flavor in pesto sauce. The essential oil and oleoresin are available, however, their use is limited due to the high cost; basil has such low volatile oil that producing the essential oil or oleoresin is expensive.

4.4 Bay Leaves (*Laurus nobilis* L.)

4.4.1 Background Information

Bay leaves, also known as laurel leaves, are native to the Mediterranean countries. Bay leaves are large, light to olive green elliptical leaves about 8 cm long and 3–4 cm wide. They are harvested by hand from evergreen trees and dried in shallow layers in the shade. The leaves have a tendency to curl and therefore are often pressed with boards to prevent this.[7]

Bay leaves were made into crowns for victorious athletes and scholars to wear in ancient Greece. In Biblical times, during the Roman Empire, and also in the Middle Ages, people associated bay leaves with goodness and saw it as a protection against evil.

4.4.2 Chemical and Physical Specifications

Bay leaves contain about 1.5%–2.5% volatile oil. The major component is cineole.[8] Oleoresin bay contains about 4%–8% volatile oil. An essential oil of bay is also available. The moisture limit set by ASTA for bay leaves is 9.0%. Ground bay moisture is usually under 7%, if ground ambiently. The major defect present in bay leaves are sticks, which may be as large as small branches when imported into the United States. When purchasing whole bay leaves as a spice processor, they are available in various forms: select, semi-select, and grinding quality. Broken leaves are considered a defect as well as holes which may be present in the leaves and can be indicative of infestation. The broken leaves are used by spice processors for grinding. Ash and acid insoluble ash levels should be kept to about 4% and 0.8%, respectively, in good quality bay leaves. See Tables 4.10 and 4.11 for a summary of typical chemical specifications for whole and ground bay leaves, including the FDA DALs for the whole leaves. Table 4.12 outlines the nutritional data for bay.

Table 4.10   Whole Bay (Laurel Leaves): Chemical and Physical Specifications.

Specification	Suggested Limits
ASTA cleanliness specifications:	
Whole dead insects, by count	2
Mammalian excreta, by mg/lb	1
Other excreta, by mg/lb	10.0
Mold, % by weight	2.00
Insect defiled/infested, % by weight	2.50
Extraneous, % by weight	0.50
FDA DALs:	
Moldy pieces by weight	Ave of 5%
or	
Insect infested pieces by weight	Ave of 5%
or	
Mammalian excreta, after process-ing	Ave of 1 mg per lb
Volatile oil[1]	1.5% min
Moisture[2]	9.0% max
Ash[1]	4.0% max
Acid insoluble ash[1]	0.8% max
Military specifications (EE-S-631J, 1981)	Max 3% of stems by weight excluding petioles
Average bulk index (mg/100 g)	N/A

[1]   These are suggested limits that the authors put together from the data collected over the past 5 years. These numbers are equivalent to the level where most quality spice will fall into.
[2]   ASTA suggested maximum moisture level.

Table 4.11 Ground Bay: Chemical and Physical Specifications.

Specification	Suggested Limits
FDA DALs	None
Volatile oil[1]	1.0% min
Moisture[1]	9.0% max
Total ash[1]	4.0% max
Acid insoluble ash[1]	0.8% max
Military specifications (EE-S-631J, 1981)	
Volatile oil (ml/100 g)	1.0 min
Moisture	7.0% max
Total ash	4.5% max
Acid insoluble ash	0.5% max
Granulation	95% min through a U.S.S. #30
Bulk index[2] (ml/100 g)	220

[1] These are suggested limits that the authors put together from data collected in the past 5 years. These numbers are equivalent to the level where most quality spice will fall into.
[2] Average bulk index. Granulation will effect number.

Table 4.12 Nutritional Composition of Bay Leaves Per 100 Grams.

Composition	USDA Handbook 8-2[1] (Crumbled)	ASTA[2]
Water (grams)	5.44	4.5
Food energy (Kcal)	313	410
Protein (grams)	7.61	7.5
Fat (grams)	8.36	8.8
Carbohydrates (grams)	74.96	75.4
Ash (grams)	3.62	3.7
Calcium (grams)	0.83	1.0
Phosphorus (mg)	113	110
Sodium (mg)	23	20
Potassium (mg)	529	600
Iron (mg)	43	53.3
Thiamine (mg)	.009	0.10
Riboflavin (mg)	.421	0.42
Niacin (mg)	2.005	2.0
Ascorbic acid (mg)	46.53	47
Vitamin A activity (RE)	618	618

[1] Composition of Foods: Spices and Herbs. USDA Agricultural Handbook 8-2. January 1977.
[2] The Nutritional Composition of Spices, ASTA Research Committee, February, 1977.

4.4.3 Import Tonnage

Bay leaves are imported primarily from Greece and Turkey. The import tonnage in 1991 is not available from the USDA since the figures actually combine bay leaves and thyme.

4.4.4 Countries of Origin

4.4.4.1 Quality Differences

The quality of bay leaves from different sources is basically equivalent. No real difference in volatile oil content or leaf quality is obvious. The only product difference is in the case of the domestic versus the imported product. Domestic bay leaves are darker green, longer and more narrow than their imported counterpart. The flavor is somewhat different. Domestic bay leaves are not really seen in the industrial market. One company does pack them for the retail and foodservice market.

4.4.4.2 Harvest Times

Both Greek and Turkish bay leaves are harvested during the same time period: August and September.

4.4.5 Commercial Uses

Bay leaves are not generally used in the whole form in the food industry. They are primarily used in this form, however, in the retail and foodservice trades. Bay leaves are a large component in pickling spices in the processed meats and pickle industry; however, bay leaves are generally in the crushed form, about $1/8-1/4$ in. in size. Ground bay is utilized in many seasoning blends and products, most often flavoring soups, stews, gravies, and meats, usually as a background flavor. Oil of bay and oleoresin bay are used in soluble pickling spices, very often in the production of corned beef.

4.5 Capsicum Spices (*Capsicum annuum* and *Capsicum frutensens* among others)

4.5.1 Background Information

The group of spices belonging to the Genus *Capsicum* are numerous. Capsicums include paprika, chili pepper, red pepper (cayenne), and bell peppers, although the latter is commonly considered and eaten as a vegetable and will not be covered in this section. The capsicums within each category also vary tremendously and the species designation is not always cut-and-dried. As a general rule, paprika belongs to the *Capsicum annuum* L. species and the red peppers and chili peppers belong to the *Capsicum frutescens* L. species.

Paprika is the ground product from the mild or sweet varieties of capsicum. Red peppers are blends of different varieties of the more pungent peppers and are sold on the basis of heat value. Red peppers vary tremendously in heat value, size, and shape. They are available ground, crushed, and whole (generally only for foodservice and for pickling spices). The term cayenne is no longer used industrially and is usually only seen in foodservice and retail products. There is no standard heat value for cayenne pepper. Purchasing red pepper on the basis of heat value results in a more consistent product.

Chili pepper is ground from larger and milder peppers usually grown in the southwestern United States and Mexico. They can be caramelized during the drying process to produce varying flavors and colors ranging from a bright red to a dark brown.

The capsicum spices are indigenous to the Western Hemisphere. Christopher Columbus found capsicum peppers in the New World and wrote about them in his journals. Capsicums were eaten by the Indians as far back as 7000 B.C., the remains of which were found in archeological sites in Mexico.[1] The plants were taken back to Europe and they spread to Asia and Africa within 150 years.[7] From these first plants come all the varieties known today. Different climates, soil conditions, and through breeding selection, capsicums with a variety of pungency, shape, and color appeared.

4.5.2 Chemical and Physical Specifications

The ASTA recommended maximum moisture level is 11% in all capsicum peppers. Peppers are very susceptible to surface mold contamination during harvesting and drying.

Volatile oil content is low in all capsicums and is not considered a specification. The pungency for the red peppers and the color value for the paprikas are the most important parameters when choosing a product. Ash and acid insoluble ash levels generally remain below 8% and 1% for red pepper and 8% and 3% for paprika.

See Tables 4.13 to 4.15 for typical chemical and physical specification levels for whole and ground chilies and paprika. Nutritional information for the capsicums can be found in Tables 4.16 through 4.18.

4.5.2.1 Paprika

The pigment responsible for the red color in capsicum peppers is capsanthin. It is a carotenoid present in all capsicums; however, it is the important buying factor in paprika. Other carotenoids present are capsorubin, zeaxanthin, lutein, kryptoxanthin, and alpha and beta carotene.[16] The pigment content increases as the fruit ripens and continues after maturity. The seeds of the paprika pod do not contain color. Color retention during storage is influenced by light and temperature. The higher the temperature in which the product is stored, the faster the loss of pigment in paprika. Refrigerated storage is desirable if the product is to be kept for an extended length of time. Another factor influencing color retention is the moisture level of the spice itself. Too low a moisture content can cause the color to fade. Optimum moisture content is considered to be 12%.[1] The color value of paprika is

Table 4.13   Whole Capsicum Pods (Chilies): Chemical and Physical Specifications.

Specification	Suggested Limits
ASTA cleanliness specifications:	
Whole dead insects, by count	4
Mammalian excreta, by mg/lb	1
Other excreta, by mg/lb	8.0
Mold, % by weight	3.00
Insect defiled/infested, % by weight	2.50
Extraneous, % by weight	0.50
FDA DALs:	
Insect infested and/or moldy pods by weight or	Ave of 3%
Mammalian excreta per pound, identified as to source when possible	Ave of 1 mg
Volatile oil	N/A
Moisture[1]	11.0% max
Ash	8.0% max
Acid insoluble ash	1.0% max

[1] ASTA suggested maximum moisture level.

usually expressed in ASTA color value. This is the extractable color present in the paprika. Surface color does not determine the amount of color contributed to a food product. If there are two paprikas and one looks redder than the other, it may actually have less extractable color. The extractable color is that which will show up in a finished food product. Common paprika ASTA colors available in the industry are 85, 100, 120, and 150. Color can also be expressed in Color Units which are 40 times the ASTA color. The latter is generally used to describe the oleoresin paprika products. For example, oleoresins are available in 40,000, 80,000, and 100,000 Color Units as a general rule. This translates to 1,000, 2,000, and 2,500 ASTA color values. Oleoresins are extracted to produce 100,000 or greater color unit products which are then blended down to the lower concentrations for ease of use in food plants and to standardize the color to a known common value.

4.5.2.2 Red Pepper (Cayenne)

The pungent component of red peppers is capsaicin (8-methyl-N-vanillyl-6-enamide). It is a white crystalline substance which is insoluble in water, and perceptible in dilutions of 1 in 15–17 million.[17] It does not have any taste or odor of its own. The level of capsaicin varies widely in capsicum peppers, from less than 0.05% in paprika to 0.1% in the mildly pungent types to as high as 1.3% in the hottest chilies.[1] In practice, the level of pungency is determined by the Scoville heat unit method, an organoleptic test for determining pungency of red peppers, or the

Table 4.14   Ground Capsicum (Not Including Paprika):
Chemical and Physical Specifications.

Specification	Suggested Limits
FDA DALs (6 subsamples):	
Insect fragments	Ave of 50 or more/25 grams
or	
Rodent hairs	Ave of 6 or more/25 grams
or	
Howard mold count	Ave of 20%
Volatile oil	N/A
Moisture	11.0% max
Total ash	8.0% max
Acid insoluble ash	1.0% max
Military specifications (EE-S-631J, 1981) for *crushed* red pepper	
Volatile oil (ml/100 g)	N/A
Moisture	10.0% max
Total ash	8.0% max
Acid insoluble ash	1.0% max
Granulation	98% min through a U.S.S. #4
	85% min through a U.S.S. #8
	95% min on a U.S.S. #20
Scoville Pungency	30,000–55,000
Bulk index[1]—ground (ml/100 g)	200
—crushed	235

[1]   Average bulk index. Granulation will effect number.

HPLC method to determine the same. See Chapter 3 for a description of these two methods. The Scoville heat values for red peppers available industrially are generally 20,000, 40,000, and 60,000. The Scoville heat for a specific red pepper variety as grown ranges from about 10,000 to 120,000. The different heat value peppers are then blended to produce a specific product. As a general rule, the higher the heat value, the lower the red surface color of the ground red pepper.

An oleoresin is an extract of red pepper with a very concentrated pungency. The products available industrially are usually 200,000, 500,000, and 1 million Scoville Heat Units. They are extracted in a concentrated form and blended down to produce a product which is less concentrated and easier to use. Oleoresins can be blended with oil to keep them decolorized, but are sometimes blended with paprika extractive to increase the red color.

Other capsaicinoids present in red peppers also contribute to the pungency of the same, the second highest percent being dihydrocapsaicin.[1] Analytical methods usually fail to take other compounds which contribute pungency into account, and therefore do not measure total pungency. Organoleptic methods, however, measure

Table 4.15 Ground Capsicum (Paprika): Chemical and Physical Specifications.

Specification	Suggested Limits
FDA DALs (6 subsamples):	
Insect fragments	Ave of 75 or more/25 grams
or	
Rodent hairs	Ave of 11 or more/25 grams
or	
Howard mold count	Ave of 16%
Volatile oil	N/A
Moisture	11.0% max
Total ash	8.0% max
Acid insoluble ash	3.0% max
Military specifications	
(EE-S-631J, 1981)	
Volatile oil (ml/100 g)	N/A
Moisture	12.0% max
Total ash	10.5% max
Acid insoluble ash	2.5% max
Granulation	95% min through a U.S.S. #30
Extractable color	110
Bulk index[1] (ml/100 g)	160

[1] Average bulk index. Granulation will effect number.

Table 4.16 Nutritional Composition of Red Pepper Per 100 Grams.

Composition	USDA Handbook 8-2[1]	ASTA[2]
Water (grams)	8.05	6.0
Food energy (Kcal)	318	420
Protein (grams)	12.01	16.0
Fat (grams)	17.27	15.5
Carbohydrates (grams)	56.63	54.3
Ash (grams)	6.04	8.0
Calcium (grams)	.148	0.1
Phosphorus (mg)	293	320
Sodium (mg)	30	10
Potassium (mg)	2,014	2,100
Iron (mg)	7.80	9.9
Thiamine (mg)	.328	.520
Riboflavin (mg)	.919	.930
Niacin (mg)	8.701	13.6
Ascorbic acid (mg)	76.44	29
Vitamin A activity (RE)	4,161	3,140

[1] Composition of Foods: Spices and Herbs. USDA Agricultural Handbook 8-2. January 1977.
[2] The Nutritional Composition of Spices, ASTA Research Committee, February, 1977.

Table 4.17 Nutritional Composition of Paprika Per 100 Grams.

Composition	USDA Handbook 8-2[1]	ASTA[2]
Water (grams)	9.54	7.0
Food energy (Kcal)	289	390
Protein (grams)	14.76	14.0
Fat (grams)	12.95	10.4
Carbohydrates (grams)	55.74	60.3
Ash (grams)	7.02	8.6
Calcium (grams)	.177	0.2
Phosphorus (mg)	345	300
Sodium (mg)	34	20
Potassium (mg)	2,344	2,400
Iron (mg)	23.59	23.1
Thiamine (mg)	.645	.600
Riboflavin (mg)	1.743	1.360
Niacin (mg)	15.32	15.3
Ascorbic acid (mg)	71.12	59
Vitamin A activity (RE)	6,060	5,800

[1] Composition of Foods: Spices and Herbs. USDA Agricultural Handbook 8-2. January 1977.
[2] The Nutritional Composition of Spices, ASTA Research Committee, February, 1977.

the pungency perceived, which would be the total of all components contributing to the heat level. Organoleptic methods such as the Scoville Heat Unit are difficult to reproduce between laboratories. Pungency levels vary in the same variety, by geographical region, and in maturity levels. Purseglove et al.[1] give a good review of capsicum sources and relative capsaicin contents.

Table 4.18 Nutritional Composition of Chili Pepper Per 100 Grams.

Composition	ASTA[1]
Water (grams)	6.5
Food energy (Kcal)	415
Protein (grams)	14.0
Fat (grams)	14.1
Carbohydrates (grams)	58.2
Ash (grams)	7.2
Calcium (grams)	0.1
Phosphorus (mg)	320
Sodium (mg)	10
Potassium (mg)	2,100
Iron (mg)	9.9
Thiamine (mg)	.590
Riboflavin (mg)	1.660
Niacin (mg)	14.2
Ascorbic acid (mg)	64
Vitamin A activity (RE)	5,180

[1] The Nutritional Composition of Spices, ASTA Research Committee, February, 1977.

Capsaicin does not seem to be present in the seeds of peppers, although there is still some controversy over this, and is higher in the fleshy part than in the pericarp portion of the pepper. Further information in this area is given in an excellent review by Maga.[16]

4.5.2.3 Chili Pepper

Chili pepper is the dried ground product of the milder peppers generally grown in the American Southwest and Mexico. The two types of chilies used for chili peppers are Ancho and Anaheim peppers. Chili pepper is usually a blended product of different chilies to get the exact flavor profile and color desired. Chili peppers are often caramelized to get a burnt flavor note and a surface browned color. They are available in a wide variety of products, from a bright red to a deep brown. Common heat values for chili pepper are mild, about 1,000 Scoville heat units. Surface color is the most important color factor for this type of pepper.

Chili powder is a blend of chili pepper with salt, red pepper, cumin, oregano, and garlic and onion. This seasoning will be discussed in Chapter 7.

4.5.3 Import Tonnage

Capsicums are either imported or grown domestically. The hottest varieties of red peppers come from Africa, India, China, and Pakistan. Paprika is generally imported from Hungary and Spain or grown domestically in California. Chili peppers are grown domestically, mainly in New Mexico and in Mexico. Table 4.19 gives total imports for the capsicums.

4.5.4 Countries of Origin

4.5.4.1 Quality Differences

Paprika: Paprika is either grown domestically or imported most commonly from Spain, Morocco, and Hungary. In recent years, the quality and consistency of the domestic paprika has exceeded that of the imported. All paprika, whether imported or produced domestically, is ground at the source, versus other spices which are shipped whole and ground by spice processors in the United States.[18] Historically, Hungarian paprika has been known for its high quality. Now the U.S. produces the most consistent paprika. The surface color of domestic paprika is usually a deeper red than its Hungarian and Spanish counterparts. Domestic paprika is also unique in the fact that the fruits are usually diced before mechanical drying, and then ground. Spanish and Hungarian paprika are dried in the whole form and then ground. Many manufacturers are now also mechanically drying paprika both in Spain and Hungary. The advantage of the domestic source of paprika is the fact that it is not subject to price increases due to political upheaval, as well as the fact that the product is extremely consistent due to the technological advances of the domestic industry. At one point, Spanish paprika became very expensive, was hard to get, and was not consistent. Hungarian paprika has been difficult to get in recent years.

Table 4.19 Volume of Capsicums Imported and Grown Domestically
              (In Millions of Pounds).

	Paprika	Capsicum: Anaheim & Ancho	Capsicum: Other Whole
Domestic (1990 Data)	21.0 100% California	101.7 21.9% New Mexico 8.1% California	Unavailable
Imported (1990 Data)	9.1 46.4% Spain 14.7% Hungary 12.8% Mexico 12.2% Morrocco	3.3 96.2% Mexico	25.8 30.4% China 23.7% India 16.2% Mexico 14.0% Pakistan

Red pepper: Many red peppers are imported into the United States; however, the finish grinding and blending is done on a large scale in California. Since the pungency varies so much from origin, variety, and even from crop to crop, it has become common practice for manufacturers to buy imported chilies and grind to blend their own red pepper. The domestic producers also grow some of their own milder red peppers for blending, and dry them artificially, although some smaller growers still sun dry. The imported peppers are sun dried.

   Chili pepper: Most chili pepper production for domestic use is done in the United States. Ancho and Anaheim chilies are grown in New Mexico and Mexico, artificially dried and ground in the United States. The quality and consistency of these products is very high.

4.5.4.2 Harvest Times

Imported paprika (Hungarian and Spanish) is harvested in August to September. Domestic is harvested in October through December. Red peppers from India are harvested in two different growing seasons, March through April and September through October. Chinese chilies are harvested from August through December. Those imported from Turkey and Pakistan, as well as those grown in the United States are harvested in the fall.

4.5.5 Commercial Uses

Red pepper is used in a large variety of products, often in the meat and pickling industry in the form of crushed red pepper or ground red pepper. Any product that has some heat or pungency uses red pepper, generally in the ground form or as oleoresins such as in processed meats, snack foods, and sauces. The list is endless.

   Paprika is used even more extensively. Since it has a bright red color with an extremely mild flavor, it is used whenever a red to orange color is desired such as in processed meats, snack foods, sauces, gravies, salad dressings, and entrees. Chili pepper is used primarily in the manufacture of chili powder, but is also used alone in foods with a Mexican or Southwest flavor.

4.6 Caraway Seed (*Carum carvi* L.)

4.6.1 Background Information

Caraway seed is the fruit of an herb of the parsley family. Each seed is a half of the fruit and is about 0.5 cm long, tan to brown, and curved with five lighter colored ridges along the length of the seed. Caraway is native to Europe and Western Asia. It has been used and cultivated in Europe since the Middle Ages.[7]

4.6.2 Chemical and Physical Specifications

Caraway seeds can contain about 1.5%–3.5% volatile oil. The main component of the essential oil is carvone, at about 50%–60%. The flavor closely resembles dill seed, which also contains carvone in high levels. Caraway also contains limonene, dihydrocarvone, dihydrocarveol, carveol, acetaldehyde, methyl alcohol, furfural, and diacetyl.[3] An essential oil is commercially available, although an oleoresin is common not.

ASTA suggested moisture limits are 11% maximum. Ash and acid insoluble ash are generally less than 6% and often less than 0.5%, respectively. More information on chemical and physical specifications, including the FDA DALs for whole caraway can be found in Tables 4.20 and 4.21. Nutritional composition is listed in Table 4.22.

Table 4.20 Whole Caraway: Chemical and Physical Specifications.

Specification	Suggested Limits
ASTA cleanliness specifications:	
Whole dead insects, by count	4
Mammalian excreta, by mg/lb	3
Other excreta, by mg/lb	10.0
Mold, % by weight	1.00
Insect defiled/infested, % by weight	1.00
Extraneous, % by weight	0.50
FDA DALs (Condimental seed):	
Adulteration with Mammalian excreta	Ave of 3 mg per lb
Volatile oil[1]	1.5% min
Moisture[2]	11.0% max
Ash[1]	6.0% max
Acid insoluble ash[1]	0.5% max
Average bulk index (mg/100 g)	180

[1] These are suggested limits that the authors put together from the data collected over the past 5 years. These numbers are equivalent to the level where most quality spice will fall into.
[2] ASTA suggested maximum moisture level.

Table 4.21   Ground Caraway: Chemical and Physical Specifications.

Specification	Suggested Limits
FDA DALs	None
Volatile oil[1]	1.0% min
Moisture[1]	11.0% max
Total ash[1]	6.0% max
Acid insoluble ash[1]	0.5% max
Military specifications (EE-S-631J, 1981)	
Volatile oil (ml/100 g)	2.0 min
Moisture	10.0% max
Total ash	8.0% max
Acid insoluble ash	1.0% max
Granulation	95% min through a U.S.S. #30
Bulk index[2] (ml/100 g)	190

[1] These are suggested limits that the authors put together from data the authors collected in the past 5 years. These numbers are equivalent to the level where most quality spice will fall into.
[2] Average bulk index. Granulation will effect number.

Table 4.22   Nutritional Composition of Caraway Seed Per 100 Grams.

Composition	USDA Handbook 8-2[1] (Seed)	ASTA[2]
Water (grams)	9.88	6.0
Food energy (Kcal)	333	465
Protein (grams)	19.77	21.0
Fat (grams)	14.59	23.1
Carbohydrates (grams)	49.9	43.5
Ash (grams)	5.87	5.6
Calcium (grams)	.689	.70
Phosphorus (mg)	568	500
Sodium (mg)	17	20
Potassium (mg)	1,351	1,900
Iron (mg)	16.23	8.5
Thiamine (mg)	.383	.38
Riboflavin (mg)	.379	.38
Niacin (mg)	3.606	8.1
Ascorbic acid (mg)	—	ND[3]
Vitamin A activity (RE)	36	36

[1] Composition of Foods: Spices and Herbs. USDA Agricultural Handbook 8-2. January 1977.
[2] The Nutritional Composition of Spices, ASTA Research Committee, February, 1977.
[3] ND = Not detected.

4.6.3 Import Tonnage

Caraway is imported into the United States primarily from The Netherlands. The total amount of product imported to the U.S. in 1991 was 8.1 million pounds, 70.1% from The Netherlands, 15.6% from Hungary, and 3.5% each from Denmark and Egypt. The monetary value of caraway imported into the United States in 1991 was $2.9 million.[6]

4.6.4 Countries of Origin

4.6.4.1 Quality Differences

The Netherlands is the most well known source, but other countries do produce an equivalent quality product.

4.6.4.2 Harvest Times

Caraway is harvested during the summer months. The Netherlands generally harvests a few months later than Egypt.

4.6.5 Commercial Uses

Caraway is used in the whole form in rye and other specialty breads. It is often used in foods with an Eastern European heritage. Caraway seed is used whole in sauerkraut and pork roasts. Ground caraway seed is seldom used in the food industry, although it does find use in some specialty ethnic baked goods and in some sausages. The main food use of caraway oil is in the sausage industry.

4.7 Cardamom (*Elettaria cardamomum* Maton)

4.7.1 Background Information

Cardamom seed, the dried fruit of a plant of the ginger family, is unique since it is actually a seed pod containing 6–8 brown to black highly flavored irregular round seeds. The pod itself is green to light tan in color and about 2–3 cm long and 1 cm wide. The seeds contained within are about 0.25 cm in diameter. Whole cardamom is available in three forms according to Purseglove et al.[19]:

1. *Whole green cardamoms*—mature fruit picked when green and the color preserved by artificially drying.
2. *Whole tan colored cardamoms*—sun dried product, causing the green color to fade. Sun drying is also used when the crop matures too long and loses its green color before drying.
3. *Whole bleached cardamoms*—mature fruits picked tan and bleached with sulfur dioxide fumes. This product is a premium product, costing about 5 times the level of the whole green cardamoms.

Cardamom is also available to spice processors as a decorticated product. This is undesirable since it will lose its volatile oil very quickly without the protective coating of the pod. Cardamom is native to Southern India and Ceylon. It is now also grown and exported from Guatemala. Most cardamom is sold ground in the United States. The whole pod containing the seeds is usually ground. In Middle Eastern countries where cardamom coffee is very popular, the whole green cardamom is the most desirable product. The green pods suggest freshness since they will fade to tan as they age.

Cardamom too, has a long history. The Greeks imported it in 400 B.C. and by 100 A.D., India was exporting cardamom to the Romans.[7]

4.7.2 Chemical and Physical Specifications

Cardamom can contain between 2% and 10% essential oil, although a level of 3%–8% is more common. This is based on grinding the whole pod. The seeds contain the highest percent of volatile oil—about 11%. The pods contain only about 1%. The seeds are about 60%–80% by weight of the whole cardamom.[19] The volatile oil contains about 25%–40% of cineole, 30%–40% alpha-terpinyl acetate and about 1%–2% limonene. At least 15 other compounds have been identified[3] including linalyl acetate, linalool, borneol, alpha-terpineol, alpha-pinene, limonene, and myracene.[19]

The essential oil of cardamom is available, although it is not generally used in high quantities. An oleoresin of cardamom is available in the food industry and generally contains between 45% and 70% volatile oil.

ASTA recommends 12% maximum moisture in the whole pod. Ash levels normally range from 4% to 9% and acid insoluble ash can be as high as 2%. Recommended chemical and physical specifications of whole and ground cardamom can be found in Tables 4.23 and 4.24. Nutritional information is outlined in Table 4.25.

4.7.3 Import Tonnage

Cardamom is primarily imported into the U.S. from Guatemala and a small amount from India. The Guatemalan imports were 81% and the Indian imports were 8.5% of the 1991 total import tonnage of 370,000 pounds. The dollar value for this volume was about $650,000.[6]

4.7.4 Countries of Origin

4.7.4.1 Quality Differences

No significant quality differences are noted between different origins. There are two different types of cardamom: Malabar and Mysore which do have some quality differences, but both are native to India and should not provide much difference in a ground product.

4.7.4.2 Harvest Times

Cardamom is harvested in Guatemala and India from September to October.

Table 4.23 Whole Cardamom: Chemical and Physical Specifications.

Specification	Suggested Limits
ASTA cleanliness specifications:	
Whole dead insects, by count	4
Mammalian excreta, by mg/lb	3
Other excreta, by mg/lb	1.0
Mold, % by weight	1.00
Insect defiled/infested, % by weight	1.00
Extraneous, % by weight	0.50
FDA DALs	None
Volatile oil[1]	3.0% min
Moisture[2]	12.0% max
Ash[1]	10.0% max
Acid insoluble ash[1]	2.0% max
Average bulk index (mg/100 g)	
Bleached	320
Green	250

[1] These are suggested limits that the authors put together from the data collected over the past 5 years. These numbers are equivalent to the level where most quality spice will fall into.
[2] ASTA suggested maximum moisture level.

Table 4.24 Ground Cardamom: Chemical and Physical Specifications.

Specification	Suggested Limits
FDA DALs	None
Volatile oil[1]	3.0% min
Moisture[1]	12.0% max
Total ash[1]	10.0% max
Acid insoluble ash[1]	2.0% max
Military specifications	
(EE-S-631J, 1981)	
(Decorticated Cardamom)	
Volatile oil (ml/100 g)	3.0 min
Moisture	12.0% max
Total ash	7.0% max
Acid insoluble ash	3.0% max
Granulation	95% min through a U.S.S. #40
Bulk index[2] (ml/100 g)	190

[1] These are suggested limits that the authors put together from data the authors collected in the past 5 years. These numbers are equivalent to the level where most quality spice will fall into.
[2] Average bulk index. Granulation will effect number.

Table 4.25 Nutritional Composition of Cardamom Seed Per 100 Grams.

Composition	USDA Handbook 8-2[1] (Ground)	ASTA[2]
Water (grams)	8.28	8.0
Food energy (Kcal)	311	360
Protein (grams)	10.76	10.0
Fat (grams)	6.70	2.9
Carbohydrates (grams)	68.47	74.2
Ash (grams)	5.78	4.7
Calcium (grams)	.383	0.3
Phosphorus (mg)	178	210
Sodium (mg)	18	10
Potassium (mg)	1,119	1,200
Iron (mg)	13.97	11.6
Thiamine (mg)	.198	.18
Riboflavin (mg)	.182	.23
Niacin (mg)	1.102	2.3
Ascorbic acid (mg)	—	ND[3]
Vitamin A activity (RE)	trace	ND[3]

[1] Composition of Foods: Spices and Herbs. USDA Agricultural Handbook 8-2. January 1977.
[2] The Nutritional Composition of Spices, ASTA Research Committee, February, 1977.
[3] ND = Not detected.

4.7.5 Commercial Uses

Cardamom is used whole in the pod in pickling spices. The ground product is utilized in bakery products and in processed meats. It is not used to a large extent in the United States. It is, however, used extensively in the Middle Eastern countries, most often added whole to flavor coffee. In fact, prices on the world market fell dramatically in 1991 due to the lack of demand from the Middle East as a consequence of the Persian Gulf War.

4.8 Celery Seed (*Apium graveolens* L.)

4.8.1 Background Information

Celery seed is the fruit of an herb of the parsley family. The fruit itself is two united carpels which each produce a single seed. This seed is small, about 1–2 mm in length, oval, and greenish brown. The plant variety which produces celery seeds is not the same variety as common celery eaten as a vegetable in the United States. The seeds are from a wild celery species native to Europe, commonly called "small-age." Domestic celery seed is, however, produced from Pascal celery, the same which is eaten as a vegetable in the United States.[20] Domestic celery seed is seldom available industrially.

Celery has been used since the Greek and Roman periods, mostly as a medicinal plant.[7] Using celery seeds as a spice did not materialize until the early 1800s, usually as an ingredient in pickling spices.

4.8.2 Chemical and Physical Specifications

Celery contains 1.5%–3% volatile oil, primarily containing about 60%–70% d-limonene and 10%–20% β-selinene.[21] The characteristic celery odor is thought to be due to oxygenated compounds present in the oil (sedanolide and sedanonic acid anhydride).[3] Essential oil of celery seed is available; however, the most common extractive form is the oleoresin due to its fuller flavor. This product contains 12%–16% volatile oil.

ASTA suggested moisture levels are 10% maximum. Ash and acid insoluble ash should run under 10% and 2%, respectively. See Tables 4.26 and 4.27 for a summary of typical chemical and physical specifications including the FDA DAL's for whole celery. Table 4.28 outlines the available nutritional data for celery seed.

4.8.3 Import Tonnage

The total amount of celery imported into the United States for 1991 was 5.85 million pounds, 93% from India and 5.8% from China. The monetary value this represents is $1.9 million.[6]

Table 4.26 Whole Celery: Chemical and Physical Specifications.

Specification	Suggested Limits
ASTA cleanliness specifications:	
Whole dead insects, by count	4
Mammalian excreta, by mg/lb	3
Other excreta, by mg/lb	3.0
Mold, % by weight	1.00
Insect defiled/infested, % by weight	1.00
Extraneous, % by weight	0.50
FDA DALs (Condimental Seed):	
Adulteration with mammalian excreta	Ave of 3 mg per lb
Volatile oil[1]	1.5% min
Moisture[2]	10.0% max
Ash[1]	10.0% max
Acid insoluble ash[1]	2.0% max
Average bulk index (mg/100 g)	195

[1] These are suggested limits that the authors put together from the data collected over the past 5 years. These numbers are equivalent to the level where most quality spice will fall into.

[2] ASTA suggested maximum moisture level.

Table 4.27   Ground Celery: Chemical and Physical Specifications.

Specification	Suggested Limits
FDA DALs	None
Volatile oil[1]	1.0% min
Moisture[1]	10.0% max
Total ash[1]	10.0% max
Acid insoluble ash[1]	2.0% max
Military specifications (EE-S-631J, 1981)	
Volatile oil (ml/100 g)	2.0 min
Moisture	10.0% max
Total ash	14.0% max
Acid insoluble ash	2.0% max
Granulation	95% min through a U.S.S. #55
Nonvolatile ether extract	12.0% min
Bulk index[2] (ml/100 g)	190

[1]   These are suggested limits that the authors put together from data the authors collected in the past 5 years. These numbers are equivalent to the level where most quality spice will fall into.
[2]   Average bulk index. Granulation will effect number.

Table 4.28   Nutritional Composition of Celery Seed Per 100 Grams.

Composition	USDA Handbook 8-2[1] (Seed)	ASTA[2]
Water (grams)	6.04	5.0
Food energy (Kcal)	392	450
Protein (grams)	18.07	18.0
Fat (grams)	25.27	22.8
Carbohydrates (grams)	41.35	43.8
Ash (grams)	9.27	10.2
Calcium (grams)	1.767	1.8
Phosphorus (mg)	547	550
Sodium (mg)	160	170
Potassium (mg)	1,400	1,400
Iron (mg)	44.9	44.9
Thiamine (mg)	—	.41
Riboflavin (mg)	—	.49
Niacin (mg)	—	4.4
Ascorbic acid (mg)	17.14	17
Vitamin A activity (RE)	5	5

[1]   Composition of Foods: Spices and Herbs. USDA Agricultural Handbook 8-2. January 1977.
[2]   The Nutritional Composition of Spices, ASTA Research Committee, February, 1977.

4.8.4 Countries of Origin

4.8.4.1 Quality Differences

Celery seed is primarily imported from India but some is imported from China. Quality differences are not a factor in celery origins.

4.8.4.2 Harvest Times

Indian celery is harvested during the summer months and Chinese celery in October to December.

4.8.5 Commercial Uses

Celery seed is an ingredient in pickling spices. Ground celery is used in a large variety of products. Meat dishes, snack foods, gravies, and sauces all contain ground celery seed at low levels, providing a flavor enhancing effect. The oleoresin is also used in a large variety of food items. Chicken gravies, boullions, and soups would not taste like chicken without the inclusion of celery and/or its oleoresin.

4.9 Cinnamon and Cassia

4.9.1 Background Information

The most common species of cinnamon and cassia are listed below. All four are listed in the Code of Federal Regulations as GRAS (21 CFR 182.10):

Cinnamomum verum Presl (syn *Cinnamomum zeylanicum* Blume)
Cinnamomum cassia Presl
Cinnamomum loureirii Nees
Cinnamomum burmannii Blume

Cinnamon and cassia have a long history. Rosengarten[7] states that this spice was mentioned numerous times in the Bible, most notably in Exodus 30:23–25 and Ezekiel 29:19. He also claims that the ancient Egyptians imported cinnamon for embalming and the Chinese used cinnamon close to 2700 years B.C. These historical references have now been brought under scrutiny by Purseglove et al.[1]

Cinnamon and cassia are the bark of evergreen trees; however, there are multiple species of the trees. In the past, cinnamon and cassia have been separated into two distinct species: *C. verum* as cinnamon and the *C. cassia, C. loureirii,* and *C. burmannii* species representing cassia. In order to avoid confusion, this book will refer to each species by their botanical name rather than as "cassia" or "cinnamon" since each does have their own unique characteristics. These species are the products that are most commonly in commercial trade. Many other species are available, although not to any extent in international trade. Both cinnamon and cassia species can be called cinnamon in the United States. This book will use the two terms interchangeably. Other countries mandate one name or the other in labeling. Cinnamon and cassia are reddish brown to tan in color, depending on the species. The "whole" spice consists of long slender quills of bark.

Cassia is harvested by peeling off the bark on trees and allowing it to curl up in quills as it dries. Quills are graded, cut, and sold by size. It should be noted that as the bark curls up, insects can crawl inside. The pieces of whole cinnamon must therefore be cracked and checked for dead or live insects. The FDA DALs require cinnamon bark to contain an average of less than 5% insect infested pieces by weight.

Grinding quality cassia is the broken pieces of bark that come from small twigs and branches of the trees. This product looks like small chips of bark, anywhere from $1/8$ to 4 in. in length and about a $1/4$ to a $1/2$ in. in width.

4.9.2 Species Identification

4.9.2.1 *Cinnamomum verum* Presl

Cinnamomum verum Presl is known in the industry as Ceylon cinnamon, Seychelles cinnamon, or "true cinnamon." It is lighter in color and milder in flavor than the other varieties that will be discussed. This product is seldom imported into the United States, but is imported into Great Britain and other countries. Cinnamon leaf oil is derived from this species and is unique in that it contains eugenol (clove-like flavor) as its major constituent: 70%–90%. The cinnamic aldehyde (cinnamon-like flavor) content is very low: less than 5%. The other major species contain cinnamic aldehyde as the major component of the leaf oils. The bark oil of *C. verum* contains about 60% cinnamic aldehyde and 10% eugenol. Other components are eugenol acetate, and small amounts of aldehydes, ketones, alcohols, esters, and terpenes.

4.9.2.2 *Cinnamomum loureirii* Nees

Cinnamomum loureirii Nees is also known as Saigon or Vietnamese cassia. It is grown primarily in Vietnam and has not been a viable source for import into the United States since the Vietnamese War. Some cinnamon on the market is beginning to be called Saigon-type cinnamon, which is probably a *C. cassia* species. Saigon was once known in the industry for its premium quality product. This may explain the Saigon-type designation. *C. loureirii* contains cinnamic aldehyde as its major steam volatile oil constituent. In 1991 there was literally no product imported from Vietnam. Some may be coming into the United States, however, through other ports.

4.9.2.3 *Cinnamomum cassia* Presl

Cinnamomum cassia Presl is also known as Chinese cassia, Canton cassia, or a variety of other geographical designations in China. It is often described as having a sweeter flavor than the other varieties and can contain a very high volatile oil content. *C. cassia* is the source for cassia oil, which contains about 85%–90%

cinnamic aldehyde. The cinnamon leaf oil from this species also contains a high percent of cinnamic aldehyde.

4.9.2.4 *Cinnamomum burmannii* Blume

Cinnamomum burmannii Blume is also known as Korintji or Batavia cinnamon. It is grown in Indonesia, mainly on the island of Padang. This type of cinnamon is the most common product imported and sold in the United States today. It is a high-quality product, with volatile oils ranging from 1% to 3.5%. Korintje cinnamon is bought on the basis of volatile oil content. The higher the volatile oil, the higher the price. It is generally graded to A, B, and C grades, with A being the best quality and C being the poorest quality. Korintje A is the long quills taken from the main trunk of the tree. It usually has the highest volatile oil since it is taken from the thicker bark from lower parts of the tree. Korintje B is from side branches of the tree, and Korintje C is generally the broken pieces of the bark which has the lowest volatile oil content. Cinnamon sticks, or quills, are purchased by size: 12, 6, or 3 in. The small pieces of chips are bought to produce ground cinnamon. This product is usually from the small branches of the tree or broken pieces from when the quills are harvested and dried.

   C. burmannii Blume is distinguishable from other species since it has a high percent of mucilaginous substances or gums present. The level runs about 8%–9% versus 0.73%–2.9% of other species.[22] A quick method to determine mucilage content is to mix the cassia in question 1 to 1 with hot water. *C. burmannii* Blume will ball up and actually be able to be rolled into a ball, whereas the other species will simply produce a thick suspension of cinnamon.

4.9.3 Chemical and Physical Specifications

Cinnamon or cassia is purchased in the food industry on the basis of oil content. Three volatile oil specs are recommended: 1.5%–2.0%, 2.0%–2.5%, and 2.5%–3.0%, using the lower number in the range as minimums. The higher the oil content, the higher the price of the cinnamon. The heat of grinding is very destructive to volatile oil content of cinnamon. Cryogenic grinding, however, does retain more volatiles.[23] Components of the volatile oils were previously discussed under each species.

   The essential oil comes in three main forms: oil of cassia (from the bark), oil of cassia leaf, and, in a limited supply, oleoresin of cassia which can be derived from any of the species and usually contains 25%–40% volatile oil. Other cassia oils are available, usually as artificial cassia oil or cassia oil WONF (with other natural flavors). These products have some degree of added flavors to them.

   ASTA has set suggested moisture levels to be at 14% for all *Cinnamomum* species. Most good quality cinnamon should have ash and acid insoluble ash levels less than 5% and 1%, respectively. Insect fragment levels, mandated by the FDA DALs, must be less than 400 per 5 grams in the ground spice. Physical and chemical specifications, including FDA DALs for cinnamon can be found in Tables 4.29 and 4.30. Nutritional information can be found in Table 4.31.

Table 4.29   Whole Cassia or Cinnamon: Chemical and Physical Specifications.

Specification	Suggested Limits	
	Cassia	Cinnamon
ASTA cleanliness specifications:		
Whole dead insects, by count	2	2
Mammalian excreta, by mg/lb	1	1
Other excreta, by mg/lb	1.0	2.0
Mold, % by weight	5.00	1.00
Insect defiled/infested, % by weight	2.50	1.00
Extraneous, % by weight	0.50	0.50
FDA DALs (6 subsamples):		
Insect infested pieces by weight or	Ave of 5%	
Moldy pieces by weight or	Ave of 5%	
Mammalian excreta identified as to source when possible	1 mg per lb	
Volatile oil[1]	Varies by quality typical 1.5%–3.0%	
Moisture[2]	14.0% max	
Ash[1]	5.0% max	
Acid insoluble ash[1]	1.0% max	
Average bulk index (mg/100 g)	N/A	

[1]   These are suggested limits that the authors put together from the data collected over the past 5 years. These numbers are equivalent to the level where most quality spice will fall into.
[2]   ASTA suggested maximum moisture level.

4.9.4 Import Tonnage

The total amount of cinnamon and cassia imported to the United States in 1991 was 30.6 million pounds, with a monetary value of $26.3 million.[6] 90.3% was from Indonesia (*C. burmannii* or Korintje), 4.2% from Sri Lanka, and 3.8% from China (*C. cassia*).

4.9.5 Countries of Origin

This topic was covered under the species description section.

4.9.5.1 Harvest Times

C. cassia Presl is harvested in China in March and April. *C. burmannii* Blume is harvested in Indonesia year-round.

Table 4.30   Ground Cinnamon: Chemical and Physical Specifications.

Specification	Suggested Limits
FDA DALs (6 subsamples)	
Insect fragments	Ave of 400 or more/50 g
or	
Rodent hairs	Ave of 11 or more/50 g
Volatile oil[1]	Varies by Quality Typical 1.5%–3.0%
Moisture[1]	14.0% max
Total ash[1]	5.0% max
Acid insoluble ash[1]	1.0% max
Military specifications (EE-S-631J, 1981)	
Korintji cinnamon	
Volatile oil (ml/100 g)	1.5 min
Moisture	11.0% max
Total ash	5.0% max
Acid insoluble ash	2.0% max
Granulation	95% min through a U.S.S. #60
Bulk index[2] (ml/100 g)	165

[1]   These are suggested limits that the authors put together from data the authors collected in the past 5 years. These numbers are equivalent to the level where most quality spice will fall into.
[2]   Average bulk index. Granulation will effect number.

Table 4.31   Nutritional Composition of Cinnamon Per 100 Grams.

Composition	USDA Handbook 8-2[1] (data for *C. verum* & *C. cassia* combined)	ASTA[2]
Water (grams)	9.52	10.0
Food energy (Kcal)	261	355
Protein (grams)	3.89	4.5
Fat (grams)	3.18	2.2
Carbohydrates (grams)	79.85	79.8
Ash (grams)	3.55	3.5
Calcium (grams)	1.228	1.6
Phosphorus (mg)	61	50
Sodium (mg)	26	10
Potassium (mg)	500	400
Iron (mg)	38.07	4.1
Thiamine (mg)	.077	.14
Riboflavin (mg)	.14	.21
Niacin (mg)	1.30	1.9
Ascorbic acid (mg)	28.46	40
Vitamin A activity (RE)	26	26

[1]   Composition of Foods: Spices and Herbs. USDA Agricultural Handbook 8-2. January 1977.
[2]   The Nutritional Composition of Spices, ASTA Research Committee, February, 1977.

4.9.6 Commercial Uses

Whole cassia is available as 3, 6, or 12 in. quills, as chips, and as a ground product. The stick cinnamon is sold primarily to specialty foodservice and retail industries to be used in products like mulling spices. The chips are also used in tea infusions or spiced cider blends.

The ground cinnamon market is very large in the United States. Most of the cinnamon imported is ground. This product is sold on an industrial level for primarily baked goods: cinnamon rolls, danish, breads, muffins, cookies, etc. Cinnamon and cassia in baked goods must not be put in the dough if it is of the raised variety, but rather must be put between layers as in a cinnamon roll. The cinnamic aldehyde and/or eugenol present in the volatile oil of the spice are both antifungal agents and may destroy the yeast. Cinnamon leaf and cassia oils are used in processed meats, condiments such as ketchup, and also in bakery items.

Cassia may be adulterated, either declared or undeclared, with cinnamic aldehyde (artificial flavor) or with cassia oil (natural flavor) to bring the volatile oil to a higher level. This is a much more inexpensive way to get the cinnamon "bite" than with the natural cinnamon oil present in the spice. If this adulteration is suspected and is not labeled, the purchaser can have tests performed at an outside laboratory to determine volatile oil and percent cinnamic aldehyde.

4.9.6.1 Shelf Life and Storage Conditions

Cassia volatile oil is very volatile and is lost very quickly from the ground spice. Whole cinnamon does not lose its volatile oil as fast. When ground cinnamon is stored in bulk in an ambient warehouse, a good rule of thumb is 0.1% per month loss. If the product is stored in small containers in the laboratory, which are not air tight, a loss of 0.25%–0.5% per month is more realistic. This is one product which should be stored refrigerated or frozen in the laboratory setting to insure that the flavor stays the same over extended periods of time. If formulating a new item with cassia, this may be critical.

4.10 Cloves (*Eugenia caryophyllus* Thunb, or *Syzygium aromaticum*)

4.10.1 Background Information

Cloves are the dried unopened flower bud of an evergreen tree belonging to the Myrtle family and indigenous to the Moluccas or Spice Islands in what is now eastern Indonesia. The spice is brown and resembles a nail with a large round head. Cloves must be picked just before the flowers open to have the bud present. The spice is then typically sun dried.

Cloves were known to be a spice of commerce in Alexandria and Europe in the first few centuries A.D. From 800 A.D., cloves were an important import into Europe. The Portuguese controlled the trade in the Moluccas Islands from 1514 until the Dutch took over in 1605 and held the monopoly until the early 19th century when the clove crop became established in Zanzibar from tree seedlings smuggled out of the Moluccas Islands. A more detailed account of the history of this interesting spice can be found in Rosengarten[7] and Purseglove et al.[1]

4.10.2 Chemical and Physical Specifications

Whole cloves contain a high level of volatile oil, up to 20% by weight. This can cause difficulties in grinding. The ground spice is coarser than other spices and may lump due to the high oil content. The major component is eugenol, present in about 70%–90% of the whole spice. Three essential oils are available from this spice: clove bud oil, clove stem oil, and clove leaf oil. Each has a different chemical composition and flavor. Clove bud oil, the most expensive essential oil obtained from cloves is also the best quality product. It contains from 80%–90% eugenol up to 15% eugenol acetate and 5%–12% beta-caryophyllene. The yield extracted from the buds is about 17% by weight. Clove stem oil is the next best product. The eugenol content of this essential oil is 90%–95%. Eugenol acetate and beta-caryophyllene are present in lower amounts than in the bud oil. The yield extracted is about 5%–7% of the stem weight. Clove leaf oil is produced from the top branches of trees which have been trimmed. The oil distilled from this portion of the plant is of a low quality and is less expensive than the stem and bud oils. The yield from the leaves is under 2% and the principle component is also eugenol (80%–88%). An oleoresin is available and contains about 40%–60% volatile oil.

The ASTA recommended moisture limit on the whole spice is 8%. Ash and acid insoluble ash are usually less than 5% and less than 0.5%, respectively. See Tables 4.32 and 4.33 for a complete summary of suggested chemical and physical specifications including the FDA DALs. See Table 4.34 for the nutritional composition of cloves.

4.10.3 Import Tonnage

Cloves are primarily imported from Madagascar (58.2%) and Indonesia (11.8%). In the past, Brazil also exported significant amounts to the U.S. These imports dropped to virtually zero in 1991. The total amount imported into the United States in 1991 was 2.5 million pounds, with a monetary value of $2.2 million.[6]

4.10.4 Countries of Origin

4.10.4.1 Quality Differences

No significant differences in the quality of cloves is evident from various origins except for Brazilian which is slightly lower in volatile oil content and is not as attractive in appearance as the Madagascar clove.

4.10.4.2 Harvest Times

Cloves are harvested in September through December, depending on the origin.

Table 4.32 Whole Cloves: Chemical and Physical Specifications.

Specification	Suggested Limits
ASTA cleanliness specifications:	
Whole dead insects, by count	4
Mammalian excreta, by mg/lb	5
Other excreta, by mg/lb	8.0
Mold, % by weight	1.00
Insect defiled/infested, % by weight	1.00
Extraneous, % by weight	1.00
A 5% Allowance for unattached clove stems over and above the tolerance for other extraneous matter is permitted.	
FDA DALs:	
Adulteration	Ave of 5%
with stems by weight	
Volatile oil[1]	16.0% min
Moisture[2]	8.0% max
Ash[1]	5.0% max
Acid insoluble ash[1]	0.5% max
Military specification (EE-S-631J)	5% or more by weight of stems
Average bulk index (mg/100 g)	240

[1] These are suggested limits that the authors put together from the data collected over the past 5 years. These numbers are equivalent to the level where most quality spice will fall into.
[2] ASTA suggested maximum moisture level.

Table 4.33 Ground Cloves: Chemical and Physical Specifications.

Specification	Suggested Limits
FDA DALs	None
Volatile oil[1]	14.0% min
Moisture[1]	8.0% max
Total ash[1]	5.0% max
Acid insoluble ash[1]	0.5% max
Military specifications (EE-S-631J, 1981)	
Volatile oil (ml/100 g)	15.0 min
Moisture	9.0% max
Total ash	6.0% max
Acid insoluble ash	0.5% max
Granulation	95% min through a U.S.S. #30
Bulk index[2] (ml/100 g)	180

[1] These are suggested limits that the authors put together from data the authors collected in the past 5 years. These numbers are equivalent to the level where most quality spice will fall into.
[2] Average bulk index. Granulation will effect number.

Table 4.34   Nutritional Composition of Cloves Per 100 Grams.

Composition	USDA Handbook 8-2[1] (Ground)	ASTA[2]
Water (grams)	6.86	5.0
Food energy (Kcal)	323	430
Protein (grams)	5.98	6.0
Fat (grams)	20.06	14.5
Carbohydrates (grams)	61.22	68.8
Ash (grams)	5.88	5.0
Calcium (grams)	.646	.7
Phosphorus (mg)	105	110
Sodium (mg)	243	250
Potassium (mg)	1,102	1,200
Iron (mg)	8.68	9.5
Thiamine (mg)	.115	.11
Riboflavin (mg)	.267	ND[3]
Niacin (mg)	1.458	1.5
Ascorbic acid (mg)	80.81	81
Vitamin A activity (RE)	53	53

[1]   Composition of Foods: Spices and Herbs. USDA Agricultural Handbook 8-2. January 1977.

[2]   The Nutritional Composition of Spices, ASTA Research Committee, February, 1977.

[3]   ND = Not detected.

4.10.5   Commercial Uses

Cloves are used in the bakery industry and the processed meats industry as a ground spice. The whole clove is used at the consumer level primarily to stud baked hams and other meats. Ground clove is included with cinnamon and nutmeg in a number of pie recipes. It is used in the processed foods industry in pickling spices for meat and pickle products. The essential oil products are used primarily in the processed meat industry: they are essential components of wiener and bologna products.

4.11   Coriander (*Coriandrum sativum* L.)

4.11.1   Background Information

Coriander is an annual herb of the parsley family native to Europe and the Mediterranean region. From this plant comes two products: (1) coriander seed—the dried ripe fruit of the plant, and (2) cilantro—the leaf of the plant. Coriander seed is tan to light brown, and round with verticle ridges. The flavor of the seed is unpleasant during its growth stage; however, upon maturing it becomes aromatic and pleasant. Cilantro has a totally different flavor, almost soap-like in character.

Coriander has a long history. It is mentioned in the Bible in Exodus 16:31 and Numbers 11:7. Purseglove et al.[19] states that coriander was used in Egypt for both medicinal and culinary purposes as early as 1550 B.C. Rosengarten[7] mentions that coriander was introduced in the New World by the early colonists in the 1600s.

4.11.2 Chemical and Physical Specifications

Coriander seed contains 0.1%–1.5% volatile oil. The principle component is d-linalool, also known as coriandrol, present at about 60%–70%. Other compounds present include pinenes, terpinenes, geraniol, vorneal, and decylaldehyde.[3] Generally, the smaller the size of the coriander seed, the more volatile oil is present. Purseglove et al.[19] give a good review of the research done in this area, as well as the change in oil level and composition during maturation. Coriander leaf, or cilantro, contains about 4% volatiles, on a wet leaf basis, primarily 2-decenal (about 46%) and 2-dodecenal (about 10%). Up to 39 other components, mainly alkanals, 2-alkenals in the C9–C16 range, and 2-aldenols were found in a recent study.[24] Coriander oil and oleoresin from the seed are available quite readily in the U.S. The oleoresin contains 5%–10% volatile oil and is not used as often as the essential oil. A product sometimes used as a substitute for coriander oil is oil of rosewood which has similar flavor characteristics. Cilantro is not generally distilled into an oil or oleoresin.

ASTA recommended maximum moisture level in coriander seed is 9%. Ash usually runs about 5%–6% and acid insoluble ash is almost always less than 1%. See Tables 4.35 and 4.36 for a summary of the chemical and physical specifications for coriander seed, including FDA DALs, Table 4.37 for the nutritional composition for coriander and Table 4.38 for the nutritional composition for cilantro.

Table 4.35 Whole Coriander: Chemical and Physical Specifications.

Specification	Suggested Limits
ASTA cleanliness specifications:	
Whole dead insects, by count	4
Mammalian excreta, by mg/lb	3
Other excreta, by mg/lb	10.0
Mold, % by weight	1.00
Insect defiled/infested, % by weight	1.00
Extraneous, % by weight	0.50
FDA DALs (Condimental Seed):	
Adulteration ` with mammalian excreta	Ave of 3 mg per lb
Volatile oil[1]	0.3% min
Moisture[2]	9.0% max
Ash[1]	6.0% max
Acid insoluble ash[1]	1.0% max
Average bulk index (mg/100 g)	285

[1] These are suggested limits that the authors put together from the data collected over the past 5 years. These numbers are equivalent to the level where most quality spice will fall into.

[2] ASTA suggested maximum moisture level.

Table 4.36 Ground Coriander: Chemical and Physical Specifications.

Specification	Suggested Limits
FDA DALs	None
Volatile oil[1]	0.2% min
Moisture[1]	9.0% max
Total ash[1]	6.0% max
Acid insoluble ash[1]	1.0% max
Military specifications (EE-S-631J, 1981)	
Volatile oil (ml/100 g)	trace
Moisture	10.0% max
Total ash	7.0% max
Acid insoluble ash	1.0% max
Granulation	95% min through a U.S.S. #30
Bulk index[2] (ml/100 g)	200

[1] These are suggested limits that the authors put together from data the authors collected in the past 5 years. These numbers are equivalent to the level where most quality spice will fall into.
[2] Average bulk index. Granulation will effect number.

Table 4.37 Nutritional Composition of Coriander Seed Per 100 Grams.

Composition	USDA Handbook 8-2[1]	ASTA[2]
Water (grams)	8.86	6.0
Food energy (Kcal)	298	450
Protein (grams)	12.37	12.0
Fat (grams)	17.77	19.6
Carbohydrates (grams)	54.99	56.5
Ash (grams)	6.02	5.3
Calcium (grams)	.709	0.8
Phosphorus (mg)	409	440
Sodium (mg)	35	20
Potassium (mg)	1,267	1,200
Iron (mg)	16.32	5.9
Thiamine (mg)	.239	.26
Riboflavin (mg)	.290	.23
Niacin (mg)	2.130	3.2
Ascorbic acid (mg)	—	ND[3]
Vitamin A activity (RE)	Trace	ND[3]

[1] Composition of Foods: Spices and Herbs. USDA Agricultural Handbook 8-2. January 1977.
[2] The Nutritional Composition of Spices, ASTA Research Committee, February, 1977.
[3] ND = Not detected.

Table 4.38   Nutritional Composition of Cilantro Per 100 Grams.

Composition	USDA Handbook 8-2[1]
Water (grams)	7.3
Food energy (Kcal)	279
Protein (grams)	21.83
Fat (grams)	4.76
Carbohydrates (grams)	52.10
Ash (grams)	14.02
Calcium (grams)	1.246
Phosphorus (mg)	481
Sodium (mg)	211
Potassium (mg)	4,466
Iron (mg)	42.46
Thiamine (mg)	1.252
Riboflavin (mg)	1.500
Niacin (mg)	10.707
Ascorbic acid (mg)	566.7
Vitamin A activity (RE)	—

[1] Composition of Foods: Spices and Herbs. USDA Agricultural Handbook 8-2. January 1977. Supplement 1990.

4.11.3 Import Tonnage

Coriander is imported into the U.S. from a variety of countries. Exporting countries and their respective percentage of imports in 1991 include Morocco (38.6%), Canada (31.6%), Romania (11%), and Bulgaria (11%), among others. 1991 saw Canadian exports to the U.S. increase by 350%. Coriander is also grown in Russia, other parts of Europe, and India, although the export trade is not great. The total volume imported for 1991 was 5.4 million pounds with a monetary value of $1.4 million.[6]

4.11.4 Countries of Origin

4.11.4.1 Quality Differences

Generally, the quality and volatile oil content is much higher in the Russian and European coriander than in other varieties. The fruits of the product grown in these areas are smaller than those grown in India. Indian coriander contains a lower linalool content and a higher ester content than its European and Russian counterparts.[19] Most of the research has been done on Indian coriander since it is a large crop in that country; however, most is used internally and not much is available for export. The differences between corianders are academic, however, when choosing an origin. The product available on the U.S. market is primarily the lower volatile oil type. The Russian and European varieties are not available as a spice in the United States because they are used primarily for the distillation of coriander oil and oleoresin.

4.11.4.2 Harvest Times

Romanian, Moroccan, and Egyptian coriander are harvested in the summer months. Coriander grown in China is harvested in August and September. Cilantro is harvested in the United States in October through February.

4.11.5 Commercial Uses

Coriander seed and its extractives are used primarily in sausage items. It is a major component in bologna and wieners along with a large variety of other sausages. Coriander seed is often used in Mexican cooking and is a component of chili powders. In addition, coriander is essential in Indian cooking and is a major ingredient in curry powders and other Indian spice mixes such as garam masalas. Whole coriander is used in pickling spices, for meats and pickles. It can be cracked and is often used on pastrami, corned beef, and roast beef as a rub on the outside of the meat. Cilantro is used as a fresh and dried leaf herb in small amounts in Indian, Vietnamese, and Mexican cooking. It is gaining popularity and is currently an important flavor in salsas.

4.12 Cumin (*Cuminum cyminum* L.)

4.12.1 Background Information

Cumin is the dried ripe fruit of an annual herb of the parsley family. It is indigenous to Egypt and the Mediterranean region. The fruit, or seed as it is commonly called, is greenish tan, long and narrow with ridges down its length. Its appearance is similar to caraway; however, it is not curved. The flavor is warm and bitter, also often described as similar to caraway. This similarity is questionable, supported by the fact the essential oil components are so dissimilar.

Cumin was used in Biblical times; it is mentioned in Matthew 23:23 along with mint, anise, or dill and also in Isaiah 28:27. The interesting point to note in the latter verse is that the harvesting of cumin is mentioned. Rosengarten[7] states cumin was mentioned in a list of medicinal plants used in Egypt in Ebers Papyrus at about 1550 B.C.

4.12.2 Chemical and Physical Specifications

Cumin contains 2%–5% volatile oil, most commonly running between 2% and 3.5%. The major component is cumaldehyde (or cuminic aldehyde). Other compounds present include dihydrocuminaldehyde, cuminyl alcohol, *dl*-pinene, *p*-cumene, and dipentene.[3] A recent study found that cumin essential oil, held for 12 months, had only a small amount of deterioration; however, the deterioration that did occur was a decrease in cuminic aldehyde and an increase in terpinene, *b*-pinene, *P*-cymene, linalyl acetate, and cuminyl alcohol.[9]

Cumin essential oil is available and used in the food industry. The oleoresin is not used as much; however, it is available and contains a volatile oil content in the 7%–15% range.

The recommended moisture limit suggested by ASTA is 9%. Typical ash and acid insoluble ash levels are 5%–8% and 0.2%–1%, respectively. Chemical and physical specification suggestions, as well as the FDA DALs for whole cumin are available in Tables 4.39 and 4.40. One interesting thing to note is that the FDA DALs for cumin include ash and acid insoluble ash. This is due to common adulteration in this spice with sand and grit. The nutritional composition of cumin is listed in Table 4.41.

4.12.3 Import Tonnage

Cumin is imported from a wide variety of countries. It is grown all across the Middle East and India but is mainly exported to the U.S. from the Middle Eastern countries. Many countries grow and harvest cumin, but do not export to any appreciable amount since they use so much internally. The main countries exporting to the United States are Pakistan and Turkey. Iranian cumin was hard to get in the period

Table 4.39 Whole Cumin: Chemical and Physical Specifications.

Specification	Suggested Limits
ASTA cleanliness specifications:	
Whole dead insects, by count	4
Mammalian excreta, by mg/lb	3
Other excreta, by mg/lb	5.0
Mold, % by weight	1.00
Insect defiled/infested, % by weight	1.00
Extraneous, % by weight	0.50
Ash	9.5% max
Acid insoluble ash	1.5% max
FDA DALs:	
Adulteration with sand & grit	Ave of 9.5% ash and/or 1.5% AIA
Volatile oil[1]	2.5% min
Moisture[2]	9.0% max
Ash[1]	8.0% max
Acid insoluble ash[1]	1.0% max
Average bulk index (mg/100 g)	240
Military specification (EE-S-631J, 1981) Harmless extraneous vegetable matter	5% by weight

[1] These are suggested limits that the authors put together from the data collected over the past 5 years. These numbers are equivalent to the level where most quality spice will fall into.
[2] ASTA suggested maximum moisture level.

Table 4.40 Ground Cumin: Chemical and Physical Specifications.

Specification	Suggested Limits
FDA DALs	None
Volatile oil[1]	2.0% min
Moisture[1]	9.0% max
Total ash[1]	8.0% max
Acid insoluble ash[1]	1.0% max
Military specifications (EE-S-631J, 1981)	
Volatile oil (ml/100 g)	2.2 min
Moisture	9.0% max
Total ash	9.5% max
Acid insoluble ash	2.0% max
Bulk index[2] (ml/100 g)	185

[1] These are suggested limits that the authors put together from data the authors collected in the past 5 years. These numbers are equivalent to the level where most quality spice will fall into.

[2] Average bulk index. Granulation will effect number.

from 1979 to 1980 due to the Hostage Crisis, however, there were other sources that became available rather quickly. The United States imports virtually no Iranian cumin anymore. The total import data for the year 1991 was 8.85 million pounds with a monetary value of $5.5 million. The breakdown by country of origin is as follows: Pakistan 51.5%, Turkey 21.9%, China 8.9%, and India 6.6%.[6]

Table 4.41 Nutritional Composition of Cumin Seed Per 100 Grams.

Composition	USDA Handbook 8-2[1]	ASTA[2]
Water (grams)	8.06	6.0
Food energy (Kcal)	375	460
Protein (grams)	17.81	18.0
Fat (grams)	22.27	23.8
Carbohydrates (grams)	44.24	44.6
Ash (grams)	7.62	7.7
Calcium (grams)	.931	0.9
Phosphorus (mg)	499	450
Sodium (mg)	168	160
Potassium (mg)	1,788	2,100
Iron (mg)	66.35	47.8
Thiamine (mg)	.628	.730
Riboflavin (mg)	.327	.380
Niacin (mg)	4.579	2.5
Ascorbic acid (mg)	7.71	17
Vitamin A activity (RE)	127	127

[1] Composition of Foods: Spices and Herbs. USDA Agricultural Handbook 8-2. January 1977.

[2] The Nutritional Composition of Spices, ASTA Research Committee, February, 1977.

4.12.4 Countries of Origin

4.12.4.1 Quality Differences

Cumin is grown in a wide variety of countries. The quality is consistent from source to source. This spice is one which can be easily bought on chemical specifications without much regard to the origin.

4.12.4.2 Harvest Times

Cumin is harvested in March and April in India and in June and July in Iran and Turkey. Chinese cumin is harvested in August and September.

4.12.5 Commercial Uses

Cumin is used commercially to flavor many ethnic products. It is an essential component of Mexican foods, along with chili pepper and oregano. Cumin use is prevalent in many Latin American cuisines. Indian cooking also uses a large amount of cumin. It is an essential component of curries. Cumin is used to some extent in barbecue sauces and barbecue flavored snack foods. Generally, in these applications it provides a subtle background flavor note. Cumin is mainly used in the food industry in the ground form.

4.13 Dill Seed and Dill Weed (*Anethum sowa* and *Anethum graveolens* L.)

4.13.1 Background Information

Dill seed and dill weed both come from the same plant. It is an annual belonging to the parsley family, native to the Mediterranean region. The "seed" is the ripe fruit of the plant, actually formed by two united carpels. The "weed" is the leaves or greens of the plant. Dill seeds are oval and brown to tan. The flavor of this spice is similar to caraway: carvone is the main constituent of each. The dill seed currently being imported into the U.S. from India, however, is not *Anethum graveolens* but rather *Anethum sowa,* a species native to northern India. This type of dill is characterized by a larger, flatter tan colored seed with a yellow colored frame around the edge. This type of dill is typically imported into the U.S. as the whole seed.[25]

Dill is another spice which has its roots in early history. It is mentioned in Matthew 23:23 in the Bible and was cultivated by Greeks and Romans. This early history is based on the assumption that the term "aneth" referred to dill.[25] Dill is known to have been used extensively in the Middle Ages in England and the Scandinavian countries. In fact, the name dill comes from an Old Norse word, *dilla,* meaning "lull," since they used it to quiet crying babies.[7,25]

4.13.2 Chemical and Physical Specifications

Dill seed contains 2%–5% volatile oil, typically 2%–3%. Its main constituent is carvone, present at the 40%–50% level. Other components are d-limonene and phellandrene. A recent study, meant to identify odorants in dill seed and dill weed, also found eugenol and vanillin present in the seed.[26] Dill weed contains 0.3%–1.5% volatile oil, the chief constituent also being carvone. This explains the flavor similarity to caraway. The same study as previously mentioned, however, found that the chief odor constituents in dill weed are methyl 2-methylbutanoate, alpha-phellandrene, dill ether, and myristicin. Dill seeds are typically stronger in flavor than dill weed, due to the higher level of carvone present. Dill weed oil, dill seed oil, and oleoresin dill are all available. The weed oil is used most often, although it is weaker in carvone content than the seed oil. The oleoresin dill is also extracted from the seed, although it is not commonly used or available.

The ASTA recommended maximum moisture level in the whole dill seed is 10%. The dill weed moisture should be in the 10% range. Ash and acid insoluble ash for dill seed is 5%–8% and less than 1%, respectively. The chemical and physical suggested specifications for dill seed can be found in Tables 4.42 and 4.43 and for dillweed in Table 4.45. Nutritional information for the seed can be found in Table 4.44 and for the weed in Table 4.46.

4.13.3 Import Tonnage

Dill seed is mainly imported from India. In 1991, the total amount imported to the United States was 1.2 million pounds with a monetary value of about $475,000.[6] The United States imported 68.1% of its dill seed from India and 16.7% from Pakistan. Dill weed is generally imported from Egypt or grown domestically. The 1991 volumes are unavailable.

Table 4.42 Whole Dill Seed: Chemical and Physical Specifications.

Specification	Suggested Limits
ASTA cleanliness specifications:	
Whole dead insects, by count	4
Mammalian excreta, by mg/lb	3
Other excreta, by mg/lb	2.0
Mold, % by weight	1.00
Insect defiled/infested, % by weight	1.00
Extraneous, % by weight	0.50
FDA DALs (Condimental Seed):	
Adulteration with mammalian excreta	Ave of 3 mg per lb
Volatile oil[1]	2.5% min
Moisture[2]	10.0% max
Ash[1]	8.0% max
Acid insoluble ash[1]	1.0% max
Average bulk index (mg/100 g)	215

[1] These are suggested limits that the authors put together from the data collected over the past 5 years. These numbers are equivalent to the level where most quality spice will fall into.
[2] ASTA suggested maximum moisture level.

Table 4.43   Ground Dill Seed: Chemical and Physical Specifications.

Specification	Suggested Limits
FDA DALs	None
Volatile oil[1]	2.0% min
Moisture[1]	10.0% max
Total ash[1]	8.0% max
Acid insoluble ash[1]	1.0% max
Military specifications (EE-S-631J, 1981)	None
Bulk index[2] (ml/100 g)	190

[1]   These are suggested limits that the authors put together from data the authors collected in the past 5 years. These numbers are equivalent to the level where most quality spice will fall into.
[2]   Average bulk index. Granulation will effect number.

Table 4.44   Nutritional Composition of Dill Seed Per 100 Grams.

Composition	USDA Handbook 8-2[1]	ASTA[2]
Water (grams)	7.70	6.5
Food energy (Kcal)	305	435
Protein (grams)	15.98	13.0
Fat (grams)	14.53	17.9
Carbohydrates (grams)	55.17	56.4
Ash (grams)	6.62	6.0
Calcium (grams)	1.516	1.6
Phosphorus (mg)	277	210
Sodium (mg)	20	10
Potassium (mg)	1,186	1,100
Iron (mg)	16.32	11.8
Thiamine (mg)	.418	.42
Riboflavin (mg)	.284	.28
Niacin (mg)	2.807	.28
Ascorbic acid (mg)	—	ND[3]
Vitamin A activity (RE)	5	5

[1]   Composition of Foods: Spices and Herbs. USDA Agricultural Handbook 8-2. January 1977.
[2]   The Nutritional Composition of Spices, ASTA Research Committee, February, 1977.
[3]   ND = Not detected.

4.13.4 Countries of Origin

4.13.4.1 Quality Differences

Dill seed imported from India is most likely *Anethum sowa*. This has become the norm in the spice industry in the United States. This product is generally ground or used whole in pickling spices. *Anethum graveolens*, on the other hand, is grown in Egypt where it is harvested as dillweed. *A. graveolens* is also grown to be harvested as dillweed domestically, mainly in California. The product grown in the U.S. is generally a brighter green color, has a fresher flavor, and is cleaner microbiologically since it is mechanically dried rather than sun dried as it is in Egypt. The Egyptian product also has insect infestation at times. During storage, both types of dillweed will fade.

Dillweed oil is produced in the United States, mainly in the northwest and in western Canada. Dillseed oil is imported from Europe and India.

Table 4.45 Whole Dillweed: Chemical and Physical Specifications.

Specification	Suggested Limits
Volatile oil[1]	0.3% min
Moisture[2]	10.0% max
Ash[1]	10.0% max
Acid insoluble ash[1]	2.0% max
Military specifications (EE-S-631J, 1981)	
Volatile oil (ml/100 g)	0.2 min
Moisture	9.0% max
Ash	15.0% max
Acid insoluble ash	2.0% max
Granulation	50% min on a U.S.S. #50
Average bulk index (mg/100 g)	550

[1] These are suggested limits that the authors put together from the data collected over the past 5 years. These numbers are equivalent to the level where most quality spice will fall into.
[2] ASTA suggested maximum moisture level.

Table 4.46 Nutritional Composition of Dillweed Per 100 Grams.

Composition	USDA Handbook 8-2[1]
Water (grams)	7.30
Food energy (Kcal)	253
Protein (grams)	19.96
Fat (grams)	4.36
Carbohydrates (grams)	55.82
Ash (grams)	12.56
Calcium (grams)	1.784
Phosphorus (mg)	543
Sodium (mg)	208
Potassium (mg)	3,308
Iron (mg)	48.77
Thiamine (mg)	.418
Riboflavin (mg)	.284
Niacin (mg)	2.807
Ascorbic acid (mg)	—
Vitamin A activity (RE)	—

[1] Composition of Foods: Spices and Herbs. USDA Agricultural Handbook 8-2. January 1977. Supplement 1990.

4.13.4.2 Harvest Times

Indian dill seed is harvested in February through May. Egyptian dillweed is harvested in January through April, and domestic dillweed is harvested twice: once in the spring, and once in the fall.

4.13.5 Commercial Uses

The major commercial use of dill is in the form of dillweed oil, used in the pickle industry to make dill pickles. Dill seed is used whole in pickling spices for pickles and for meats. Dillweed is growing tremendously in use in recent years. It has found use in sauces, on fish and chicken, and in salad dressings. Historically, dillweed has been used extensively in Scandinavian and German cuisines.

4.14 Fennel Seed (*Foeniculum vulgare* Mill)

4.14.1 Background Information

Fennel seed is the dried fruit of an herb of the parsley family native to Europe. The seed is light green to gray, about 0.75 cm long, and curved. There are a number of varieties of fennel, one a vegetable with a taste similar to celery, and a bitter fennel used in liqueurs. The fennel seed we use as a spice is from garden fennel.

Fennel has been used for centuries, most often as the plant itself. It was often hung over doorways to ward off evil spirits. Fennel was used in ancient Greece and Rome, and in fact the English word "marathon" is derived from the Greek word for fennel. A famous battle took place on a field of fennel in which an athlete named Pheidippides ran 150 miles to Sparta to request help. This is where we get the word marathon.[27]

4.14.2 Chemical and Physical Specifications

Fennel contains 1%–3% of a volatile oil which is composed of about 50%–60% anethole and about 20% d-fenchone. The flavor of fennel is similar to anise but less sweet and more "green." Anethole is also the major component of anise. Other compounds present in fennel are d-α-pinene, d-α-phellandrene, dipentene, methyl chavicol, feniculun, anisaldehyde, and anisic acid.[3] Some of these compounds are also present in anise. Oil of fennel is commonly available. An oleoresin is also available with a volatile oil content of only about 3%–6%.

The ASTA recommended moisture specification in whole fennel is 10%. Ash and acid insoluble ash levels are generally 6%–9% and less than 1%, respectively. Excreta can be a problem in fennel, compounded by the fact that the shape and weight of the seeds are very similar to rodent excreta so cleaning can be difficult. Chemical and physical specifications, including FDA DALs, can be found in Tables 4.47 and 4.48. Nutritional analysis of fennel is listed in Table 4.49.

Table 4.47   Whole Fennel: Chemical and Physical Specifications.

Specification	Suggested Limits
ASTA cleanliness specifications:	
Whole dead insects, by count	[1]
Mammalian excreta, by mg/lb	[1]
Other excreta, by mg/lb	[1]
Mold, % by weight	1.00
Insect defiled/infested, % by weight	1.00
Extraneous, % by weight	0.50
FDA DALs:	
Mammalian excreta	20% or more
and/or insects	of subsamples
or	
Mammalian excreta	Ave of 3 mg per lb
Volatile oil[2]	1.5% min
Moisture[3]	10.0% max
Ash[2]	9.0% max
Acid insoluble ash[2]	1.0% max
Average bulk index (mg/100 g)	210

[1]   If more than 20% of the subsamples contain any rodent, other excreta, or whole insects, or an average of 3 mg/lb of mammalian excreta, the lot must be reconditioned.
[2]   These are suggested limits that the authors put together from the data collected over the past 5 years. These numbers are equivalent to the level where most quality spice will fall into.
[3]   ASTA suggested maximum moisture level.

Table 4.48   Ground Fennel: Chemical and Physical Specifications.

Specification	Suggested Limits
FDA DALs	None
Volatile oil[1]	1.0% min
Moisture[1]	10.0% max
Total ash[1]	9.0% max
Acid insoluble ash[1]	1.0% max
Military specifications (EE-S-631J, 1981)	
Volatile oil (ml/100 g)	1.0 min
Moisture	8.0% max
Total ash	10.0% max
Acid insoluble ash	1.0% max
Granulation	95% min through a U.S.S. #25
Bulk index[2] (ml/100 g)	210

[1]   These are suggested limits that the authors put together from data the authors collected in the past 5 years. These numbers are equivalent to the level where most quality spice will fall into.
[2]   Average bulk index. Granulation will effect number.

Table 4.49 Nutritional Composition of Fennel Seed Per 100 Grams.

Composition	USDA Handbook 8-2[1]	ASTA[2]
Water (grams)	8.81	6.0
Food energy (Kcal)	345	370
Protein (grams)	15.80	9.5
Fat (grams)	14.87	10.0
Carbohydrates (grams)	52.29	60.8
Ash (grams)	8.22	13.4
Calcium (grams)	1.196	1.3
Phosphorus (mg)	487	480
Sodium (mg)	88	90
Potassium (mg)	1,694	1,700
Iron (mg)	18.54	11.1
Thiamine (mg)	.408	.41
Riboflavin (mg)	.353	.36
Niacin (mg)	6.050	6.0
Ascorbic acid (mg)	—	ND[3]
Vitamin A activity (RE)	14	14

[1] Composition of Foods: Spices and Herbs. USDA Agricultural Handbook 8-2. January 1977.
[2] The Nutritional Composition of Spices, ASTA Research Committee, February, 1977.
[3] ND = Not detected.

4.14.3 Import Tonnage

The total amount of fennel imported into the United States for the year 1991 was 9.9 million pounds, with a dollar value of about $4.5 million.[6] The majority of these imports come from Egypt (59.9%), India (19.8%), and Taiwan (11%).

4.14.4 Countries of Origin

4.14.4.1 Quality Differences

Fennel is imported primarily from India and Egypt. There are some slight differences in quality, with Indian generally possessing a higher volatile oil content and a more uniform size and shape than the Egyptian product. The differences are slight. In the case of ground fennel, the uniformity of seeds does not matter. As long as a volatile oil content is met, the two origins should have equivalent functionalities.

4.14.4.2 Harvest Times

Indian fennel is harvested in February and March. Egyptian fennel is harvested in June. August and September is the harvest time for Turkish fennel.

4.14.5 Commercial Uses

By far the most common use of fennel is in pizza sauces and toppings. Fennel in the whole, cracked, and ground form all contribute the distinctive flavor in pizza meat toppings. Another important use for fennel in the processed meat industry is in Italian sausage. The consumption of fennel has increased dramatically in the past few years. Oil of fennel is also used in all the above types of products.

4.15 Fenugreek (or Foenugreek) (*Trigonella foenum-graecum* L.)

4.15.1 Background Information

Fenugreek is the seed of an annual herb, unique in the spices in that it belongs to the bean, or *Leguminosae* family. It is native to southeastern Europe and parts of Asia. Ten to twenty seeds grow in a long narrow pod, much like peas. The seeds themselves are about 0.5 cm in diameter and are irregularly shaped, very hard, and tan or mustard colored. The flavor of fenugreek is similar to maple syrup, although it does have a strong bitter undertone.

Fenugreek usage is very old. Rosengarten[7] states that it was used for medicinal purposes by the ancient Egyptians and is mentioned in medical writings in their tombs. Historically, the main usage of Fenugreek was medicinal rather than as a flavor; it is still used medicinally in many parts of the world.

4.15.2 Chemical and Physical Specifications

Very little work has been done on fenugreek seed, most likely since it is not used much in the United States as a ground spice. The volatile oil content of Fenugreek is very small: less than 0.02% according to Parry.[3] Other analysis shows a volatile oil content of 0.2%–0.5%. Fenugreek also contains fixed oils at about 5%–7%. Ash is generally no more than 2%–3% and acid insoluble ash is usually less than 0.25%. A suggested moisture limit for this spice is 12% maximum. Tables 4.50 and 4.51 have chemical and physical specifications for fenugreek. Nutritional data can be found in Table 4.52.

4.15.3 Import Tonnage

The import tonnage for fenugreek is not available from the U.S.D.A.

4.15.4 Countries of Origin

4.15.4.1 Quality Differences

No large differences in quality can be noted from the different exporting countries.

4.15.4.2 Harvest Times

Fenugreek is harvested in Morocco during July and August and in India during June and July.

Table 4.50   Whole Fenugreek: Chemical and Physical Specifications.

Specification	Suggested Limits
ASTA cleanliness specifications:	None
FDA DALs:	None
Volatile oil[1]	0.25% min
Moisture[2]	12.0% max
Ash[1]	3.0% max
Acid insoluble ash[1]	0.25% max
Average bulk index (mg/100 g)	120

[1]   These are suggested limits that the authors put together from the data collected over the past 5 years. These numbers are equivalent to the level where most quality spice will fall into.
[2]   ASTA suggested maximum moisture level.

4.15.5   Commercial Uses

Fenugreek is used in the United States as a spice and as a flavoring. The spice is used mainly in curry powders, chutneys, and some other Indian foods. The extract is used primarily in the flavor industry as a major component of imitation maple flavor. In other countries, fenugreek is used medicinally as a digestive aid and to promote lactation in both women and in cows. This usage may be based on some fact: fenugreek contains diosgenin, a compound used as a starting material for sex hormones in the pharmaceutical industry.[7]

Table 4.51   Ground Fenugreek: Chemical and Physical Specifications.

Specification	Suggested Limits
FDA DALs	None
Volatile oil[1]	0.25% min
Moisture[1]	12.0% max
Total ash[1]	4.0% max
Acid insoluble ash[1]	0.5% max
Military specifications (EE-S-631J, 1981)	
Volatile oil (ml/100 g)	—
Moisture	9.5% max
Total ash	5.0% max
Acid insoluble ash	1.0% max
Granulation	95% min through a U.S.S. #25
Bulk index[2] (ml/100 g)	190

[1]   These are suggested limits that the authors put together from data the authors collected in the past 5 years. These numbers are equivalent to the level where most quality spice will fall into.
[2]   Average bulk index. Granulation will effect number.

Table 4.52   Nutritional Composition of Fenugreek Seed Per 100 Grams.

Composition	USDA Handbook 8-2[1]
Water (grams)	8.84
Food energy (Kcal)	323
Protein (grams)	23.00
Fat (grams)	6.41
Carbohydrates (grams)	58.35
Ash (grams)	3.40
Calcium (grams)	.176
Phosphorus (mg)	296
Sodium (mg)	67
Potassium (mg)	770
Iron (mg)	33.53
Thiamine (mg)	.322
Riboflavin (mg)	.366
Niacin (mg)	1.640
Ascorbic acid (mg)	3.00
Vitamin A activity (RE)	—

[1] Composition of Foods: Spices and Herbs. USDA Agricultural Handbook 8-2. January 1977. Supplement 1990.

4.16 Ginger (*Zingiber officinale* Roscoe)

4.16.1 Background Information

Ginger is the rhizosome of a plant native to southern Asia. It is a perennial plant, but is usually grown as an annual for harvesting as a spice. The whole rhizosomes of commerce are about 4–5 in. long and tan colored. They are often called "hands" or "fingers" due to their shape. The word ginger is derived from a Sanskrit word meaning "shaped like a horn."

Ginger has been grown by the Chinese for centuries. Rosengarten[7] states that ginger is mentioned in the writings of Confucius from about 500 B.C. It is also known to be one of the first spices known in Europe, appearing in writings in the eleventh century. By the 14th century, it was second only to black pepper in popularity. Ginger was successfully introduced to the New World and, by about 1650, Jamaica, Santo Domingo, and Barbados were all exporting ginger back to Europe.

Gingerbread and ginger ale (ginger sprinkled on top of ale), were popular in Europe in the 1500s and 1800s, respectively.

Ginger is available in a variety of forms. The unpeeled type has an outer "cork" skin still intact on the rhizosome, whereas the peeled types have either had the skin removed completely or simply scraped off. The rough scraped type usually only has had part of the skin removed, generally that which is on the flat sides of the fingers.

Ginger can also be bleached with acid or with lime, resulting in a light colored product. Ginger "splits" are also available. These are rhizosomes split in half lengthwise to quicken the drying time. Various countries treat the ginger rhizosomes differently. The United States commonly imports the unpeeled varieties from India.

Ginger oil and ginger oleoresin are both available. The oleoresin contains the pungent components and has a volatile oil content of about 25%–30%. It is dark brown and very viscous. An African-type ginger oleoresin is also available, which is typically more pungent than the Jamaican or Cochin type. Ginger oil contains the volatile component only with no pungency present.

4.16.2 Chemical and Physical Specifications

Ginger contains 1.5%–3.0% volatile oil, typically 2.0%. The volatile oil is composed mainly of sesquiterpene hydrocarbons. This group of compounds contributes about 50%–66% of the volatile oil. Oxygenated sesquiterpenes are present at up to 17% and the remainder is composed of monoterpene hydrocarbons and oxygenated monoterpenes. Of the sesquiterpene hydrocarbons, about 20%–30% is (−)-α-zingiberene, up to 12% (−)-β-bisabolene, up to 19% (+)-ar-curcumene and up to 10% farnesene.[1] A sensory study completed in 1975[28] showed that β-sesquiphellandrene and ar-curcumene were the major contributors to the "ginger" flavor, whereas α-terpineol and citral contributed a lemony flavor. The high lemon flavor and high citral content is apparent in Australian ginger. This product contains up to 19.3% citral versus up to 4% in other sources. Purseglove[1] states that this could be due to the controlled mechanical drying of the ginger grown in Australia. This type of drying may not flash off these lower boiling compounds as readily as sun drying does. It has also been noted that Cochin ginger ground under cryogenic conditions retains more of a lemon-like flavor character. These citral and terpineol components may be flashed off more in ambient grinding whereas in cryogenic grinding they are retained.

There have been numerous studies concerning the pungent components of ginger and what contributes to that pungency. It has been thought that the pungency was due to three compounds: gingerol, shogoal, and zingerone. In the last 25 years, however, more research has been done by Connel and Sutherland[29,30] and the following seems to be the case, as described by Purseglove: fresh ginger contains gingerol, which can be described as a series of compounds with the general structure, 1-(4'-hydroxy-3'-methoxyphenyl)-5-hydroxyalkan-3-ones. They are mainly condensation products of zingerone with saturated straight chain aldehydes of chain lengths 6, 8, and 10. These are considered [6], [8], and [10] gingerols. The presence of zingerone and shogoals in fresh extract is nonexistent. These compounds were found after storage and seem to be formed by the action of heat. They may, therefore, form during the drying process. Both zingerone and shogoals are less pungent than the gingerols. It seems, therefore, that ginger can lose its pungency during storage and under excessive heat treatment.[1] Ginger and oleoresin are both available commercially.

Ash should be less than 5% and acid insoluble ash should be less than 1%. Moisture limits set by ASTA are 12%. Tables 4.53 and 4.54 lists suggested chemical and physical specifications, including FDA DALs. Nutritional information can be found in Table 4.55.

Table 4.53 Whole Ginger: Chemical and Physical Specifications.

Specification	Suggested Limits
ASTA cleanliness specifications:	
Whole dead insects, by count	4
Mammalian excreta, by mg/lb	3
Other excreta, by mg/lb	3.0
Mold, % by weight	[1]
Insect defiled/infested, % by weight	[1]
Extraneous, % by weight	1.00
FDA DALs:	
Moldy and/or insect infested pieces	Ave of 3% by weight
Mammalian excreta	Ave of 3 mg per lb
Volatile oil[2]	2.0% min
Moisture[3]	12.0% max
Ash[2]	5.0% max
Acid insoluble ash[2]	1.0% max
Average bulk index (mg/100 g)	N/A

[1] 3% moldy pieces and/or insect infested pieces by weight.
[2] These are suggested limits that the authors put together from the data collected over the past 5 years. These numbers are equivalent to the level where most quality spice will fall into.
[3] ASTA suggested maximum moisture level.

Table 4.54 Ground Ginger: Chemical and Physical Specifications.

Specification	Suggested Limits
FDA DALs	None
Volatile oil[1]	1.5% min
Moisture[1]	12.0% max
Total ash[1]	5.0% max
Acid insoluble ash[1]	1.0% max
Military specifications (EE-S-631J, 1981)	
Volatile oil (ml/100 g)	1.5 min
Moisture	12.0% max
Total ash	7.0% max
Acid insoluble ash	1.0% max
Crude fiber	8.0% max
Starch	42.0% max
Granulation	95% min through a U.S.S. #30
Bulk index[2] (ml/100 g)	210

[1] These are suggested limits that the authors put together from data the authors collected in the past 5 years. These numbers are equivalent to the level where most quality spice will fall into.
[2] Average bulk index. Granulation will effect number.

Table 4.55 Nutritional Composition of Ginger Per 100 Grams.

Composition	USDA Handbook 8-2[1] (Ground)	ASTA[2]
Water (grams)	9.38	7.0
Food energy (Kcal)	347	380
Protein (grams)	9.12	8.5
Fat (grams)	5.95	6.4
Carbohydrates (grams)	70.79	72.4
Ash (grams)	4.77	5.7
Calcium (grams)	.116	0.1
Phosphorus (mg)	148	150
Sodium (mg)	32	30
Potassium (mg)	1,342	1,400
Iron (mg)	11.52	11.3
Thiamine (mg)	.046	.050
Riboflavin (mg)	.185	.130
Niacin (mg)	5.155	1.90
Ascorbic acid (mg)	—	ND[3]
Vitamin A activity (RE)	15	15

[1] Composition of Foods: Spices and Herbs. USDA Agricultural Handbook 8-2. January 1977.
[2] The Nutritional Composition of Spices, ASTA Research Committee, February, 1977.
[3] ND = Not detected.

4.16.3 Import Tonnage

The import tonnage for ginger in the year 1991, including whole fresh and dried was 16.4 million pounds, 12% imported from the Cochin area of India, 15.7% from Indonesia, and 11% from China. The total imports from Jamaica in 1991 were only 32,000 pounds. The dollar value this tonnage represents is $8.1 million.[6]

4.16.4 Countries of Origin

4.16.4.1 Quality Differences

Jamaican ginger has been considered the best quality ginger for years. However, very little is imported into the United States and the cost has become prohibitive. If Jamaica is the origin on your specification, chances are you are not getting Jamaican ginger. Cochin ginger in recent times has become our most popular source. It comes from the Cochin port on the Malabar coast of India. It is ginger which is unpeeled, washed, and dried. Australian ginger does have quality differences as described previously; however, it is rarely imported into the United States.

4.16.4.2 Harvest Times

Cochin ginger is harvested in January through April and Chinese ginger is harvested in January and February. Jamaican ginger is also harvested in the winter and early spring months.

4.16.5 Commercial Uses

Ginger is not used in the food industry in the whole form. It is, however, used in the cracked form in pickling spices for meats and pickles. Ginger is available fresh and preserved in brine or syrup; however, these forms are not generally used in the food industry.

Ginger in the ground form is used in a variety of bakery products such as gingerbread, spice cake, and carrot cake in combination with nutmeg, allspice, and cinnamon. Ginger is also used extensively in oriental dishes. Ground ginger, oleoresin ginger, and ginger oils are also used in the processed meats industry in a variety of sausages. Oleoresin ginger is a major flavor component of ginger ale.

4.17 Mace and Nutmeg (*Myristica fragrans* Houtt)

4.17.1 Background Information

Mace and nutmeg are from the same tree: a large evergreen tree native to the Moluccas Islands and the East Indian Archipelago. The fruit of the tree has a fleshy exterior, inside of which is a large seed encased in a shell. Covering the shell is a lacy, netlike covering, or aril, scarlet to crimson in color. This is the mace. Under this covering is the shell containing the nutmeg seed. The nutmeg seeds are quite large, about 4 cm long and 2 cm wide, brown, and oval in shape.

The fruit is harvested by separating the nutmeg and mace in one piece from the fleshy part of the fruit. The mace is later detached, flattened by hand or with boards and sun dried. During drying, mace turns from its bright scarlet or crimson color to a paler orange. East Indian mace is exported in this orange form. Mace grown in the West Indies is cured after drying. This consists of storing the product in the dark for a period of about 4 months. During this time, the color changes to a pale orange to yellow color and the brittleness of the mace increases.

Nutmeg seeds are dried in the shell by the sun or artificially with fires for about 1 week. In the West Indies, nutmeg is air dried very slowly, often taking as long as 8 weeks. When the nutmeg is dry, it rattles in its shell. Nutmeg is stored this way and either shelled mechanically or by hand prior to grading and exporting. The yield of dried mace to nutmeg is about 10%.

Nutmeg and mace were popular and well known in Europe by the 12th century. By the 16th century, the Portuguese had moved into the Moluccas islands and created a monopoly in the nutmeg and mace trade. In 1602, the Portuguese were driven out by the Dutch, who along with the clove trade, had a strict monopoly in nutmeg and mace for about 200 years. The Dutch limited production by restricting it to certain areas and destroying all nutmeg trees in other areas. The monopoly was broken in the late 1700s by the French who smuggled seedling trees into Mauritius and by the British, who occupied the Moluccas Islands during 1796–1802. Nutmeg production was introduced into the British West Indies, Trinidad, and Grenada in the early 19th century.

Oleoresins and essential oils are both available, the oleoresin of nutmeg containing 33%–35% volatile oil and the oleoresin mace containing 10%–15% volatile oil.

The essential oil is usually extracted from worm-eaten nutmegs. This has a twofold advantage. The first is that these nutmegs are cheaper, but secondly, and perhaps more importantly, these nutmegs have a higher percent of volatile oil. The worms eat the starch and fixed oils in the nutmeg and leave the volatile oil, thus increasing that percentage by weight.

4.17.2 Chemical and Physical Specifications

Nutmeg contains about 25%–40% fixed oils. Mace contains 20%–35% fixed oils.[1] Nutmeg, however, contains 90% saturated acid, with myristic acid being the major component: 70%–90%. Mace contains a much higher ratio of unsaturated acids, about 60% of the fixed oils. Salzer[31] felt the coarser flavor of nutmeg is due to the higher saturated fatty acid content because the more solid the fat, the more it modifies the impression of the flavor on the tongue. Another view is that the difference in flavor between nutmeg and mace is due to their fixed, rather than their volatile oils.

Nutmeg contains a high level of volatile oil, about 6%–15%. The composition is about 61%–88% monoterpene hydrocarbons, mainly α- and β-pinene and sabinene, 5%–15% oxygenated monoterpenes, and 2%–18% aromatic ethers, consisting mainly of myristicin. The myristicin is formed from the hydrolysis of its glycerol ester: myristic acid. Myristicin is considered the main flavor component of nutmeg. It is also a hallucinogenic narcotic and can cause fatalities if taken in high enough dosages.[32,33] During storage, the volatile oil of nutmeg decreases, as well as the percent of myristicin which hydrolyses to myrisitic acid.[34]

Mace contains an even higher level of volatile oil, 15%–25%, similar to nutmeg, however it has been studied less. Dann, Mathews, and Robinson[35] completed a study in 1977 which showed a flavor difference between nutmeg and mace from the same tree.

Moisture levels should be no greater than 8.0% in either nutmeg or mace. Ash and acid insoluble ash need to be 2%–3% and less than 0.5% in nutmeg and 2.0%–5.0% and less than 0.5% in mace. Nutmeg and mace, because of their high volatile oils, should not be ground too fine due to lumping of the product. A top screen specification of 95% through U.S.S. #20 or 25 is desirable.

See Tables 4.56 through 4.59 for a summary of the chemical and physical specifications of nutmeg and mace and Tables 4.60 and 4.61 for nutritional information.

4.17.3 Import Tonnage

Nutmeg and mace are mainly imported from the East Indies. Of 4.2 million pounds of nutmeg imported to the United States in 1991, 69% was from Indonesia and 22% from Singapore. Mace imports for 1991 were less than 400,000 pounds, although 88% were from Indonesia. The dollar value of the nutmeg imports was $3.0 million and mace was only $420,000.[6]

Table 4.56   Whole Nutmeg: Chemical and Physical Specifications.

Specification	Suggested Limits	
ASTA cleanliness specifications:	Broken	Whole
Whole dead insects, by count	4	4
Mammalian excreta, by mg/lb	5	0
Other excreta, by mg/lb	1.0	0.0
Mold, % by weight	[1]	[2]
Insect defiled/infested, % by weight	[1]	[2]
Extraneous, % by weight	0.50%	0.00
FDA DALs:		
Insect infested and/or moldy pieces by count	Ave of 10%	
Volatile oil[3]	7.0% min	
Moisture[4]	8.0% max	
Ash[3]	3.0% max	
Acid insoluble ash[3]	0.5% max	
Average bulk index (mg/100 g)	N/A	

[1] Broken—Not > 5% mold/insect defiled, combined by weight.
[2] Whole—Not > 10% insect infested &/or moldy pieces, with a maximum of 5% insect defiled pieces by count.
[3] These are suggested limits that the authors put together from the data collected over the past 5 years. These numbers are equivalent to the level where most quality spice will fall into.
[4] ASTA suggested maximum moisture level.

Table 4.57   Ground Nutmeg: Chemical and Physical Specifications.

Specification	Suggested Limits
FDA DALs (6 subsamples):	
Insect fragments	Ave of 100 or more/10 g
or	
Rodent hairs	Ave of 1 or more/10 g
Volatile oil[1]	6.0% min
Moisture[1]	8.0% max
Total ash[1]	3.0% max
Acid insoluble ash[1]	0.5% max
Military specifications (EE-S-631J, 1981)	
Volatile oil (ml/100 g)	7.5 min
Moisture	8.0% max
Total ash	3.0% max
Acid insoluble ash	0.5% max
Nonvolatile ether extract	25.0% min
Granulation	95% min through a U.S.S. #20
Bulk index[2] (ml/100 g)	180

[1] These are suggested limits that the authors put together from data the authors collected in the past 5 years. These numbers are equivalent to the level where most quality spice will fall into.
[2] Average bulk index. Granulation will effect number.

Table 4.58   Whole Mace: Chemical and Physical Specifications.

Specification	Suggested Limits
ASTA cleanliness specifications:	
Whole dead insects, by count	4
Mammalian excreta, by mg/lb	3
Other excreta, by mg/lb	1.0
Mold, % by weight	2.00
Insect defiled/infested, % by weight	1.00
Extraneous, % by weight	0.50
FDA DALs:	
Insect infested and/or moldy pieces by weight	Ave of 3%
Mammalian excreta	Ave of 3 mg per lb
Foreign matter through a 20 mesh sieve	Ave of 1.5%
Volatile oil[1]	15.0% min
Moisture[2]	8.0% max
Ash[1]	5.0% max
Acid insoluble ash[1]	0.5% max
Average bulk index (mg/100 g)	N/A

[1] These are suggested limits that the authors put together from the data collected over the past 5 years. These numbers are equivalent to the level where most quality spice will fall into.
[2] ASTA suggested maximum moisture level.

Table 4.59   Ground Mace: Chemical and Physical Specifications.

Specification	Suggested Limits
FDA DALs	None
Volatile oil[1]	14.0% min
Moisture[1]	8.0% max
Total ash[1]	5.0% max
Acid insoluble ash[1]	0.5% max
Military specifications (EE-S-631J, 1981)	
Volatile oil (ml/100 g)	12.0 min
Moisture	6.0% max
Total ash	3.5% max
Acid insoluble ash	0.5% max
Nonvolatile ether extract	20.0–35.0
Granulation	95% min through a U.S.S. #20
Bulk index[2] (ml/100 g)	205

[1] These are suggested limits that the authors put together from data the authors collected in the past 5 years. These numbers are equivalent to the level where most quality spice will fall into.
[2] Average bulk index. Granulation will effect number.

Table 4.60 Nutritional Composition of Nutmeg Per 100 Grams.

Composition	USDA Handbook 8-2[1] (Ground)	ASTA[2]
Water (grams)	6.23	4.0
Food energy (Kcal)	525	565
Protein (grams)	5.84	7.0
Fat (grams)	36.31	38.9
Carbohydrates (grams)	49.29	47.3
Ash (grams)	2.34	2.0
Calcium (grams)	.184	0.2
Phosphorus (mg)	213	200
Sodium (mg)	16	10
Potassium (mg)	350	400
Iron (mg)	3.04	2.2
Thiamine (mg)	.346	.360
Riboflavin (mg)	.057	.250
Niacin (mg)	1.299	9.4
Ascorbic acid (mg)	—	ND[3]
Vitamin A activity (RE)	10	10

[1] Composition of Foods: Spices and Herbs. USDA Agricultural Handbook 8-2. January 1977.
[2] The Nutritional Composition of Spices, ASTA Research Committee, February, 1977.
[3] ND = Not detected.

Table 4.61 Nutritional Composition of Mace Per 100 Grams.

Composition	USDA Handbook 8-2[1] (Ground)	ASTA[2]
Water (grams)	8.17	4.5
Food energy (Kcal)	475	565
Protein (grams)	6.71	8.0
Fat (grams)	32.38	38.8
Carbohydrates (grams)	50.51	46.1
Ash (grams)	2.23	2.3
Calcium (grams)	.252	0.2
Phosphorus (mg)	110	110
Sodium (mg)	80	70
Potassium (mg)	463	500
Iron (mg)	13.90	11.3
Thiamine (mg)	.312	.370
Riboflavin (mg)	.448	.560
Niacin (mg)	1.350	1.2
Ascorbic acid (mg)	—	ND[3]
Vitamin A activity (RE)	80	80

[1] Composition of Foods: Spices and Herbs. USDA Agricultural Handbook 8-2. January 1977.
[2] The Nutritional Composition of Spices, ASTA Research Committee, February, 1977.
[3] ND = Not detected.

4.17.4 Countries of Origin

4.17.4.1 Quality Differences

Nutmeg and mace (although not as commonly) are designated as East Indian or West Indian. There is some chemical composition validity to the differences in origin. West Indian Nutmeg is low in α-pinene and myristicin and high in β-pinene and sabinene. East Indian nutmeg is higher in myristicin. This may be why the East Indian origin is often considered stronger in flavor: due to the higher level of myristicin. Baldry et al.[36] confirmed this in taste panels of the essential oils. These differences are important especially when purchasing the essential oil. The differences are less apparent in ground spice.

4.17.4.2 Harvest Times

Mace and nutmeg are harvested throughout the year.

4.17.5 Commercial Uses

Nutmeg is used in the food industry at a far greater level than mace. Both spices are used in the baking industry in all sorts of sweet bakery goods. Nutmeg complements cinnamon and is often found in combination with that spice.

Another large use of nutmeg is in the processed meats industry. Many sausages get their flavor from nutmeg, mace, and their corresponding essential oils and oleoresins. The major flavor component of wieners and bologna is nutmeg. When dark specks are not desired, the essential oil and oleoresin are used. Nutmeg can also improve the flavor of white sauces at low levels.

4.18 Marjoram (*Origanum marjorana* L.; also formerly called *Marjorana hortensis* Moench)

4.18.1 Background Information

Marjoram is a low bushy plant belonging to the mint family and grown as an annual. The leaves are grayish green, narrow, and about 1 cm long. Marjoram is native to the Mediterranean region and Western Asia. It has often been mistaken for oregano in botanical classification.

Marjoram has been used as a flavoring agent since the ancient Greek and Roman eras. The Greeks felt it was a symbol of happiness and that if grown on a grave, the deceased would be eternally happy.[7] Marjoram was popular during the Middle Ages as a medicine and as a culinary herb in England during the 16th century.

4.18.2 Chemical and Physical Specifications

Marjoram contains 0.7%–3% volatile oil which is about 40% terpines, composed mainly of terpen-4-ol and α-terpineol. In 1990, Paakkonen, Malmstedn, and Hyvonen[15b] found that elevated storage temperatures decreased the marjoram quality during long-term storage. An essential oil and an oleoresin are both commercially available. The oleoresin contains only about 5%–10% volatile oil.

The recommended ASTA moisture limit is 10%. Ash is usually between 10% and 15% and acid insoluble ash is usually less than 5%. Tables 4.62 and 4.63 outline typical chemical and physical specifications, including FDA DALs. Nutritional information is located in Table 4.64.

4.18.3 Import Tonnage

Import tonnage for 1991 is not available from the U.S.D.A.

4.18.4 Countries of Origin

4.18.4.1 Quality Differences

No appreciable differences in quality from origin to origin is noted. French marjoram is reputed to be a higher quality product; however, this is not necessarily true.

Table 4.62 Whole Marjoram: Chemical and Physical Specifications.

Specification	Suggested Limits	
ASTA cleanliness specifications:		
Whole dead insects, by count	3	
Mammalian excreta, by mg/lb	1	
Other excreta, by mg/lb	10.0	
Mold, % by weight	1.00	
Insect defiled/infested, % by weight	1.00	
Extraneous, % by weight	1.00	
FDA Dals (6 subsamples):	Unprocessed	Processed
Insect infested &/or moldy pieces by weight	Ave of 5%	—
Mammalian excreta per lb, identified as to source when possible	Ave of 1 mg	—
Insect fragments &/or rodent hairs per 10 gram subsample	—	Ave of 250 / Ave of 2
Volatile oil[1]	1.0% min	
Moisture[2]	10.0% max	
Ash[1]	15.0% max	
Acid insoluble ash[1]	5.0% max	
Federal specification (EE-S-631J, 1981)	<10% of stems by weight	
Average bulk index (mg/100 g)	660	

[1] These are suggested limits that the authors put together from the data collected over the past 5 years. These numbers are equivalent to the level where most quality spice will fall into.
[2] ASTA suggested maximum moisture level.

Table 4.63   Ground Marjoram: Chemical and Physical Specifications.

Specification	Suggested Limits
FDA DALs (6 subsamples):	
Insect fragments	Ave of 1175 or more/10 g
or	
Rodent hairs	Ave of 8 or more/10 g
Volatile oil[1]	0.8% min
Moisture[1]	10.0% max
Total ash[1]	15.0% max
Acid insoluble ash[1]	5.0% max
Military specifications (EE-S-631J, 1981)	
Volatile oil (ml/100 g)	0.6 min
Moisture	10.0% max
Total ash	15.0% max
Acid insoluble ash	4.0% max
Nonvolatile ether extract	20–35
Granulation	95% min through a U.S.S. #30
Bulk index[2] (ml/100 g)	270

[1] These are suggested limits that the authors put together from data the authors collected in the past 5 years. These numbers are equivalent to the level where most quality spice will fall into.
[2] Average bulk index. Granulation will effect number.

Table 4.64   Nutritional Composition of Marjoram Per 100 Grams.

Composition	USDA Handbook 8-2[1]	ASTA[2]
Water (grams)	7.64	6.5
Food energy (Kcal)	271	365
Protein (grams)	12.66	12.5
Fat (grams)	7.04	6.8
Carbohydrates (grams)	60.56	64.4
Ash (grams)	12.10	9.7
Calcium (grams)	1.990	2.5
Phosphorus (mg)	306	230
Sodium (mg)	77	110
Potassium (mg)	1,522	1,400
Iron (mg)	82.71	72.7
Thiamine (mg)	.289	.290
Riboflavin (mg)	.316	.320
Niacin (mg)	4.120	4.1
Ascorbic acid (mg)	51.43	51
Vitamin A activity (RE)	807	807

[1] Composition of Foods: Spices and Herbs. USDA Agricultural Handbook 8-2. January 1977.
[2] The Nutritional Composition of Spices, ASTA Research Committee, February, 1977.

4.18.4.2 Harvest Times

Marjoram grown in Egypt is harvested in March through July. French marjoram is harvested in September to November and domestically grown marjoram is harvested in June to September.

4.18.5 Commercial Uses

Marjoram is used in many foods where a well-rounded herb note is desired. Soups, sauces, and salad dressings often contain marjoram. It has been used as a substitute for oregano when prices go up for that spice. Marjoram is used in italian herb blends and is often a component of pizza and spaghetti sauce mixes. It is used in the whole and ground forms, and infrequently as an essential oil or oleoresin.

4.19 Mustard Seed (*Brassica hirta* Moench, and *Brassica juncea*)

4.19.1 Background Information

Mustard seed is a very small tan to brown seed, about 3 mm in diameter. *Brassica hirta* refers to white or yellow mustard and *Brassica juncea* refers to the oriental or brown mustard. Another species, *Brassica nigra* is black mustard, but is not used in any appreciable amount in the United States.

Mustard seed has been used for centuries. It is mentioned in the Bible in Matthew 13:31, Mark 4:30, and Luke 13:18. All of these scriptures describe Jesus's parable: "The Kingdom of Heaven is like a tiny mustard seed planted in a field. It is the smallest of all seeds, but becomes the largest of plants, and grows into a tree where birds can come and find shelter."

The volatile oil of mustard, allylisothiocyanate is available. It is hot and biting, similar to horseradish in flavor. It is very volatile and must be used with extreme caution.

4.19.2 Chemical and Physical Specifications

Mustard is unique in the spices in that it has an important chemical reaction which takes place and contributes to flavor. The pungency characteristics of the two species (*B. hirta* and *B. juncea*) must be described separately. Both species contain an enzyme, myrosinase which reacts with glycosidic compounds in the presence of moisture to release the pungency. The difference between the two species is the components responsible for the reaction and the end products produced. The reactions are described in Figure 4.1. These reactions are responsible for the pungent odor and hot biting flavor in mustard, primarily in the *B. juncea* species (brown and oriental mustards). An illustration of this principle is the pungency generated when mixing oriental mustard flour with water to make hot mustard sauce. Upon sitting, the mustard sauce becomes very hot and pungent. Temperatures greater than 100 °F

(a) *Brassica hirta:* (X = SINAPINE)

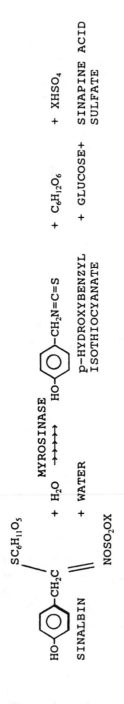

(b) *Brassica juncea:*

Figure 4.1 Chemical reactions of mustard. (a) Sinalbin in the presence of water reacts with myrosinase to form p-hydroxybenzyl isothiocyanate (sharp taste without pungent aroma), glucose and sinapine acid sulfate. (b) Sinigrin in the presence of water reacts with myrosinase to form allylisothiocyanate (pungent irritating odor = mustard oil), glucose, and postassium bisulfate.

will inactivate the enzyme, as well as a pH below 5.0.[37] To ensure pungency release, acid or heat should be added after a few minutes to allow it to develop. If, however, the mustard is added to an acidic media or to a liquid in which temperatures are greater than 100 °F, no pungency will develop since the enzyme will be inactivated immediately.

Mustard seeds contain 28%–36% fixed oil. The protein content of mustard seed is about 30%–40%. This is important in the processed meats industry as a protein source. Nutritional data for mustard seed can be found in Table 4.65. Moisture levels recommended by ASTA are 11% maximum.

If whole or ground yellow (*B. hirta*) mustard is purchased, it is generally described as #1, #2, or #3 grade. This designation refers to the number of dark seeds present, as well as other characteristics. The higher the number of dark seeds, the lower the quality and the higher the grade number. This is important in the meat industry where large amounts of ground mustard is used. Dark specks are not desirable in products such as bologna and wieners. The grading of mustard by the Canadian Grain Grading Guide is used to classify #1, #2, or #3 mustard seeds. This grading system is listed in Table 4.66.

Finally, mustard seed also contains a natural mucilaginous substance in the bran of the seed. It is a cold water swelling, linear acidic polysaccharide which exhibits thickening and emulsification properties.[38] One company is currently marketing mustard bran for this purpose.

Table 4.65 Nutritional Composition of Mustard Seed Per 100 Grams.

Composition	USDA Handbook 8-2[1] (Yellow)	ASTA[2] (Powder)
Water (grams)	6.86	3.0
Food energy (Kcal)	469	580
Protein (grams)	24.94	32
Fat (grams)	28.76	42.6
Carbohydrates (grams)	34.94	18.5
Ash (grams)	4.51	4.0
Calcium (grams)	.521	0.3
Phosphorus (mg)	841	790
Sodium (mg)	5	10
Potassium (mg)	682	700
Iron (mg)	9.98	8.3
Thiamine (mg)	.543	.65
Riboflavin (mg)	.381	.45
Niacin (mg)	7.890	8.5
Ascorbic acid (mg)	—	22
Vitamin A activity (RE)	6	6

[1] Composition of Foods: Spices and Herbs. USDA Agricultural Handbook 8-2. January 1977.
[2] The Nutritional Composition of Spices, ASTA Research Committee, February, 1977.

Table 4.66   Grades of Canadian Mustard Seed—Primary Grade Determinants.

Grade	Class	Degree of Soundness	Standard of Cleanliness
No. 1 Canada	Not less than 99.5% of one class.	Reasonable well matured, sweet, of good natural colour. May contain not over 1.5% damaged seeds, including not over 0.1% heated.	May contain not more than 0.3% of other seeds that are conspicuous and that are not readily separable from mustard seed, including not over 0.1% of conspicuous seeds that are distinctly detrimental to quality, such as cow cockle.
No. 2 Canada	Not less than 98% of one class.	Fairly well matured, sweet. May contain not over 3% damaged seeds, including not over 1.5% distinctly green seeds, and not over 0.2% heated.	May contain not more than 0.5% of other seeds that are conspicuous and that are not readily separable from mustard seed, including not over 0.2% of conspicuous seeds that are distinctly detrimental to quality, such as cow cockle.
No. 3 Canada	Not less than 95% of one class.	May contain not over 5% damaged seeds, including not over 0.5% heated, and not over 3.5% of distinctly green seeds and heated in combination. May have the natural odour associated with low quality seed, but shall not have any odour that would indicate serious deterioration or contamination.	May contain not more than 0.7% of other seeds that are conspicuous and that are not readily separable from mustard seed, including not over 0.3% of conspicuous seeds that are distinctly detrimental to quality, such as cow cockle.

4.19.3 Import Tonnage

Almost 122 million pounds of mustard seed was imported into the United States in 1991. 99.9% of this volume was from Canada.[6] The dollar value of this amount of mustard was about $17.4 million, which shows that mustard is probably the most inexpensive spice. In addition, another 16.7 million pounds was produced in the United States, primarily in North and South Dakota. It is also grown in Montana, Washington, Oregon, and California.

4.19.4 Countries of Origin

4.19.4.1 Quality Differences

Mustard is one of the few spices which grows in the northern climates. It is cultivated in the Northern Plains of the United States and in Canada. The quality of seed and the species are the most important factors for purchasing mustard.

4.19.4.2 Harvest Times

Mustard seed is harvested in August and September.

4.19.5 Commercial Uses

Mustard seed is available in three forms: whole, ground, and flour. The whole seed is mainly used in pickling spices, both for pickles and in the meat industry. The whole seed is also purchased by prepared mustard manufacturers who wet mill the product. Vinegar, salt, and spices including turmeric for color are added to produce prepared mustard. Grinding the whole mustard seed produces ground mustard. This product is used in the processed meats industry by sausage producers due to the high protein content. The product may only be used in cooked sausages. Fresh sausages must use a mustard which has been treated with heat to destroy the myrosinase. Otherwise, the enzyme reacts with the meat protein, producing an off flavor. Mustard flour is produced by milling the seed after the husk or bran is removed. It is specially milled to produce a very fine product. Generally, the companies which mill mustard flour mix various amounts of yellow and brown seeds to produce the exact flavor profile desired. Mustard flour is not produced by every spice company, but mainly by specialty producers who have the proper milling equipment. Mustard flour is used by salad dressing manufacturers and in oriental hot mustard sauces.

4.20 Oregano (*Origanum vulgare*–Mediterranean, and *Lippia graveolens* or *Lippia berlandieri*–Mexican)

4.20.1 Background Information

True oregano—*Origanum vulgare* (a leafy perennial herb of the mint family indigenous to the Mediterranean region) has often been confused with marjoram. The flavor is similar and the botanical classification has often been confused over the years. Oregano was frequently called "wild marjoram," thus increasing the confusion. Today, due to its popularity, this confusion is waning.

Oregano has been used and known since the ancient Greek and Roman eras as a spice for flavoring foods.[7] This is a difference from other spices in this era which were used primarily for medicinal purposes.

Oregano became popular in the U.S. after World War II and growth has remained high. In the 1960s, the volume imported was 1.5 million pounds.[39] The volume imported in 1991 was almost 12 million pounds.[6] Both the essential oil and oleoresin are available commercially. The oleoresin contains 25%–30% volatile oil.

4.20.2 Chemical and Physical Specifications

Mediterranean oregano has a volatile oil level of about 2.0%. Mexican oregano has a higher volatile oil content. When it is in short supply and only a low volatile oil product is available, sometimes adulteration at the source with a different species of oregano which is silvery grey in color and very high in volatile oil occurs. Other adulteration products in times of short supply include other species of *Origanum* which are similar, but often have a more minty and less bitter flavor. Oregano can also be adulterated with sumac, which is processed in close proximity to oregano. A test for detection of sumac adulteration consists of examination of the oregano in question under 30–100× magnification. Oregano leaves contain visible oil glands and jointed hairs where the sumac does not contain oil glands and the hairs are single celled. Under further examination, sumac contains oxalate crystals under polarized light magnification.

The major component of the volatile oil of oregano is thymol and carvacrol. The Mexican type of oregano has a higher percent of thymol, and a lower percent of carvacrol than Mediterranean oregano. The variation between lot to lot is enormous; however, averages show the above statement to be a generalization. Thymol ranged from 0.9% to 26.7% in Greek oregano and between 0.7% to 40% in Mexican oregano. Carvacrol ranged from 32% to 85% in Greek oregano and 15% to 41% in Mexican oregano. Limited analysis of Turkish oregano has shown a low level of thymol but a level of carvacrol similar to Greek oregano.[40] At least 20 other components have been found to be present in the volatile oil of oregano.

The moisture limit recommended by ASTA is 10%. Ash and acid insoluble ash levels can be quite high in oregano. There is often foreign matter present in the spice, especially in the whole form. This spice should be cleaned before grinding. Often spice processors sell whole Greek and Turkish oregano in "original bags," thus eliminating the need for cleaning. In some cases, the loss from cleaning this spice can be as high as 30%–50%. If purchasing oregano in original bags, the quality of the product is much lower and the price will be less expensive than if buying cleaned oregano. Typical ash and acid insoluble ash levels in uncleaned oregano can be as high as 10.0% and 2.5%.

A summary of typical chemical and physical specifications can be found in Tables 4.67 and 4.68. Nutritional information is found in Table 4.69.

4.20.3 Import Tonnage

11.8 million pounds of oregano was imported into the United States in 1991, representing $10.2 million. 44.6% was from Turkey, 35% from Mexico and only 8.2% from Greece.[6]

4.20.4 Countries of Origin

4.20.4.1 Quality Differences

If purchasing *Origanum vulgare,* a "Mediterranean" oregano description is sufficient. The variations between Turkish and Greek are not enough to warrant a specific origin. In addition, when the product is not available from one source, it is easy to change to the other. Mexican oregano is a different story. This product is not the same species as Greek and Turkish oregano. It is actually either *Lippia graveolens* or *Lippia berlandieri.* This type of "oregano" has larger leaves, is darker in

Table 4.67   Whole Oregano: Chemical and Physical Specifications.

Specification	Suggested Limits		
ASTA cleanliness specifications:			
Whole dead insects, by count	3		
Mammalian excreta, by mg/lb	1		
Other excreta, by mg/lb	10.0		
Mold, % by weight	1.00		
Insect defiled/infested, % by weight	1.00		
Extraneous, % by weight	1.00		
FDA DALs			
(whole plant, unprocessed):			
Insect infested &/or moldy pieces by weight	Ave of 5%		
Mammalian excreta, identified as to source, when possible	Ave of 1 mg per lb		
Volatile oil[1]	Mexican	Greek	Turkish
	3% min	2% min	2% min
Moisture[2]	10.0% max		
Ash[1]	10.0% max		
Acid insoluble ash[1]	2.5% max		
Average bulk index (mg/100 g)	500		

[1] These are suggested limits that the authors put together from the data collected over the past 5 years. These numbers are equivalent to the level where most quality spice will fall into.
[2] ASTA suggested maximum moisture level.

color and has a higher volatile oil content—up to 4%. It may be time for the spice industry to separate the Mediterranean and Mexican oregano by introducing a different common name to substitute for Mexican oregano to stop confusion and promote the fact that they are two completely different species, not even from the same genus.

4.20.4.2 Harvest Times

Regardless of origin or species, oregano is harvested from late summer to early fall.

4.20.5 Commercial Uses

Mediterranean oregano is used primarily in Italian flavored products, in combination with either basil or marjoram. It is used in sauces, meat dishes, pizzas, and a variety of other products, across all food categories.

Mexican oregano is used primarily in Mexican foods—chili, taco meat, burritos, and others. It has a harsher flavor which complements these products. In fact, a combination of oregano and cumin often gives a flavor typically identifiable as Mexican.

Table 4.68 Ground Oregano: Chemical and Physical Specifications.

Specification	Suggested Limits		
FDA DALs (6 subsamples):	Ground	Crushed	
Insect fragments	Ave of 1250/10 g	Ave of 300/10 g	
or			
Rodent hairs	Ave of 5/10 g	Ave of 2/10 g	
Volatile oil[1]	Mexican	Greek	Turkish
	2.0% min	1.5% min	1.5% min
Moisture[1]	10.0% max		
Total ash[1]	10.0% max		
Acid insoluble ash[1]	2.5% max		
Military specifications (EE-S-631J, 1981)			
Volatile oil (ml/100 g)	2.0 min		
Moisture	10.0% max		
Total ash	9.5% max		
Acid insoluble ash	2.0% max		
Granulation			
(Regular)	95% min through a U.S.S. #30		
(Coarse)	95% min through a U.S.S. #20		
Bulk index[2] (ml/100 g)	240		

[1] These are suggested limits that the authors put together from data the authors collected in the past 5 years. These numbers are equivalent to the level where most quality spice will fall into.
[2] Average bulk index. Granulation will effect number.

Table 4.69 Nutritional Composition of Oregano Per 100 Grams.

Composition	USDA Handbook 8-2[1] (Ground)	ASTA[2]
Water (grams)	7.16	8.0
Food energy (Kcal)	306	360
Protein (grams)	11.00	12.0
Fat (grams)	10.25	6.4
Carbohydrates (grams)	64.43	64.9
Ash (grams)	7.15	9.0
Calcium (grams)	1.576	1.7
Phosphorus (mg)	200	200
Sodium (mg)	15	20
Potassium (mg)	1,669	1,700
Iron (mg)	44.00	53.3
Thiamine (mg)	.341	.340
Riboflavin (mg)	—	ND[3]
Niacin (mg)	6.220	6.2
Ascorbic acid (mg)	—	ND[3]
Vitamin A activity (RE)	690	690

[1] Composition of Foods: Spices and Herbs. USDA Agricultural Handbook 8-2. January 1977.
[2] The Nutritional Composition of Spices, ASTA Research Committee, February, 1977.
[3] ND = Not detected.

The two types of oregano are utilized in dishes where the herb is grown. The Mediterranean type typically in Italian foods and the Mexican type in Mexican foods. On the west coast, however, the Mexican variety is much more prevalent and is often sold as oregano, regardless of origin.

4.21 Parsley [*Petroselinum cripsum* (Mill.) Nym.]

4.21.1 Background Information

Parsley is usually included as a spice; however, the FDA has classified it as a vegetable and therefore it must be labeled on ingredient statements as "parsley" rather than included in the term "spices." There is more than one variety of parsley; however, that which is cultivated most often is *Petroselinum cripsum*. This variety is commonly known as the Curled Leaf variety, which is grown primarily as an annual in California. The plants are cut and harvested, the stems removed, and the leaves are dried mechanically, causing a very dark green color. The product is then sold in flakes, which are about $1/4$ in. in size. Parsley is also available in a variety of other, smaller sizes such as a $-10+30$ or a $-8+40$ granulation.

According to Rosengarten,[7] parsley was used by the ancient Greeks and Romans. The Greeks used it to crown athletes but also believed it was a symbol of death, and therefore often spread it over graves. The Romans, on the other hand, used it as a food, often eaten with lettuce. During medieval times, parsley was felt to be evil and brought bad luck. Parsley was brought to England in the 16th century and followed the colonists to the new world.

4.21.2 Chemical and Physical Specifications

The volatile oil of parsley is very low, about 0.05%. This makes the inclusion of this on a specification irrelevant. This 0.05% volatile oil can be extracted and sold as an essential oil and is available, although seldom used.

Moisture levels should be kept at no more than 5.0%. Parsley is not typically tested for ash and acid insoluble ash.

Specifications for this product usually include a percentage of brown and yellow leaves and amount of stems present, since these are both detrimental attributes. These should be no more than 0.3% each. The bulk index of parsley flakes is variable and very high, generally ranging from 1200–1800 ml/100 grams.

Nutritional information for parsley can be found in Table 4.70.

4.21.3 Import Tonnage

Parsley is generally not imported into the United States, but rather grown domestically. Domestic production figures are not available.

Table 4.70   Nutritional Composition of Parsley Per 100 Grams.

Composition	USDA Handbook 8-2[1]	ASTA[2]
Water (grams)	9.02	4.0
Food energy (Kcal)	276	355
Protein (grams)	22.42	22.0
Fat (grams)	4.43	5.6
Carbohydrates (grams)	51.66	54.3
Ash (grams)	12.47	14.1
Calcium (grams)	1.468	1.2
Phosphorus (mg)	351	310
Sodium (mg)	452	540
Potassium (mg)	3,805	3,600
Iron (mg)	97.86	14.5
Thiamine (mg)	.172	.170
Riboflavin (mg)	1.230	1.230
Niacin (mg)	7.929	7.9
Ascorbic acid (mg)	122.04	392
Vitamin A activity (RE)	2,334	2,330

[1]   Composition of Foods: Spices and Herbs. USDA Agricultural Handbook 8-2. January 1977.
[2]   The Nutritional Composition of Spices, ASTA Research Committee, February, 1977.

4.21.4 Countries of Origin

4.21.4.1 Quality Differences

Parsley is grown domestically and supplies most of the need in the United States. It is a very high-quality product since it is mechanically dried and harvested in a very modern manner.

4.21.4.2 Harvest Times

Parsley is harvested domestically from May to August.

4.21.5 Commercial Uses

Parsley is used in a large variety of products, anywhere a green leafy piece is desired. It is usually used as a visual and does not contribute much flavor, just a grassy green note if used at a high enough level. Parsley is used in sauces, soups, pasta dishes, snack food seasonings, among others. It is often used in "herb and . . ." products, being the visual green rather than the herbs. It is the green part of sour cream and onion seasoning, not the onion as most people think.

4.22 Pepper—White and Black (*Piper nigrum* L.)

4.22.1 Background Information

White and black pepper are both from the same plant—*Piper nigrum*, which is indigenous to the Malabar Coast of Southern India. Black pepper is the unripe dried fruit, while white pepper is the mature berry in which the hull is removed. Black pepper berries are round, about 0.75–1.0 cm in diameter, black to dark brown in color and shrivelled in appearance. White pepper is a round berry, smooth and off-white to grey in appearance. Green peppercorns are immature berries. These are usually freeze dried or mechanically air dried and are quite fragile and expensive. Pepper is grown on vines which can produce fruit for up to 50 years. The vines are usually supported by trees in the wild or wooden stakes if the vines are cultivated. The berries grow in clusters of about 50 berries in the shape of long spikes.

Black pepper is harvested by hand when the berry is green and dried in the sun on the spikes. They are heaped in piles to promote a browning reaction caused by fermentation, turning the berries dark, and then raked to allow uniform drying. Black pepper is very susceptible to mold formation. During drying, the berries shrivel and turn black, thus turning into the black pepper we are used to.

White pepper is harvested differently. The berries are picked when ripe and they are bright red. They are removed from the spikes and packed into bags and soaked in slow running water. This loosens the pericarp or hull from the core of the berry. After 1–2 weeks of soaking, the berries are trampled to remove the rest of the hull and the cores are washed and sun-dried. Due to the process, white pepper is even more susceptible to mold formation than black pepper. White pepper can have internal mold growth while black pepper only has a surface mold contamination problem.[1]

Pepper has a long history. It was mentioned as far back as 1000 B.C. in ancient Sanskrit literature. During the Middle Ages, pepper was common and used primarily for seasoning and masking flavors in salted preserved meat. It was highly prized, and often used as money for rent, taxes, and dowries.[7] The search for pepper was the reason for a search for a sea route to India.

Black pepper oleoresin and essential oil are both available. The oleoresin varies from source and is available in a variety of strengths in regard to volatile oil and piperine content. Black pepper essential oil is not used much in the food industry. A white pepper oleoresin is available, along with a decolorized black pepper oleoresin. These too, are not used to any great extent.

4.22.2 Chemical and Physical Specifications

There are two main components of black and white pepper: the volatile oil and the pungent components, commonly known as piperine. The volatile oil level in black pepper is usually higher than in white pepper. The hull of the pepper contains fiber and some essential oil. This essential oil is removed during processing into white pepper. Black pepper contains about 0.6%–2.6% volatile oil,[1] depending on the source, but usually contains 2.0%–5.0% in good quality pepper berries. White pepper contains 1.0%–3.0% volatile oil. The maturity of the berry can influence volatile oil content. The volatile oil content increases up to the level in a green peppercorn, and then decreases with maturity.[1] The essential oil contains a large number of compounds—nearly 100 different components have been identified in various studies. The main components present are α-pinene, β-pinene, 1-αphellandrene, β-caryophyllene, limonene, and sabine-delta-3-carene. It has been shown that during storage, not only is some volatile oil lost, but some oxidation of the volatile oil also occurs.

The main pungency component of pepper is piperine. There has been some debate over the years as to whether piperine was the component which caused pungency or not since it was first isolated in 1820. There is a very interesting history on the chemistry of piperine and related compounds which is too detailed to relate here. If interested, Purseglove[1] and Govindarajan[41] do excellent jobs covering this area.

Piperine is the trans, trans form of 1-piperoylpiperidine. Other minor pungent alkaloids present are piperettine, piperyline, piperolein A and B, and piperanine. It is uncertain, however, how these other components measure up against piperine in a sensory assessment of pungency. Piperine content increases with the maturity of the berry.[1]

Piperine can occur in four isomers when synthesized. The structure of piperine is shown in Figure 4.2.

The isomers have different configurations at the double bonds as follows:

Piperine	*trans-trans*
Isopiperine	*cis-trans*
Isochavicine	*trans-cis*
Chavicine	*cis-cis*.

None of the isomers have the high pungency level of piperine. It has been suggested that there is a slow photoisomerization of piperine to its isomers during storage, thus decreasing its pungency.[42] Mori, Yamamoto, and Komei,[43] Yamamoto, Tonari, and Mori,[44] and Grewe et al.,[45] as reported by Giovandran, found no indication of the presence of the other isomers in pepper extracts or in black pepper. Giovandran, therefore, feels that piperine, being the most stable isomer, is the predominant pungent constituent of pepper and the presence of the other isomers occurring naturally in pepper is doubtful.

Chemical methods for determining piperine content are many and give varying results. For example, nonvolatile ether extract is generally used in pepper to give an assessment of pungency. It is now known, however, to have no correlation with piperine content.[1,41] The Kjeldahl method of determining piperine was the first method and is currently an ASTA method. It measures all nitrogen-containing substances. Piperine is the major nitrogen-containing substance in pepper; however, it could be and sometimes was adulterated with nitrogen-containing products like urea to boost the "piperine" content. A second ASTA method is a photocolorimetric procedure which quantitatively tests for the methylenedioxy group on the piperine molecule. This method, too has been criticized, since other compounds having the methylenedioxy group such as piperettine, will also react and thus give a falsely high reading.[46] The relative pungency of compounds such as piperettine is unknown. Newer methods include UV spectroscopy, and high-pressure liquid chromatography (HPLC).[47]

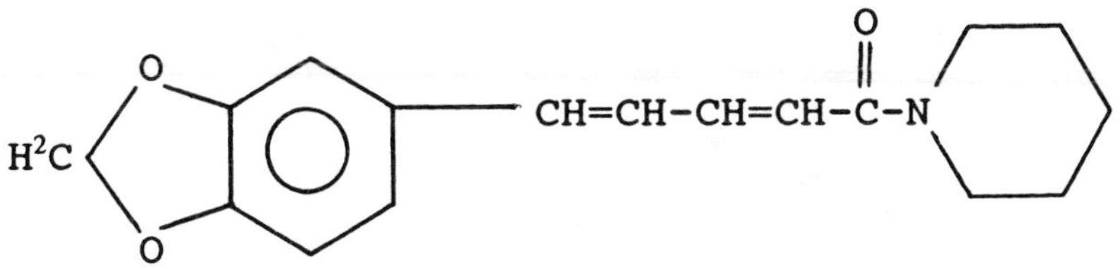

Figure 4.2 The structure of piperine.

The microbiological flora of black and white pepper is high. Total plate counts can be as high as 40 million per gram. *Aspergillus, Penicillium* and *Salmonella* have all been found in pepper. Kiss and Farkas[13] report that black pepper can also be high in *Bacillus cereus* and *Clostridium perfringens*. Brazilian black pepper was blocklisted from import to the United States for a period of time in the 1980s due to Salmonella contamination.

Pepper is one of the only spices which contains high levels of lipase activity. Black and white pepper have a lipase activity of about 2.1 versus other spices which have a lipase activity of about 0.001–0.13 (as percentage lauric acid).[48] Free fatty acids are formed by the hydrolysis of triglycerides by the lipase present in black and white pepper. When high levels of lauric acid are formed, as in fats such as palm and coconut oils, a "soapy" flavor results.

ASTA recommended moisture levels are 12% for black pepper and 14% for white pepper. White pepper is higher since it does have more moisture present from the processing method.

Ash and acid insoluble ash levels should be less than 5% and 0.5%, respectively, in black pepper and less than 1.5% and 0.3%, respectively, in white pepper. A summary of typical chemical and physical specifications can be found in Tables 4.71 through 4.74. Nutritional information is in Tables 4.75 and 4.76.

4.22.3 Import Tonnage

Black pepper is the largest imported spice into the United States at about 85.6 million pounds in 1991 with a dollar value of about $52.2 million.[6] It comes mainly from Indonesia (29.2%), India (5.9%), Brazil (38%), and Malaysia (21%). Indian imports have decreased in recent years. A lot of pepper is still produced in India; however, it is being exported to countries other than the U.S. and/or used internally. White pepper imports for 1991 were 11.4 million pounds with a dollar value of about $7.1 million. 95.4% of this white pepper comes to the U.S. from Indonesia (Muntok white pepper).

4.22.4 Countries of Origin

4.22.4.1 Quality Differences

Black peppers do exhibit some differences by source. The names given to the pepper in the industry are usually designated by the port where the pepper is shipped from.

Table 4.71   Whole Black Pepper: Chemical and Physical Specifications.

Specification	Suggested Limits
ASTA cleanliness specifications:	
Whole dead insects, by count	2
Mammalian excreta, by mg/lb	1
Other excreta, by mg/lb	5.0
Mold, % by weight	[1]
Insect defiled/infested, % by weight	[1]
Extraneous, % by weight	1.00
FDA DALs:	
Insect infested and/or moldy pieces by weight	Ave of 1%
Mammalian excreta	Ave of 1 mg per lb
Foreign matter pickings and siftings by weight	Ave of 1%
Volatile oil[2]	2.0% min
Moisture[3]	12.0% max
Ash[2]	5.0% max
Acid insoluble ash[2]	0.5% max
Average bulk index (mg/100 g)	165

[1]   1% moldy and/or infested pieces by weight.
[2]   These are suggested limits that the authors put together from the data collected over the past 5 years. These numbers are equivalent to the level where most quality spice will fall into.
[3]   ASTA suggested maximum moisture level.

Malabar black pepper is from the Malabar coast in Southwestern India. Malabar is generally an aromatic pepper with a high piperine level. Tellicherry is a type of Malabar. It is a grade designation for the large berries. Lampong black pepper is from Indonesia, mainly from the island of Sumatra. Lampong is a district of Southeastern Sumatra. This berry is smaller than Indian with a thin shell, often making it ideal for machine decortication. The pepper itself is high in volatiles and piperine, very similar to Indian. Sarawak pepper is from Malaysia, along the northwestern coast of Borneo. Sarawak tends to be milder in flavor and pungency. This type of pepper is not often imported to the United States, but more often imported to other countries. Brazilian pepper is a newer source. Its quality was often thought to be lower than the Indonesian and Indian varieties; however, that has improved in recent years. The pepper from Brazil has a smoother surface and a blacker appearance, with the core exhibiting a brighter white color. When ground this pepper looks less green and more white. It generally has a lower volatile oil than pepper from India and Indonesia.

White pepper is most commonly imported from Bangka, Indonesia and is called Muntok white pepper from the name of the port from where it is shipped.

Black peppers do have some differences based on origin as described above. The

practice of specifying a specific origin is decreasing. Even though there are differences, the variation within each source is high. By specifying a certain origin you
are only increasing your costs and would be better off specifying a certain volatile
oil and piperine content.

4.22.4.2 Harvest Times

Brazilian and Indonesian (Lampong) black pepper is harvested in August and September. Indian (Malabar) black pepper is harvested in January and February. Malay-
sian pepper is harvested in April through June. Muntok white pepper is generally
harvested in June and July.

4.22.5 Commercial Uses

Black pepper is used in almost any application where spice is used, with the
exception of baked goods. Its use is universal in sauces, gravies, processed meats,

Table 4.72 Ground Black Pepper: Chemical and Physical Specifications.

Specification	Suggested Limits
FDA DALs (6 subsamples):	
Insect fragments	Ave of 475 or more/50 g
or	
Rodent hair fragments	Ave of 2 or more/50 g
Volatile oil[1]	1.5% min
Moisture[1]	12.0% max
Total ash[1]	5.0% max
Acid insoluble ash[1]	0.5% max
Military specifications	
(EE-S-631J, 1981)	
Volatile oil (ml/100 g)	2.0 min
Moisture	12.0% max
Total ash	7.0% max
Acid insoluble ash	1.0% max
Crude fiber	12.5% max
Nonvolatile methylene chloride extract	7.5% min
Starch	30.0% max
Granulation	70% min through U.S.S. #30
	or
	95% min through U.S.S. #16
	95% min on U.S.S. #35
Bulk index (ml/100 g)	Varies with granulation

[1] These are suggested limits that the authors put together from data the authors collected in the past 5 years. These numbers are equivalent to the level where most quality spice will fall into.

Table 4.73   Whole White Pepper: Chemical and Physical Specifications.

Specification	Suggested Limits
ASTA cleanliness specifications:	
Whole dead insects, by count	2
Mammalian excreta, by mg/lb	1
Other excreta, by mg/lb	1.0
Mold, % by weight	[1]
Insect defiled/infested, % by weight	[1]
Extraneous, % by weight	0.50
FDA DALs:	
Insect infested &/or moldy pieces by weight	Ave of 1%
Mammalian excreta	Ave of 1 mg per lb
Foreign matter pickings and siftings by weight	Ave of 1%
Volatile oil[2]	1.5% min
Moisture[3]	14.0% max
Ash[2]	1.5% max
Acid insoluble ash[2]	0.3% max
Average bulk index (mg/100 g)	150

[1]   1% Moldy and/or infested pieces by weight.
[2]   These are suggested limits that the authors put together from the data collected over the past 5 years. These numbers are equivalent to the level where most quality spice will fall into.
[3]   ASTA suggested maximum moisture level.

poultry, snack foods, batters, and breadings. White pepper is utilized to a lesser degree. It has a slightly different flavor than black, often described as musty. This product is used in processed meats and in applications where dark specking is not desired. Another choice for this latter application is the use of oleoresin black pepper to get the flavor and heat of pepper without the dark specking. Oleoresin black pepper is used in many processed foods in the U.S. It is probably the most widely used oleoresin.

4.23 Rosemary (*Rosmarinus officinalis* L.)

4.23.1 Background Information

Rosemary is the leaves of a small evergreen shrub belonging to the mint family and indigenous to the Mediterranean region. The leaves are narrow, about 2 cm long, and resemble curled pine needles. In fact, the flavor can be described as reminiscent of pine. An essential oil is available as well as an unflavored extract. The oleoresin contains only 2%–4% volatile oil.

Rosemary was revered in ancient Greece for its association with memory and became a symbol of faithfulness to lovers. During Medieval times, rosemary was

Table 4.74 Ground White Pepper: Chemical and Physical Specifications.

Specification	Suggested Limits
FDA DALs (6 subsamples):	
Insect fragments	Ave of 475 or more/50 g
or	
Rodent hair fragments	Ave of 2 or more/50 g
Volatile oil[1]	1.5% min
Moisture[1]	14.0% max
Total ash[1]	1.5% max
Acid insoluble ash[1]	0.3% max
Military specifications	
(EE-S-631J, 1981)	
Volatile oil (ml/100 g)	1.0 min
Moisture	15.0% max
Total ash	3.0% max
Acid insoluble ash	0.3% max
Crude fiber	5.0% max
Starch	52.0% max
Nonvolatile methylene chloride extract	7.5% min
Granulation	95% min through a U.S.S. #40
Bulk index[2] (ml/100 g)	180

[1] These are suggested limits that the authors put together from data the authors collected in the past 5 years. These numbers are equivalent to the level where most quality spice will fall into.

[2] Average bulk index. Granulation will effect number.

Table 4.75 Nutritional Composition of Black Pepper Per 100 Grams.

Composition	USDA Handbook 8-2[1]	ASTA[2]
Water (grams)	10.51	8.0
Food energy (Kcal)	255	400
Protein (grams)	10.95	10.0
Fat (grams)	3.26[3]	10.2
Carbohydrates (grams)	64.81	66.5
Ash (grams)	4.33	4.6
Calcium (grams)	.437	0.4
Phosphorus (mg)	173	160
Sodium (mg)	44	10
Potassium (mg)	1,259	1,200
Iron (mg)	28.86	17.0
Thiamine (mg)	.109	.070
Riboflavin (mg)	.240	.210
Niacin (mg)	1.142	0.8
Ascorbic acid (mg)	—	ND[4]
Vitamin A activity (RE)	19	19

[1] Composition of Foods: Spices and Herbs. USDA Agricultural Handbook 8-2. January 1977.

[2] The Nutritional Composition of Spices, ASTA Research Committee, February, 1977.

[3] Piperine subtracted from lipid value.

[4] ND = Not detected.

Table 4.76   Nutritional Composition of White Pepper Per 100 Grams.

Composition	USDA Handbook 8-2[1]	ASTA[2]
Water (grams)	11.42	9.5
Food energy (Kcal)	296	395
Protein (grams)	10.40	12.0
Fat (grams)	2.12[3]	8.0
Carbohydrates (grams)	68.61	69.0
Ash (grams)	1.59	1.0
Calcium (grams)	.265	0.2
Phosphorus (mg)	176	150
Sodium (mg)	5	10
Potassium (mg)	73	100
Iron (mg)	14.31	6.9
Thiamine (mg)	.022	.020
Riboflavin (mg)	.126	.130
Niacin (mg)	.212	.2
Ascorbic acid (mg)	—	ND[4]
Vitamin A activity (RE)	Trace	ND[4]

[1] Composition of Foods: Spices and Herbs. USDA Agricultural Handbook 8-2. January 1977.
[2] The Nutritional Composition of Spices, ASTA Research Committee, February, 1977.
[3] Piperine subtracted from lipid value.
[4] ND = Not detected.

thought to be a protector from evil. Rosemary was also used for flavor in salting meats for preservation during the Middle Ages in Europe.[7]

4.23.2 Chemical and Physical Specifications

Rosemary contains about 0.5%–2.0% volatile oil. Major components found by gas chromatography analysis are α-pinene (7%–25%), d-linalool (14%–17%), and camphene (2%–10%).[3] These values can vary from origin and from lot to lot within each origin.

Rosemary extract has been known for some time to have antioxidant properties[49] in food products. In addition, it has recently been found to possess some anti-microbial activity. These subjects will be discussed more fully in Chapter 6.

ASTA recommended maximum moisture levels for rosemary is 10%. Ash and acid insoluble ash should be 8% and 1%, respectively. The major foreign matter present in this spice are small pieces of branches from the plant itself. Typical chemical and physical specifications can be found in Tables 4.77 and 4.78. Nutritional data is located in Table 4.79.

4.23.3 Import Tonnage

Import tonnage information for rosemary is not available from the U.S.D.A.

Table 4.77 Whole Rosemary: Chemical and Physical Specifications.

Specification	Suggested Limits
ASTA cleanliness specifications:	
Whole dead insects, by count	2
Mammalian excreta, by mg/lb	1
Other excreta, by mg/lb	4.0
Mold, % by weight	1.00
Insect defiled/infested, % by weight	1.00
Extraneous, % by weight	0.50
FDA DALs (leafy spices):	
Insect infested and/or moldy pieces by weight	Ave of 5%
Mammalian excreta, after processing, identified as to source when possible	Ave of 1 mg per lb
Volatile oil[1]	1.5% min
Moisture[2]	10.0% max
Ash[1]	8.0% max
Acid insoluble ash[1]	1.0% max
Average bulk index (mg/100 g)	475

[1] These are suggested limits that the authors put together from the data collected over the past 5 years. These numbers are equivalent to the level where most quality spice will fall into.
[2] ASTA suggested maximum moisture level.

Table 4.78 Ground Rosemary: Chemical and Physical Specifications.

Specification	Suggested Limits
FDA DALs	None
Volatile oil[1]	0.8% min
Moisture[1]	10.0% max
Total ash[1]	8.0% max
Acid insoluble ash[1]	1.0% max
Military specifications (EE-S-631J, 1981)	
Volatile oil (ml/100 g)	1.1 min
Moisture	9.0% max
Total ash	9.0% max
Acid insoluble ash	0.2% max
Granulation	95% min through a U.S.S. #35
Bulk index[2] (ml/100 g)	310

[1] These are suggested limits that the authors put together from data the authors collected in the past 5 years. These numbers are equivalent to the level where most quality spice will fall into.
[2] Average bulk index. Granulation will effect number.

Table 4.79   Nutritional Composition of Rosemary Per 100 Grams.

Composition	USDA Handbook 8-2[1]	ASTA[2]
Water (grams)	9.31	5.5
Food energy (Kcal)	331	440
Protein (grams)	4.88	4.5
Fat (grams)	15.22	17.4
Carbohydrates (grams)	64.06	66.4
Ash (grams)	6.53	6.0
Calcium (grams)	1.280	1.5
Phosphorus (mg)	70	70
Sodium (mg)	50	40
Potassium (mg)	955	1,000
Iron (mg)	29.25	33.0
Thiamine (mg)	.514	.510
Riboflavin (mg)	—	ND[3]
Niacin (mg)	1.000	1.0
Ascorbic acid (mg)	61.22	61
Vitamin A activity (RE)	313	310

[1]   Composition of Foods: Spices and Herbs. USDA Agricultural Handbook 8-2. January 1977.

[2]   The Nutritional Composition of Spices, ASTA Research Committee, February, 1977.

[3]   ND = Not detected.

4.23.4 Countries of Origin

4.23.4.1 Quality Differences

Rosemary is imported primarily from Portugal, Yugoslavia, and France. In 1992, the availability of rosemary from Yugoslavia was badly hindered due to the internal conflicts in that country. No strong origin differences between sources are apparent.

4.23.4.2 Harvest Times

Rosemary is harvested in France in August and in Portugal and Yugoslavia during June and July.

4.23.5 Commercial Uses

Rosemary as a spice is not used in large amounts industrially in the United States. The main flavoring use is as a ground product in sauces or blended with other herbs in cheeses and other items. Rosemary oil is used in processed meats for flavoring. A deflavored and deodorized rosemary extract is used in the food industry as a natural antioxidant in recent years, replacing the more traditional phenolic antioxidants.

4.24 Saffron (*Crocus sativus* L.)

4.24.1 Background Information

Saffron is the stigmas of the purple autumn crocus of the iris family native to the Mediterranean area. It is the most expensive spice due to its labor intensive harvesting. Each plant has three dark orange to reddish brown stigmas, or thread-like filaments, which are handpicked and dried on trays to produce saffron. To compound the labor expense, saffron loses 80% of its weight during drying. 250,000 stigmas (75,000 crocus plants) are required to produce one pound of dried saffron. Saffron has a bitter flavor and is most valued for its yellow color.

Saffron is referred to in Solomon 4:13–14 in the Bible. The Greeks and Romans sprinkled saffron on the floors of theaters as a perfume. By the 13th century, saffron was introduced into Europe. Between 1350 and 1800, there was strict enforcement of nonadulteration laws of the product. In fact, those who did tamper with it were burned alive for punishment.[7] By the 1500s, saffron was being cultivated in England.

4.24.2 Chemical and Physical Specifications

Not much information on the chemical components of saffron is available. In fact, moisture, ash, and acid insoluble ash recommended levels are not available. Few, if any suppliers analyze these components due to the cost of saffron.

Saffron does contain less than 1% of an essential oil; however, most buyers purchase saffron for its yellow color, although the use of artificial colors and turmeric have far outweighed the use of saffron due to cost considerations. The primary chemical constituents of saffron are 2,2,6-trimethyl-4,6-cyclohexadienal, crocin (the coloring agent), and picrocrocin (thought to be responsible for the bitter flavor).[50]

The nutritional data for saffron can be found in Table 4.80.

Table 4.80 Nutritional Composition of Saffron Per 100 Grams.

Composition	USDA Handbook 8-2[1]
Water (grams)	11.90
Food energy (Kcal)	310
Protein (grams)	11.43
Fat (grams)	5.85
Carbohydrates (grams)	65.37
Ash (grams)	5.45
Calcium (grams)	.111
Phosphorus (mg)	252
Sodium (mg)	148
Potassium (mg)	1,724
Iron (mg)	11.10
Thiamine (mg)	—
Riboflavin (mg)	—
Niacin (mg)	—
Ascorbic acid (mg)	—
Vitamin A activity (RE)	—

[1] Composition of Foods: Spices and Herbs. USDA Agricultural Handbook 8-2. January 1977. Supplement 1990.

4.24.3 Import Tonnage

The importation of saffron is very small, due to the high cost. In 1991, 7337 pounds were imported, 96% from Spain, mostly from the LaMancha region in the central portion of the country. The wholesale cost of saffron was about $460/pound, with a retail value of about $750/pound.

4.24.4 Countries of Origin

4.24.4.1 Quality Differences

Spain is the primary producer. Other products which have been tried as substitutes for saffron have large quality discrepancies. Safflower is one of those items which is sometimes sold as saffron.

4.24.4.2 Harvest Times

Saffron is harvested in Spain in October and November.

4.24.5 Commercial Uses

Saffron is rarely, if ever, used in the industrial food market. Occasionally, saffron is used by foodservice and retail customers in products such as arroz con pollo and yellow rice which traditionally use saffron. Otherwise, industrial use has been replaced with turmeric or artificial colors.

4.25 Sage (*Salvia officinalis* L.)

4.25.1 Background Information

Sage is a bushy perennial of the mint or Labiate family native to the Mediterranean region. The plant has large, elliptical leaves, ranging from 5 to 7 cm long. They are silver-grey to green and velvety, or hairy to the touch.

Sage was used by the ancient Greek and Romans as a medicinal herb. In the Middle Ages, sage was used to treat cholera, the common cold, fevers, and epilepsy.

In England during the 16th century, sage was infused as a tea and drunk in place of tea leaves which were not introduced to Europe until later. Colonial Americans used sage both medicinally and as a culinary herb very frequently.

Sage is available as an essential oil and oleoresin. The oleoresin contains 30%–35% volatile oil.

4.25.2 Chemical and Physical Specifications

Sage contains about 1.5%–2.5% volatile oil. Major components are thujone, borneol, and cineole.[3] Analysis of selected lots of Dalmatian and Albanian Sage showed that thujone and *d*-linalool content to be at 17%–26%, and 19%–29% respectively. *d*-Camphor ranged from 3% to 13% and 1,8-cineole from 5% to

10%.[40] These percentages vary by source and are only an indication of major chemical components of sage oil.

ASTA recommended moisture limits for sage is 10% maximum. Ash and acid insoluble ash should be less than 10% and 1%, respectively.

Sage often has a high amount of extraneous material present at import. It comes in bales. Large rocks, cigarette butts, and even an occasional tennis shoe have been found in the product. When grinding, care must be taken since sage fires, due to the volatile oil constituents in the product, can occur. Branches and twigs are common in sage. Often branches with the leaves still attached are in the bales.

Sage is also known to have antioxidant and antimicrobial activity. Further information in this area can be found in Chapter 6.

Typical chemical and physical specifications can be found in Tables 4.81 and 4.82. Nutritional data is included in Table 4.83.

4.25.3 Import Tonnage

Five million pounds of sage was imported into the United States in 1991, representing $4.6 million.[6] 65% of this figure came from Albania, 17.8% from the Dalmatian area of Yugoslavia, and only 3% from Turkey. These figures are due to change drastically for 1992 and beyond due to the internal ethnic conflicts in Yugoslavia.

Table 4.81 Whole Sage: Chemical and Physical Specifications.

Specification	Suggested Limits
ASTA cleanliness specifications:	
Whole dead insects, by count	2
Mammalian excreta, by mg/lb	1
Other excreta, by mg/lb	4.0
Mold, % by weight	1.00
Insect defiled/infested, % by weight	1.00
Extraneous, % by weight	0.50
FDA DALs (unprocessed):	
Insect infested and/or moldy pieces by weight	Ave of 5%
Mammalian excreta identified as to source when possible	Ave of 1 mg per lb
Volatile oil[1]	1.5% min
Moisture[2]	10.0% max
Ash[1]	10.0% max
Acid insoluble ash[1]	1.0% max
Military specification (EE-S-631J, 1981)	10% by weight of stems, excluding petioles
Average bulk index (mg/100 g)	950

[1] These are suggested limits that the authors put together from the data collected over the past 5 years. These numbers are equivalent to the level where most quality spice will fall into.
[2] ASTA suggested maximum moisture level.

Table 4.82   Ground/Rubbed Sage: Chemical and Physical Specifications.

Specification	Suggested Limits
FDA DALs (6 subsamples):	
Insect fragments	Ave of 200 or more/10 g
or	
Rodent hairs	Ave of 9 or more/10 g
Volatile oil[1]	1.0% min
Moisture[1]	10.0% max
Total ash[1]	10.0% max
Acid insoluble ash[1]	1.0% max
Military specifications	
(EE-S-631J, 1981)	
Volatile oil (ml/100 g)	1.0 min
Moisture	9.0% max
Total ash	10.0% max
Acid insoluble ash	1.0% max
Granulation—Ground	95% min through a U.S.S. #20
Granulation—Rubbed	95% min through a U.S.S. #20
	95% min on a U.S.S. #40
Bulk index[2] (ml/100 g)	
Ground	370
Rubbed	530

[1]   These are suggested limits that the authors put together from data the authors collected in the past 5 years. These numbers are equivalent to the level where most quality spice will fall into.
[2]   Average bulk index. Granulation will effect number.

Table 4.83   Nutritional Composition of Sage Per 100 Grams.

Composition	USDA Handbook 8-2[1] (Ground)	ASTA[2]
Water (grams)	7.96	5.5
Food energy (Kcal)	315	415
Protein (grams)	10.62	10.0
Fat (grams)	12.74	14.1
Carbohydrates (grams)	60.73	62.3
Ash (grams)	7.95	7.7
Calcium (grams)	1.652	1.8
Phosphorus (mg)	91	90
Sodium (mg)	11	10
Potassium (mg)	1,070	1,000
Iron (mg)	28.12	27.3
Thiamine (mg)	.754	.750
Riboflavin (mg)	.336	.340
Niacin (mg)	5.720	5.7
Ascorbic acid (mg)	32.38	40
Vitamin A activity (RE)	590	590

[1]   Composition of Foods: Spices and Herbs. USDA Agricultural Handbook 8-2. January 1977.
[2]   The Nutritional Composition of Spices, ASTA Research Committee, February, 1977.

4.25.4 Countries of Origin

4.25.4.1 Quality Differences

Sage is imported primarily from Yugoslavia and Albania. Yugoslavian (Dalmatian) sage historically has been known for its high quality. Dalmatia is a region of Yugoslavia by the Adriatic Sea. It is now felt that the quality of Albanian sage is just as high and the two can be used interchangeably. Dalmatian is much higher in price than Albanian and specifying the origin will cost much more than not supplying an origin specification. In 1992, due to the conflict in Yugoslavia, quality products were very difficult to obtain. It will be interesting to see what 1993 and beyond brings.

Sage is also available from Greece and Turkey. These products are not used as much and generally have a different flavor profile. Turkish sage tends to have a higher level of extraneous material present. Heath[8] claims Greek sage is not *Salvia officinalis* L., but rather *Salvia triloba* L.

4.25.4.2 Harvest Times

Sage is harvested from July to September in Albania and Yugoslavia. Turkish sage is harvested in July and August.

4.25.5 Commercial Uses

Sage is a very popular herb. By far the major use of sage is in the processed meats industry in the United States. The major flavor component of fresh pork sausage seasoning is sage.

The extractives of sage, along with the rubbed and chopped versions, are also utilized primarily in the processed meats industry. Other forms of sage available are ground, rubbed, and chopped. The rubbed sage is basically a coarse ground sage which is very fluffy in appearance. This product, along with the chopped form, is frequently used in the processed meats industry. Sage is often sold rubbed since it is very difficult to grind it to a tiny particle size, except when cryogenically ground.

Sage is also the predominant herb in poultry seasoning. It is used in poultry items, as well as being the major flavor in prepared stuffings and seasoned croutons for stuffing. Sage is also utilized to some extent in gravies and sauces.

4.26 Savory (*Satureja hortensis* L.)

4.26.1 Background Information

Savory is an annual herb, also of the mint or Labiate family. It is native to southern Europe and the Mediterranean region and is often called Summer Savory. The leaves are narrow, elliptical, dark green, and about 0.5–1.0 cm long.

Savory was utilized by the ancient Romans as a culinary spice and was also used as a medicinal herb. It was used in England in the Middle Ages as a culinary herb.

4.26.2 Chemical and Physical Specifications

The volatile oil of savory is present at less than 1% of the herb. The major component is carvacrol, at about 25%–45%. Thymol (12%–13%) and *p*-cymene (9%–12%) are also present in appreciable amounts.[40]

Savory oil is available but seldom used. The oleoresin is generally not available.

The ASTA recommended moisture limit is 11% maximum. Ash and acid insoluble ash figures are not available. Chemical and physical data is located in Tables 4.84 and 4.85. Nutritional data for savory can be found in Table 4.86.

4.26.3 Import Tonnage

The import tonnage of savory is not available from the U.S.D.A.

4.26.4 Countries of Origin

4.26.4.1 Quality Differences

Savory is imported primarily from Yugoslavia and France. There is no major quality differences by origin. In fact, sometimes Yugoslavian savory is shipped to France and exported from there. Once again, the Yugoslavian conflict will directly affect availability of savory.

Table 4.84 Whole Savory: Chemical and Physical Specifications.

Specification	Suggested Limits
ASTA cleanliness specifications:	
Whole dead insects, by count	2
Mammalian excreta, by mg/lb	1
Other excreta, by mg/lb	10.0
Mold, % by weight	1.00
Insect defiled/infested, % by weight	1.00
Extraneous, % by weight	0.50
FDA DALs (leafy spices):	
Insect infested and/or moldy pieces by weight	Ave of 5%
Mammalian excreta, after processing, identified as to source when possible	Ave of 1 mg per lb
Volatile oil[1]	0.5% min
Moisture[2]	11.0% max
Ash[1]	N/A
Acid insoluble ash[1]	N/A
Average bulk index (mg/100 g)	520

[1] These are suggested limits that the authors put together from the data collected over the past 5 years. These numbers are equivalent to the level where most quality spice will fall into.
[2] ASTA suggested maximum moisture level.

Table 4.85 Ground Savory: Chemical and Physical Specifications.

Specification	Suggested Limits
FDA DALs	None
Volatile oil[1]	0.5% min
Moisture[1]	11.0% max
Total ash[1]	N/A
Acid insoluble ash[1]	N/A
Military specifications (EE-S-631J, 1981)	
Volatile oil (ml/100 g)	0.5 min
Moisture	11.0% max
Total ash	10.0% max
Acid insoluble ash	2.0% max
Granulation	95% min through a U.S.S. #40
Bulk index[2] (ml/100 g)	200

[1] These are suggested limits that the authors put together from data the authors collected in the past 5 years. These numbers are equivalent to the level where most quality spice will fall into.
[2] Average bulk index. Granulation will effect number.

Table 4.86 Nutritional Composition of Savory Per 100 Grams.

Composition	USDA Handbook 8-2[1] (Ground)	ASTA[2]
Water (grams)	9.00	9.0
Food energy (Kcal)	272	355
Protein (grams)	6.73	7.0
Fat (grams)	5.91	5.2
Carbohydrates (grams)	68.73	69.9
Ash (grams)	9.63	8.7
Calcium (grams)	2.132	2.2
Phosphorus (mg)	140	140
Sodium (mg)	24	20
Potassium (mg)	1,051	1,100
Iron (mg)	37.88	37.8
Thiamine (mg)	.366	.370
Riboflavin (mg)	—	ND[3]
Niacin (mg)	4.080	4.1
Ascorbic acid (mg)	—	ND[3]
Vitamin A activity (RE)	513	510

[1] Composition of Foods: Spices and Herbs. USDA Agricultural Handbook 8-2. January 1977.
[2] The Nutritional Composition of Spices, ASTA Research Committee, February, 1977.
[3] ND = Not detected.

4.26.4.2 Harvest Times

Savory is harvested in June and July in Yugoslavia and in August in France.

4.26.5 Commercial Uses

Savory is seldom used in the processed foods industry. It has been utilized to a small extent in herbed cheese products in recent years and in some Italian sauce applications at low levels. Savory also has limited use in food service applications in sauce products and in a "Fines Herbes" or other French-type herb mixtures.

4.27 Tarragon (*Artemisia dracunculus* L.)

4.27.1 Background Information

Tarragon is the leaf of a perennial herb native to southern Russia and Asia. It is a member of the sunflower (*Compositae*) family. The leaves are dark green, about 5 cm long and narrow with small rounded tips.

Tarragon gets its name from the French word "estragon" and the Spanish "taragona," which are both derived from the Greek word for dragon. The word for tarragon in Swedish and Dutch is actually "dragon." There is some confusion as to where this description comes from. The two usual theories are that it was used to treat snake bites, or that the roots of the plant are coiled and look like snakes.

Tarragon is a recent addition to the culinary herbs, historically speaking. It was introduced into England in the 16th century. By the early 1800s it was being grown in the United States.

4.27.2 Chemical and Physical Specifications

Tarragon contains 0.2%–1.5% volatile oil, containing mainly methyl chavicol (or estragole) and anethole. Parry[3] also includes ocimene, phellandrene, and *p*-methoxycinnamaldehyde as components present in tarragon. The anethole gives it an anise or licorice-like flavor. It is a quite distinctive flavor containing herbaceous and perfume-like undertones.

Ash and acid insoluble ash levels should be kept to 12% and 1%. The ASTA recommended moisture limit for tarragon is 10%. Chemical and physical recommended specifications can be found in Tables 4.87 and 4.88. Nutritional data is listed in Table 4.89.

4.27.3 Import Tonnage

The import data for 1991 is not available from the U.S.D.A.

4.27.4 Countries of Origin

4.27.4.1 Quality Differences

Tarragon comes from France and is also produced domestically, primarily in California. The French and domestic products are very similar. They are mechanically

Table 4.87   Whole Tarragon: Chemical and Physical Specifications.

Specification	Suggested Limits
ASTA cleanliness specifications:	
Whole dead insects, by count	2
Mammalian excreta, by mg/lb	1
Other excreta, by mg/lb	1.0
Mold, % by weight	1.00
Insect defiled/infested, % by weight	1.00
Extraneous, % by weight	0.50
FDA DALs (leafy spices):	
Insect infested	Ave of 5%
and/or moldy pieces by weight	
Mammalian excreta,	Ave of 1 mg per lb
after processing,	
identified as to source,	
when possible	
Volatile oil[1]	0.2% min
Moisture[2]	10.0% max
Ash[1]	12.0% max
Acid insoluble ash[1]	1.0% max
Average bulk index (mg/100 g)	725

[1]   These are suggested limits that the authors put together from the data collected over the past 5 years. These numbers are equivalent to the level where most quality spice will fall into.
[2]   ASTA suggested maximum moisture level.

Table 4.88   Ground Tarragon: Chemical and Physical Specifications.

Specification	Suggested Limits
FDA DALs	None
Volatile oil[1]	0.2% min
Moisture[1]	10.0% max
Total ash[1]	12.0% max
Acid insoluble ash[1]	1.0% max
Military specifications	
(EE-S-631J, 1981)	
Volatile oil (ml/100 g)	0.3 min
Moisture	10.0% max
Total ash	15.0% max
Acid insoluble ash	1.5% max
Granulation	100% min through a U.S.S. #40
Bulk index[2] (ml/100 g)	200

[1]   These are suggested limits that the authors put together from data the authors collected in the past 5 years. These numbers are equivalent to the level where most quality spice will fall into.
[2]   Average bulk index. Granulation will effect number.

Table 4.89   Nutritional Composition of Tarragon Per 100 Grams.

Composition	USDA Handbook 8-2[1] (Ground)	ASTA[2]
Water (grams)	7.74	4.5
Food energy (Kcal)	295	365
Protein (grams)	22.76	24.0
Fat (grams)	7.24	7.3
Carbohydrates (grams)	50.22	51.5
Ash (grams)	12.03	12.3
Calcium (grams)	1.139	1.3
Phosphorus (mg)	313	310
Sodium (mg)	62	70
Potassium (mg)	3,020	3,200
Iron (mg)	32.30	35.7
Thiamine (mg)	.251	.250
Riboflavin (mg)	1.339	1.340
Niacin (mg)	8.950	8.9
Ascorbic acid (mg)	—	ND[3]
Vitamin A activity (RE)	420	420

[1] Composition of Foods: Spices and Herbs. USDA Agricultural Handbook 8-2. January 1977.
[2] The Nutritional Composition of Spices, ASTA Research Committee, February, 1977.
[3] ND = Not detected.

dried. French tarragon is the most well-known product; however, there is not enough French tarragon for the current demand. The quality of the domestic product is equivalent; however, sometimes granulation size is not consistent in the leaf product. The usage of tarragon has increased dramatically in recent years, most notably in upscale products. In some instances it has become difficult to get the product unless it is contracted with domestic growers in advance.

4.27.4.2 Harvest Times

Tarragon is harvested in March and April in the United States and in July and August in France.

4.27.5 Commercial Uses

The volume of tarragon is small in the food industry. It is, however, growing at a very rapid rate. Tarragon is generally used in high end specialty products in the food industry such as those distributed through department stores and gourmet shops. Tarragon flavored vinegars, sauces, and salad dressings are becoming popular. Tarragon has a strong distinctive flavor and should be used in moderation. Tarragon or estragon oil is available but rarely used in the food industry. It is very expensive and is used primarily in the perfume industry.

4.28 Thyme (*Thymus vulgaris* L.)

4.28.1 Background Information

Thyme is a perennial shrub of the mint, or Labiate, family native to the Mediterranean region. The leaves of thyme are small, about 0.5 cm in length, grayish green, and very narrow. There are many species of thyme and when the supply is short, other varieties are sometimes passed for "true" or French thyme (*Thymus vulgaris*). For further information on other species of thyme, one of the many consumer herb books should be consulted since many of these species are grown in herb gardens and are used as culinary herbs. They are not considered thyme in the processed foods industry, however, and this is why they are not covered here.

Thyme was used by the ancient Greeks as a medicinal herb and by the Romans to flavor some food items. Thyme was often associated with courage and sacrifice. Roman soldiers bathed in thyme water to encourage the above. Ladies during the Middle Ages gave knights sprigs of thyme for courage.[51] Over the years, many medicinal uses of thyme have been claimed.

4.28.2 Chemical and Physical Specifications

Thyme contains 0.8%–2.0% volatile oil of which the main component is thymol, comprising from 7%–40%. Other major components are *p*-cymene (7%–42%) and *d*-linalool (1%–12%).[40] Some sources claim carvacrol to be a major component.[8,52] Russell and Olson[52] also found camphene and γ-terpinene in appreciable amounts.

Most good quality thyme ranges between 5% and 10% ash and 0.5% and 3.0% acid insoluble ash, although ash can be as high as 15%. The ASTA recommended moisture level is 10%.

The essential oil of thyme is available in two types: oil of red thyme and oil of white thyme. The red thyme is from Spanish thyme. The white thyme is a redistilled version of the red thyme and is generally smoother in flavor and more expensive. An oleoresin is also available, containing about 6%–8% volatile oil.

Chemical and physical recommended specifications are available in Tables 4.90 and 4.91. Nutritional data for thyme is listed in Table 4.92.

4.28.3 Import Tonnage

The import data for thyme from the U.S.D.A. is not available.

4.28.4 Countries of Origin

4.28.4.1 Quality Differences

French thyme is reported to be the highest quality. The availability of product from this source is very low. Spain is the major imported source of thyme. California produces a small amount of thyme for commercial use.

Table 4.90 Whole Thyme: Chemical and Physical Specifications.

Specification	Suggested Limits
ASTA cleanliness specifications:	
Whole dead insects, by count	4
Mammalian excreta, by mg/lb	1
Other excreta, by mg/lb	5.0
Mold, % by weight	1.00
Insect defiled/infested, % by weight	1.00
Extraneous, % by weight	0.50
FDA DALs:	
Whole plant (unprocessed)	
Insect infested and/or moldy pieces by weight	Ave of 5%
Mammalian excreta, identified as to source, when possible	Ave of 1 mg per lb
Unground (processed)	
Insect fragments and/or	Ave of 325 or more/25 g
Rodent hairs	Ave of 2 or more/25 g
Volatile oil[1]	0.8% min
Moisture[2]	10.0% max
Ash[1]	10.0% max
Acid insoluble ash[1]	3.0% max
Average bulk index (mg/100 g)	400

[1] These are suggested limits that the authors put together from the data collected over the past 5 years. These numbers are equivalent to the level where most quality spice will fall into.
[2] ASTA suggested maximum moisture level.

4.28.4.1 Harvest Times

Thyme is harvested in France twice a year, once in May and then again in September. Spain harvests thyme in February through June.

4.28.5 Commercial Uses

Thyme is a widely used herb. It is common in poultry flavored products such as stuffings and breadings. Thyme is used along with sage in poultry seasoning. It is used extensively in creole dishes and in some processed meat products.

Thyme oils are used in some processed meats and some sauce and prepared foods applications. The oleoresin is used very rarely.

Table 4.91   Ground Thyme: Chemical and Physical Specifications.

Specification	Suggested Limits
FDA DALs (6 subsamples):	
Insect fragments	Ave of 925 or more/10 g
or	
Rodent hairs	Ave of 2 or more/10 g
Volatile oil[1]	0.5% min
Moisture[1]	10.0% max
Total ash[1]	10.0% max
Acid insoluble ash[1]	3.0% max
Military specifications (EE-S-631J, 1981)	
Volatile oil (ml/100 g)	0.8 min
Moisture	9.0% max
Total ash	11.0% max
Acid insoluble ash	5.0% max
Granulation	95% min through a U.S.S. #30
Bulk index[2] (ml/100 g)	250

[1]   These are suggested limits that the authors put together from data the authors collected in the past 5 years. These numbers are equivalent to the level where most quality spice will fall into.
[2]   Average bulk index. Granulation will effect number.

Table 4.92   Nutritional Composition of Thyme Per 100 Grams.

Composition	USDA Handbook 8-2[1] (Ground)	ASTA[2]
Water (grams)	7.79	7.0
Food energy (Kcal)	276	340
Protein (grams)	9.10	7.0
Fat (grams)	7.43	4.6
Carbohydrates (grams)	63.94	68.3
Ash (grams)	11.74	13.2
Calcium (grams)	1.890	2.1
Phosphorus (mg)	201	200
Sodium (mg)	55	80
Potassium (mg)	814	900
Iron (mg)	123.6	135
Thiamine (mg)	.513	.510
Riboflavin (mg)	.399	.400
Niacin (mg)	4.940	4.9
Ascorbic acid (mg)	—	ND[3]
Vitamin A activity (RE)	380	380

[1]   Composition of Foods: Spices and Herbs. USDA Agricultural Handbook 8-2. January 1977.
[2]   The Nutritional Composition of Spices, ASTA Research Committee, February, 1977.
[3]   ND = Not detected.

4.29 Turmeric (*Curcuma longa* L.)

4.29.1 Background Information

Turmeric is the rhizosomes of a plant native to southern and southeast Asia and is a member of the ginger, or Zingiberaceae family. Turmeric is considered a spice by the food industry and ASTA; however, the Food and Drug Administration does consider it a color.[53] Turmeric has a peppery, musty, bitter flavor but is primarily used for its yellow coloring.

Purseglove[19] states that although traditionally *Curcuma longa* is used as the botanical name, the correct name is actually *Curcuma domestica* Val. for the plant. He contends that *Curcuma longa* is incorrectly used to describe the finger rhizo-somes and *Curcuma rotunda* is used to describe the round central rhizosomes. Due to the overwhelming amount of literature which use *Curcuma longa,* as well as the Food and Drug Administration, this book will continue this practice.

Turmeric is described in three ways: *Fingers* are the secondary branches off of the main or central bulbous rhizosome. They are about 3–8 cm in length and about 1 cm in width. The *bulbs* are the central rhizosomes and are more round in shape than the fingers. *Splits* are the bulbs which have been split in half or quarters before curing.

When turmeric is harvested, it is first cured. Curing consists of boiling the rhizosomes in water for 45–60 min. This procedure gets rid of the "raw" color, reduces drying time, gelatinizes the starch, and gives the turmeric a more uniform color.[19] Turmeric is then spread out to dry for 10–15 days. At the end of this time, the turmeric is "polished," which consists of removing the outer skin by rubbing the fingers either manually or in a polishing drum.

An oleoresin turmeric is available and contains the coloring matter, the volatile and fatty oils, and the bitter flavor components. It is standardized in color value, generally 5%–10% curcumin. The pure oleoresin contains the curcumin in a crys-talline layer and at least one major oleoresin manufacturer mixes it with either vegetable oil, polysorbate 80, propylene glycol and glycerides of fatty acids, or lecithin and mono and di-glycerides. These formulations make the oleoresin either oil dispersible, water soluble, brine soluble, or water dispersible depending on the application. An essential oil is not available.

Turmeric has a long history. Marco Polo discovered it in 1280 A.D. in China and compared it to saffron due to its coloring properties. It has been utilized over the years as a medicine. Turmeric does have some basis in fact for this practice. The curcumoid pigments have a choleretic action, which is the ability to increase the secretion of bile. In some parts of the world, curcumin is used medicinally because of this action.[20]

In 1783, turmeric was introduced into Jamaica and is still grown there today as a crop; however, the amount imported into the United States is very small.

4.29.2 Chemical and Physical Specifications

Turmeric contains two primary constituents, the coloring matter and the volatile oil. The coloring matter is a mixture of products in which curcumin is a major compo-

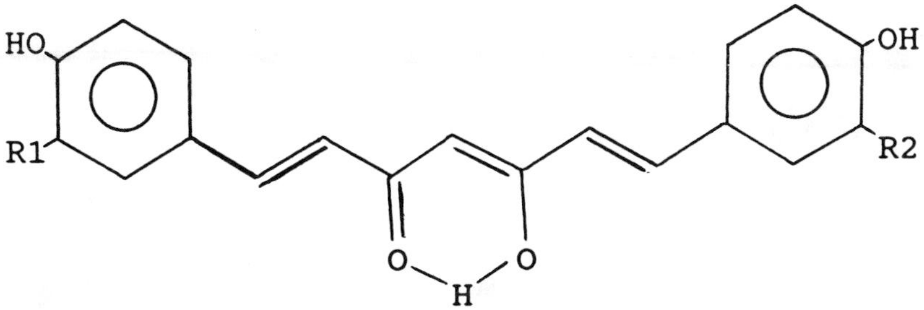

R1	R2	NAME
OMe	OMe	CURCUMIN
OMe	H	DESMETHOXYCURCUMIN
H	H	BIS-DESMETHOXYCURCUMIN

Figure 4.3 Pigments in turmeric.

nent. The other two components are desmethoxycurcumin and bis-desmethoxycurcumin. The structures are shown in Figure 4.3.

The pigments in turmeric are pH sensitive due to the unstable keto-enol structure. In acid pH's, they turn yellow-red. In an alkaline pH, they turn red-brown.[19] Turmeric is also light sensitive and will fade when exposed to light.

The volatile oil of turmeric is about 1.5%–6.0% and contains primarily oxygenated sesquiterpenes. The main components are turmerone and *ar*-turmerone (dehydroturmerone). These components comprise 50%–80% of the volatile oil.[19] The ratio of these two components are variable. Other compounds have been identified in the essential oil of turmeric; however, reproducibility of these analyses have not been demonstrated due to lack of research in this area. Volatile oil is not usually included as a specification since curcumin content is more important to the food processor.

The ASTA recommended moisture limit is 10%. Often turmeric is as low as 4%. Ash and acid insoluble ash should be kept under 8% and 1%. Suggested chemical and physical specifications for turmeric can be found in Tables 4.93 and 4.94. Nutritional analysis is located in Table 4.95.

4.29.3 Import Tonnage

Of the 4.1 million pounds of turmeric imported into the United States, the majority is imported from India (82.7%). About 8% is received from Thailand. The dollar amount represented by these figures is about $2.1 million.[6]

4.29.4 Countries of Origin

4.29.4.1 Quality Differences

India is by far the largest exporter of turmeric. There are basically two types exported from this country. The major one imported into the United States is the

Table 4.93   Whole Turmeric: Chemical and Physical Specifications.

Specification	Suggested Limits
ASTA cleanliness specifications:	
Whole dead insects, by count	3
Mammalian excreta, by mg/lb	5
Other excreta, by mg/lb	5.0
Mold, % by weight	3.00
Insect defiled/infested, % by weight	2.50
Extraneous, % by weight	0.50
FDA DALs:	None
Curcumin content[1]	5.0% min
Moisture[2]	10.0% max
Ash[1]	8.0% max
Acid insoluble ash[1]	1.0% max
Average bulk index (mg/100 g)	N/A

[1]   These are suggested limits that the authors put together from the data collected over the past 5 years. These numbers are equivalent to the level where most quality spice will fall into.
[2]   ASTA suggested maximum moisture level.

Table 4.94   Ground Turmeric: Chemical and Physical Specifications.

Specification	Suggested Limits
FDA DALs	None
Curcumin content[1]	5.0% min
Moisture[1]	10.0% max
Total ash[1]	8.0% max
Acid insoluble ash[1]	1.0% max
Military specifications (EE-S-631J, 1981)	
Volatile oil (ml/100 g)	3.5 min
Moisture	10.0% max
Total ash	8.0% max
Acid insoluble ash	0.6% max
Crude fiber	9.5% max
Color power, expressed as curcumin	5.0%–6.6%
Granulation	95% min through a U.S.S. #40
Bulk index[2] (ml/100 g)	185

[1]   These are suggested limits that the authors put together from data the authors collected in the past 5 years. These numbers are equivalent to the level where most quality spice will fall into.
[2]   Average bulk index. Granulation will effect number.

Table 4.95 Nutritional Composition of Turmeric Per 100 Grams.

Composition	USDA Handbook 8-2[1] (Ground)	ASTA[2]
Water (grams)	11.36	6.0
Food energy (Kcal)	354	390
Protein (grams)	7.83	8.5
Fat (grams)	9.88	8.9
Carbohydrates (grams)	64.93	69.9
Ash (grams)	6.02	6.8
Calcium (grams)	.182	0.2
Phosphorus (mg)	268	260
Sodium (mg)	38	10
Potassium (mg)	2,525	2,500
Iron (mg)	41.42	47.5
Thiamine (mg)	.152	.090
Riboflavin (mg)	.233	.190
Niacin (mg)	5.140	4.8
Ascorbic acid (mg)	25.85	50
Vitamin A activity (RE)	Trace	ND[3]

[1] Composition of Foods: Spices and Herbs. USDA Agricultural Handbook 8-2. January 1977.

[2] The Nutritional Composition of Spices, ASTA Research Committee, February, 1977.

[3] ND = Not detected.

Alleppey type. This product is grown in the Kerala state of India and marketed in Alleppey, thus its name. It has the highest curcumin content (5.3%–6.5%).[54] The second type of Indian turmeric is the Madras type. This product has a curcumin content of about 2.1%[54] and is mainly used in India and exported to Great Britain. A final type of turmeric is the West Indian type grown in the Caribbean, and Central and South America. This type is rarely imported into the United States. It is characterized by low curcumin and volatile oil contents.

4.29.4.2 Harvest Times

Both Alleppey and Madras turmeric are harvested in the first part of the year: January and February. Other turmerics are generally harvested in the winter months.

4.29.5 Commercial Uses

Turmeric is mainly utilized in the United States in curry powders and as a coloring agent. The main coloring agent in prepared mustard is not mustard, but turmeric. The use of ground turmeric is common in chicken bouillon and soups to give a yellow, chickeny color. It is also utilized in sauces, gravies and dry seasonings to give a yellow color. The oleoresin is used in many applications to give food a yellow color. Some examples are bakery mixes, processed cheeses, pickles, relishes, breadings, soups, beverages, confections, and sauces.

Chapter References

1. Purseglove, J.W., Brown, E.G., Green, C.L., and Robbins, S.R.J., *Spices, Volume 1*. Longman Scientific & Technical, Essex, England, 1981.

2. American Spice Trade Association, *What You Should Know About Allspice*. Englewood Cliffs, NJ, 1979.

3. Parry, J.W., *Spices Volume II, Morphology, Histology, Chemistry*. Chemical Publishing Company, New York, 1969.

4. Veek, M.E., and Russ, G.F., "Chemical and sensory properties of pimento leaf oil," *J. Food Sci* 38:1028–1031, 1973.

5. Green, C.L., and Espinosa, F., "Jamaican and Central American Pimento (Allspice; *Pimenta dioica*): Characterization of flavour differences and other distinguishing features," *Dev. Food Sci.* 18:3–20, 1988; *Food Sci. Technol. Abstr.* 21 (5): 5T45, 1989.

6. U.S.D.A., Foreign Agricultural Service, *U.S. Spice Trade*, April 1992.

7. Rosengarten, F., *The Book of Spices*. Pyramid Books, New York, 1973.

8. Heath, H.B., *Source Book of Flavors*. Van Nostrand Reinhold, New York, 1981.

9. El-Wakeil, F., Morsi, M.K.S., Farag, R.S., Shihata, A.A., Badei, A.Z.N.A., "Effects of various storage conditions on the quality of some spice essential oils," *Seifen-Ole-Fette-Wachse* 112 (10): 348–353, 1986; *Food Sci. Technol. Abstr.* 21 (4): 4T32, 1989.

10. Tjaberg, T.B., Underdal, B., and Lunde, G., "The effect of ionizing radiation on the microbiological content and volatile constituents of spices," *J. Appl. Bacteriol.* 35:473–478, 1972.

11. Vajdi, M. and Pereira, R.R., "Comparative effects of ethylene oxide, gamma irradiation and microwave treatments on selected spices," *J. Food Sci.* 38:893–895, 1973.

12. Eiss, M.I., "Irradiation of spices and herbs," *Food Technol. Aust.*, 36 (8): 362–363, 366, 370, 1984.

13. Kiss, I. and Farkas, J., "Irradiation as a method for decontamination of spices," *Food Rev. Int.* 4 (1): 77–92, 1988.

14. Narvaiz, P., Lescano, G., Kairiyama, E., Kaupert, N., "Decontamination of Spices by Irradiation," *J. Food Safety*, 10 (1): 49–61, 1989.

15a. American Spice Trade Association, *What You Should Know About Basil*. Englewood Cliffs, NJ, 1980.

15b. Paakkonen, K., Malmstedn, T., and Hyvonen, L., "Drying, Packaging, and Storage Effects on Quality of Basil, Marjoram, and Wild Marjoram," *J. Food Sci.* 55 (5): 1373–1377, 1382, 1990.

16. Maga, J.A., "Capsicum," *Crit. Rev. Food Sci. Nutr.* 6 (1): 177–199.

17. Todd, P.H., "Detection of foreign pungent compounds," *Food Technol.* 12: 468, 1958.

18. American Spice Trade Association, *What You Should Know About Paprika*. Englewood Cliffs, NJ, 1966.

19. Purseglove, J.W., Brown, E.G., Green, C.L., and Robbins, S.R.J., *Spices, Volume 2*. Longman Scientific and Technical, Essex, England, 1981.

20. American Spice Trade Association, *What You Should Know About Celery Seed*. Englewood Cliffs, NJ, 1982.

21. Cu, J.Q., Zhang, Z.J., Pu Fan, Perineau, F., Delmas, M., Gaset, A., "GC/MS and GC/FTR Analysis of the Essential Oil of Celery Seed," *J. Ess. Oil Res.* 2 (1): 1–5, 1990.

22. Stahl, W.H., Skarzynski, J.N., and Voelker, W.A., "Differentiation of certain types of cassias and cinnamons by measurement of mucilaginous character," *J. Ass. Off. Agric. Chem.* 52 (4): 741–744, 1969.

23. Pesek, C.A., Wilson, L.A., and Hammond, E.G., "Spice quality: Effect of cryogenic and ambient grinding on volatiles," *J. Food Sci.* 50:599–601, 1985.

24. Potter, T.L., and Fagerson, I.S., "Composition of coriander leaf volatiles," *J. Agric. Food Chem.* 38 (11): 2054–2056, 1990.

25. American Spice Trade Association, *What You Should Know About Dill.* Englewood Cliffs, NJ, 1986.

26. Blank, E., and Grosch, W., "Evaluation of potent odorants in dill seed and dill herb (*Anethum graveolens* L.) by aroma extract dilution analysis," *J. Food Sci.,* 56 (1): 63–66, 1991.

27. American Spice Trade Association, *What You Should Know About Fennel Seed.* Englewood Cliffs, NJ, 1981.

28. Bednarczyk, A.A., and Kramer, A., "Identification and evaluation of the flavor-significant components of ginger essential oil," *Chem. Senses Flavor* 2:377–386, 1975.

29. Connel, D.W., and Sutherland, M.D., "A re-examination of gingerol, shogoal, and zingerone. The pungent principles of ginger," *Aust. J. Chem.* 22:1033–43, 1969.

30. Connel, D.W., "The pungent principles of ginger and their importance in certain ginger products," *Food Technol. Aust.* 21:570–571, 573, 575, 1969.

31. Salzer, U.-J., "Uber die Fettsauerezusammensetzung der Lipoide einiger Gewurze," *Fette, Seifen Anstrichm.* 77:446–450, 1975.

32. Kalbhen, D.A., "Nutmeg as a narcotic," *Angew. Chem. (Int. Ed.)* 10:370–374, 1971.

33. Miloslav, Rechcigl, Jr., Ed., *CRC Handbook of Naturally Occurring Food Toxicants.* CRC Press, Boca Raton, Florida, 1983.

34. Sandford, K.J., and Heinz, D.E., "Effects of storage on the volatile constituents of nutmeg," *Phytochem.* 10:1245–1250, 1971.

35. Dann, A.E., Mathews, W.S.A., Robinson, F.V., "Studies on the yields and compositions of nutmeg and mace oils from Grenada," in *Proceedings of the Seventh International Congress of Essential Oils.* Held Oct. 1977 at Kyoto, Japan. 1977.

36. Baldry, J., Matthews, W.S., Robinson, F.V., and Nabney, J., "Chemical composition and flavour of nutmegs of different geographical origins," in *Proceedings of the IV International Congress on Food Science and Technology Vol. I,* 99–104, 1974.

37. Anonymous, *Mustard Flour.* RT French Company, 1988.

38. Weber, F.E., Taillie, S.A., and Stauffer, K.R., "Functional characteristics of Mustard Mucilage," *J. Food Sci.* 39:461–466, 1974.

39. American Spice Trade Association, *What You Should Know About Oregano.* Englewood Cliffs, NJ, 1978.

40. Rhyu, H.Y., "Gas chromatographic characterization of oregano and other selected spices of the Labiate family," *J. Food Sci.* 44:1373–1378, 1979.

41. Govindarajan, V.S., "Pepper—chemistry, technology, and quality evaluation," *Crit. Rev. Food Sci. Nutr.* 9 (1): 115–225, 1977.

42. DeCleyn, R. and Verzele, M., "Constituents of peppers. II. Piperinic acid and its isomers," *Bull. Soc. Chim. Belg.* 81:529, 1972.

43. Mori, D., Yamamoto, Y., and Komai, S., "Studies on the pungent constituents in black pepper (*Piper nigrum* L.) I. Determination of pungent principles in black pepper" (in Japanese with English summary), *J. Food Sci. Technol.* 21:466, 1974.

44. Yamamoto, Y., Tonari, K., and Mori, K., "Studies on the pungent constituents in black pepper (*Piper nigrum* L.) III. Piperine isomers" (in Japanese with English summary), *J. Food Sci. Technol.* 21:476, 1974.

45. Grewe, R., Freist, W., Newmann, J., and Kersten, S., "Uber die inhaltsstoffe des schwarzen pfeffers," *Chem. Ber.* 103:3572, 1970.

46. Genest, C., Smith, D.M., and Chapman, D.G., "A critical study of two procedures for the determination of piperine in black and white pepper," *Agric. Food Chem.* 11 (6): 508–512, 1963.

47. Galetto, W.G., Walger, D.E., and Levy, S.M., "High pressure liquid chromatographic determination of piperine in black pepper (*Piper nigrum*)" *J. Ass. Off. Anal. Chem.* 59 (5): 951–953, 1976.

48. Gross, A.F. and Ellis, P.E., "Lipase activity in spices and seasonings," *Cereal Sci. Today* 14 (10): 332–335, 1969.

49. MacNeil, J.H., and Dimic, P.S., "Use of chemical compounds and a rosemary spice extract in quality maintenance of deboned poultry meat," *J. Food Sci.* 38:1080–1081, 1973.

50. Dziezak, J.D., "Spices," *Food Technol.* 43 (1): 102–116, 1989.

51. American Spice Trade Association, *What You Should Know About Thyme.* Englewood Cliffs, NJ, 1985.

52. Russell, G.F. and Olson, K.V., "The volatile constituents of oil of Thyme," *J. Food Sci.* 37:405–407, 1972.

53. *21 Code of Federal Regulations,* 101.22 (a) (2), 1991.

54. American Spice Trade Association, *What You Should Know About Turmeric.* Englewood Cliffs, NJ, 1982.

CHAPTER

5

Spice Extractives

In most cases, the flavor of the spice can be extracted in a concentrated form and used as a flavoring. The most common forms of spice extractives used today are either volatile oils or oleoresins. These products are very useful because they can be standardized for flavor strength, eliminate the small dark particles of spices in a lightly colored product, be essentially microbiologically sterile, and eliminate all the foreign matter that can be found in ground spices.

5.1 Spice Volatile Oils

The volatile oil, also referred to as an essential oil, is generally collected by grinding the spice, boiling it in water and condensing the water and volatile oil. The volatile oil can be separated quite readily from the water. In general, the volatile oil contains the top notes of the spice flavor.

The yield of volatile oil by this method will vary from less than 0.5% to more than 16%, depending on the spice. For some spices, the volatile oil can be distilled from other parts of the plant beside the spice portion. For example, a volatile oil of clove can be distilled from the clove bud, clove stems and even the clove leaves. Although not identical in composition and strength, they all can be utilized for their clove flavor. It is important to recognize that there is a flavor difference because they sell for significant cost differences. If a specification calls for clove bud oil and a much cheaper alternative is presented, keep in mind that the product may be completely different.

Clove stem and clove leaf oils are not truly spice extractives since they did not come from the part of the plant considered to be the spice. The term natural flavor would be a correct description for these flavorings. In addition, many spice extractives have other natural flavors added (Cassia oil WONF) or can be adulterated with artificial flavors (cinnamic aldehyde added to cassia oil).

The volatile oil will generally contribute the same overall flavor of the spice unless a major portion of the flavor comes from chemicals that are not volatile—such as in black pepper, red pepper, and ginger. The volatile oil of black pepper is reminiscent of the bouquet of freshly ground black pepper. It smells like black pepper but does not contain any of the bite that black pepper is noted for. This bite, from the chemical piperine, is contained in the oleoresin. The same goes for the gingerols in ginger as well. Red pepper does not have a volatile oil and all of its bite comes from capsaicin in the oleoresin portion. For the most part, the rest of the spices can be replaced flavorwise with their respective volatile oils although the quality of the flavor will not be exactly the same since other compounds in the natural spice contribute to the flavor.

5.2 Spice Oleoresins

Spice oleoresins are obtained by grinding the spice and using a solvent, such as acetone or hexane, to extract the flavoring portion. The solvent is then removed, leaving behind the majority of the flavoring of the spice. The choice of solvent will change the composition of the oleoresin and to some degree affect the flavor of the oleoresin. As a variation on the above method of making an oleoresin, some producers will extract the volatile oil first, then proceed with the solvent extraction and add the volatile oil back at the end. The value of this system is that it is sometimes quite difficult to remove the solvent in the first case without also removing certain fractions of the volatile oil.

In either case, the resultant oleoresin can be a thick, viscous mass that is very difficult to use. In some cases, an oily layer will separate from the oleoresin that must be mixed back in before the oleoresin is used. This can be a problem in a production situation and employees must be educated about it. Using the thin oily layer on the top without thoroughly mixing it will result in significant flavor differences in the finished food product. It is because of these problems that oleoresin producers utilize a number of tricks to try to keep their oleoresins from separating or being too thick to handle. These tricks involve the addition of emulsifiers, food grade acids, vegetable oils, or even additional volatile oils.

As the above indicates, not all oleoresins are identical in strength or flavor. Some suppliers are quite adept at controlling the flavor of their oleoresins where others are not. It is desirable to purchase these items from a reputable extractive firm that can control the flavor strength and character of oils and oleoresins.

5.3 Use of Spice Extractives

Volatile oils are generally quite easy to use since they are usually water-like in consistency and mix readily into other food ingredients. The oleoresins are usually very viscous and do present problems trying to disperse them in many food systems.

Some oils, such as anise oil, can easily crystallize at a temperature slightly below room temperature. This can be taken care of by warming slowly until melted again.

Oleoresins often pose handling problems, as noted above, because of viscosity and separation problems. Oleoresins supplied in drums or pails pose interesting mixing problems. Due to their viscosity, rolling the drums or hand mixing is usually insufficient to ensure complete mixing. It is almost a necessity for mechanical mixing to ensure an adequate job. Because of their high viscosity, they do not distribute evenly or easily in food items. One way to solve this problem is to use water soluble (really water dispersable) oleoresins. These products are made by a number of manufacturers and eliminate the solubility problems because they are readily dispersible in liquids. Another problem with all of these products is the extremely small amounts that must be measured on the production room floor. One solution to all these problems is through the use of soluble seasonings. The production and use of soluble seasonings is discussed in Chapter 7.

5.4 Replacement of Spices with Oils and Oleoresins

When trying to replace a ground spice with oils and oleoresins, there are certain guidelines that can be used. For a starting point, try matching up volatile oil

Table 5.1 Typical Replacement Ratios for Ground Spice Using Oils and Oleoresins.

Spice	# Oil	# Oleoresin	Notes
Allspice	.020	.035	
Anise	.020	.050	
Basil	.005	.050	
Cardamom	.030	.015	
Caraway	.010	.050	
Celery	.010	.100	
Cinnamon	.025	.025	Oil use based on volatile oil.
Clove	.140	.050	Stem, leaf, or bud oil can be used.
Coriander	.003	.070	
Cumin	.020	.040	
Dill seed	.020	.050	
Fennel	.010	.050	
Ginger	.015	.035	
Mace	.140	.070	Nutmeg oil should be used.
Marjoram	.008	.050	
Nutmeg	.060	.080	Spice and oil must be from same origin.
Oregano	.015	.040	
Pepper, black	.015	.050	Oil does not provide piperine bite.
Rosemary	.008	.040	Oleoresin is deflavored for antioxidant.
Sage	.010	.050	
Savory	.005	.065	
Tarragon	.002	—	

Replace 1# of Ground Spice With

contents. Some experimentation will need to be done in each food system since the granulation of the spice being replaced as well as its quality will make a difference. Remember that although spice oils and oleoresins can replace the flavor of ground spices, they are not as balanced or as full flavored as the natural spice due to other flavor materials present in the spice that are not captured in the oils or oleoresins. The replacement ratios shown in Table 5.1 give a starting point to replace ground spices with the oils and oleoresins. Actual flavor replacements must be tasted in each particular application.

Suggested Reading List

1. American Spice Trade Association, *What You Should Know About Spice Extractives.* Englewood Cliffs, New Jersey, 1984.

6

Recent Spice Research

6.1 Naturally Occurring Toxicants

There are a number of naturally occurring compounds in spices, as in other food items, which are carcinogens or have some other toxic or detrimental effect. These compounds are present in low levels and are probably not a hazard in a normal diet. This section is included to make the reader aware of these compounds and the fact that they are present in the spices we eat.

Anethole, the major volatile oil component in anise and fennel has been found to have estrogenic activity. In addition, sage and parsley have also been shown to have estrogenic activity. Estrogens are a group of compounds which can produce detrimental effects on the reproductive organs of animals. This effect has been noted in some livestock; however, it presents a very low hazard to humans.[1]

Sassafras, used primarily in cajun gumbo filé seasonings, contains safrole. The sassafras leaves are safrole free. The stems contain the safrole. Seventy-five percent of sassafras oil from the stems is safrole. This compound has been shown to be a carcinogen in rodents and several of its metabolites are mutagens.[2] Black pepper also contains low levels of safrole. In addition, piperine is closely related to safrole and pepper extract has been shown to cause tumors at a variety of sites in mice.[2]

Black pepper will form nitrosamines over time in the dry state when included in a spice mixture containing nitrites, as in a meat cure. The piperidine in the pepper combines with the nitrite and forms n-nitrosopiperidine, a known nitrosamine and carcinogen. Paprika undergoes a similar reaction when combined with nitrites for long times in the dry state. In this case, N-nitroso pyrrolidine forms, also a carcinogen. The 21 CFR 170.60 states that cures containing nitrate or nitrite cannot be combined with spices or other seasonings unless a food additive petition is submitted, supported by data demonstrating that nitrosamines are not formed in the cure premix.

Nutmeg contains myristicin, a hallucinogen which is not toxic in small amounts but can cause death when taken in excess.[1,3] Recently, the National Toxicology Program stated that oleoresin turmeric shows evidence of carcinogenic activity in rats and mice, causing kidney and small intestinal tumors.[4] Other research claims an anticancer property of turmeric, probably due to curcumin.[5]

Mustard seed contains glucosinolates, which are a group of sulfur-containing glycosides which yield toxic compounds upon hydrolysis and can be harmful if consumed in sufficient quantities. White mustard (*Brassica hirta*) contains 3.3% sinalbin which forms *p*-hydroxyl benzyl-isothiocyanate, upon action of myrosinase, and readily decomposes at a high pH to yield an SCN^- ion. Brown mustard (*Brassica juncea*) contains 2.8% sinigrin which forms allylisothiocyanate. This compound is a lacrimator and causes blisters on contact with the skin. It is more toxic than the glucosinolate from white mustard. Allylisothiocyanate has been shown to be mutagenic in the Ames test,[1] and can cause chromosomal changes in hamster cells at low concentrations. It has also been shown to be carcinogenic in rats and causes embryonal death and lowered fetal weights in the rat.[1,2]

Tarragon oil is 60% estragole and basil oil is 8%–16% estragole. This compound has been shown to be a carcinogen, having mutagenicity and inducing carcinomas in selected animals.[6] The dose size in relation to its metabolism in humans has been recently addressed.[7]

6.2 Antioxidant Action of Spice Compounds

In the last 15–20 years, spice research has concentrated on two primary areas: the antioxidant and the antimicrobial activity of spices and their essential oils. First an overview of the antioxidant action of spices will be addressed.

Research on the antioxidant properties of spices have been conducted for a number of years. The earliest, most extensive research was done by Chipault et al. in 1952.[8] This research found that rosemary and sage exhibited pronounced antioxidant effects.

Further research on the antioxidant properties of rosemary has produced industrial products which are sold as natural antioxidants, which are primarily deflavored rosemary extracts. Rosemary extract has been known for some time to have antioxidant effects in foods and the antioxidant components have since been isolated and determined to be carnosol,[9] ursolic acid,[10] and rosmanol.[11] The compounds with the most antioxidant activity are carnosol and rosmanol. Recently, two additional diterpene antioxidants have been isolated and characterized—rosmaridiphenol and rosmariquinone. They have been determined to be more effective than Butylated Hydroxy Anisole (BHA), and almost as effective as Butylated Hydroxy Toluene (BHT).[12,13]

Although Chipault et al. found sage to be almost as active as rosemary for antioxidant activity, less research has been done on this spice. In fact, most natural antioxidants available commercially are extracted from rosemary. Chang et al. described a method in 1977 for preparing bland flavored antioxidants from both rosemary and sage.[14]

Al-Jalay et al.[15] evaluated the antioxidant properties of ten spices in a fermented meat sausage. Clove, allspice, and black pepper all exhibited antioxidant activity in the meat emulsions. Fresh ginger has also been found to have antioxidant activity.[16] Clove has antioxidant properties due to the gallic acid and the eugenol present.[17]

There are many more research studies available on the antioxidant capacity of spices. The above just touches the surface. Much of the research in the 1960s and 1970s was done in Japan and published in Japanese. Kramer[17] includes a concise review of this research.

6.3 Antimicrobial Action of Spice Compounds

Research on the antimicrobial action of spices can be separated into four main areas. The first type of research is basically screening studies of which spices have anti-microbial activity over a range of bacteria and yeast. More specific research is aimed at determining which spices have activity against specific food borne bacteria, generally the pathogenic varieties. This type of research begins to address more practical applications. Thirdly, there is research aimed at determining which spices have antifungal activity. Finally, research which begins to address which specific components of the spices possess the antimicrobial activity have also been done.

This section does not attempt to review all literature but simply to give an idea of what has been done in the last 5–10 years. A good review up to the early 1980s has been written by Shelef.[18]

6.3.1 Screening Studies

The first type of study is general research to determine which spices have anti-microbial activity. The most complete study tested 50 plant essential oils (22 spices) against 25 different bacteria at 4 different concentrations. The spices which were found to have the most widely inhibitory activity were bay, cinnamon, clove, thyme, marjoram, and pimento.[19] Farag et al. tested thyme, clove, caraway, cumin, rosemary, and sage essential oils against 3 gram negative, 3 gram positive, one acid fast bacterium, and one yeast. Thyme and clove were found to be very strong antimicrobial agents versus the other spices tested. The authors found a relationship between the presence of an aromatic nucleus containing a polar functional group and the antimicrobial activity.[20]

Turkish bay leaf oil was tested against a variety of bacteria, yeast, and molds. Weak antimicrobial effects were noted for this spice. Only when concentrations were increased to 0.1% were a significant amount of yeast inhibited. The molds were the least sensitive to the bay essential oil.[21] In a similar study, thyme and bay leaves were tested against three pathogenic organisms (*Salmonella typhimurium, Staphylococcus aureus,* and *Vibrio parahaemolyticus*). Thyme was found to be the most inhibitory (0.05% inhibited *S. aureus*). Bay leaves were the least active (10 times the concentration of thyme was required to inhibit *S. aureus*).[22] Other screening studies, published in the early 1980s found similar data: a variety of spices have antimicrobial properties to many different bacteria and fungi.[23-27] Many additional research studies have been published in foreign languages. Abstracts can be found in the *Food Science and Technology Abstracts.*

Comparing studies is often difficult since the conditions for screening are very different. Most studies tested different spices and different bacteria. Inhibitory levels are hard to compare since spices are natural products containing various levels of essential oil components. In some studies, essential oils are tested and, in others, ground spices are evaluated. Most of these screening studies are just that, screening for activity. More detailed studies are needed and often have been done to draw further conclusions.

6.3.2 Pathogenic Bacteria Activity

The effect of spices on specific pathogenic organisms have an important practical use in foods. A number of studies have been done to evaluate this effect. Mace, bay, and nutmeg extracts, at levels less than 125 ppm, have been shown to inhibit *Clostridium botulinum* toxin production in turkey frankfurter slurries.[28] Cinnamon, oregano, and clove oils were found to be very active, pimento and thyme were found to be active, and garlic, onion, and black pepper were found to be the least active spices in the inhibition of growth of three different strains of *Clostridium botulinum*. Inhibitory levels were in the 150–200 ppm range. An interesting point to note was the author's conclusion that the spice oils have an advantage over other antimicrobial agents in that they prevented the germination of *C. botulinum*,[29] not just growth. Ground cinnamon, clove, mustard, garlic, and onion, added at 0.5%, were found to have inhibitory effects on *Listeria monocytogenes,* with clove and cinnamon having the strongest effect.[30] Oregano, sage, and ground cloves were tested on the growth of *Campylobacter jejuni*. At 0.5%, clove inhibited growth, but both oregano and sage caused a reduction in colony forming units, with sage having the greater effect. At refrigerated temperatures, however, no decrease in colony forming units occurred, thus causing the conclusion that these spices probably would not be effective in reducing the amount of *C. jejuni* in foods stored at refrigeration temperatures.[31] Beuchat found that oregano and thyme were toxic to *Vibrio parahaemolyticus* when present in the growth media at 0.5%.[32] Other research papers which evaluate the antimicrobial effects of spices to specific pathogenic organisms are available.

A variety of research has been done to evaluate spice activity against fungi. Akgul and Kivanc (1988), evaluated ten ground spices for activity against nine foodborne fungi. Only oregano inhibited fungi growth.[33] Thyme, cumin, clove, caraway, rosemary, and sage oils were tested against *Aspergillus parasiticus* in a 1989 study. The effectiveness of the oils against this fungus were in the order listed above. The authors also found that the major components of the spice essential oils also inhibited the growth of *A. parasiticus*.[34] Benjilali et al. evaluated the antifungal properties of 6 essential oils, including species of thyme and rosemary, against 39 strains of mold. Thyme again showed the most inhibitory action.[35]

6.3.3 Antimicrobial Spice Components

Many of the above studies conclude that the inhibitory action of spices is due to the major components of the essential oils. Deans and Ritchie[19] suggest the active constituents should be chemically separated and identified. Benjilali et al.[35] felt activity was due to compounds present which are phenols. Farag and co-workers[20,34] attributed the inhibitory effects to the presence of an aromatic nucleus containing a polar functional group. In addition, the higher inhibitory spices contained phenolic OH groups.

Recent research includes a study testing thymol (thyme and oregano), eugenol (clove, pimento, and cinnamon), menthol, and anethole (from anise and fennel) on three pathogenic bacteria, *Salmonella typhimurium, Staphylococcus aureus,* and *Vibrio parahaemolyticus.* This particular study showed that each spice component inhibited the bacteria to different extents, but an overall observation was that eugenol was more active than thymol, which was more active than anethole. This study supports previous spice studies.[36] Eugenol and isoeugenol have also been shown to be sporostatic to *Bacillus subtilis* at the 0.05%–0.06% level. Gingerol and zingerone also have sporostatic activity, but at a much higher level, 0.8%–0.9%. The authors in this study felt that the inhibition effectiveness of the compound was related to the inverse of the molecular weight of the phenolic derivatives. For example, the longer the side chain on the phenolic ring structure, the less the antimicrobial activity.[37] In a related study, 0.12% ground clove and 0.02% eugenol decreased the rate and extent of germination of *Bacillus subtilis* spores.[38]

Carnosol and ursolic acid, both isolated from rosemary and shown to have antioxidant activity, were tested on six strains of foodborne bacteria and yeast. Their antimicrobial activity was compared to BHA and BHT, also known to have antioxidant and antimicrobial activity. It was shown that the carnosol and ursolic acid were effective as inhibitors at lower concentrations than the rosemary extract. In addition, carnosol was more effective than BHA or BHT and ursolic acid was more effective than BHT. The effectiveness was theorized to be due to the phenolic ring structure of these two compounds.[39]

As can be seen by a sampling of the above studies, components of the essential oils of spices do contain antimicrobial compounds. Further research is needed to isolate compounds and determine if commercialization is practical.

Chapter References

1. Miloslav, Rechcigl Jr., Ed., *CRC Handbook of Naturally Occurring Food Toxicants.* CRC Press, Boca Raton, Florida, 1983.

2. Ames, Bruce N., "Dietary Carcinogens and Anticarcinogens," *Science,* 221:1256–1264, 1983.

3. Kalbhen, D.A., "Nutmeg as a Narcotic," *Angew. Chem. (Int. Ed.)* 10:370–374, 1971.

4. Anonymous, "Turmeric Oleoresin shows 'Equivocal Evidence' of Carcinogenesis. *Food Chemical News,* 34 (18) pp. 46, 1992.

5. Kuttan, R., Bhanumathy, P., Nirmala, K., and George, M.C., "Potential Anticancer Activity of Turmeric (*Curcuma longa*)," *Cancer Lett.* 29 (2): 197–202, 1985.

6. Tateo, F., Santamaria, L., Bianchi, L., Bianchi, A., "Basil oil and Tarragon Oil: Composition and Genotoxicity Evaluation," *J. Ess. Oil Res.* 1:111–118, 1989.

7. Caldwell, A.A., Hutt, A.J., and Smith, R.L., "Metabolism of estragole in rat and mouse and influence of dose size on excretion of the proximate carcinogen 1'-hydroxyestragole," *Chem. Toxic.* 25 (11): 799–806, 1987.

8. Chipault, J.R., Mizumo, G.R., Hawkins, J.M., Lundberg, W.O., "The Antioxidant Properties of Natural Spices," *Food Res.* 17:46–55, 1952.

9. Brieskorn, C.H., Fuchs, A., Bredenberg, J.B., McChesney, J.D., and Wenkert, E., "The structure of carnosol," *J. Org. Chem.* 29:2293–2298, 1964.

10. Wu, J.W., Lee, M-H., Jo, C-T., and Chang, S.S., "Elucidation of the chemical structures of natural antioxidants isolated from Rosemary," *J. Amer. Oil Chem. Soc.* 59:339–345, 1982.

11. Inatani, R., Nakatani, N., Fuwa, H., Seto, H., "Structure of a new antioxidative phenolic diterpene isolated from Rosemary (*Rosemarinus officinalis* L.)," *Agric. Biol. Chem.* 46:1661–1666, 1982.

12. Houlihan, C.M., Ho, C-T., and Chang, S.S., "Elucidation of the Chemical Structure of a Novel Antioxidant, Rosmaridiphenol, Isolated from Rosemary," *J. Am. Oil Chem. Soc.* 61:1036–1040, 1984.

13. Houlihan, C.M., Ho, C-T., and Chang, S.S., "The Structure of Rosmariquinone—A New Antioxidant Isolated from *Rosmarinus officinalis* L," *J. Am. Oil Chem. Soc.* 62:96–98, 1985.

14. Chang, S.S., Ostric-Matijasevic, B., Hsieh, O.A.L., and Huang, C-L., "Natural Antioxidants from Rosemary and Sage," *J. Food Sci.* 42:1102–1106, 1977.

15. Al-Jalay, B., Blank, G., McConnell, B., and Al-Khayat, M., "Antioxidant Activity of Selected Spices Used in Fermented Meat Sausage," *J. Food Protect.* 50:25–27, 1987.

16. Lee, Y.B., Kim, Y.S., and Ashmore, C.R., "Antioxidant Property in Ginger Rhizome and Its Application to Meat Products," *J. Food Sci.* 51:20–23, 1986.

17. Kramer, R.E., "Antioxidants in Clove," *J. Am. Oil Chem. Soc.* 62:111–113, 1985.

18. Shelef, L.A., "Antimicrobial effects of spices," *J. Food Safety* 6:29–44, 1983.

19. Deans, S.G. and Ritchie, G., "Antibacterial properties of plant essential oil," *Int. J. Food Micro.* 5:165–180, 1987.

20. Farag, R.S., Daw, Z.Y., Hewedi, F.M., and El-Baroty, G.S.A., "Antimicrobial Activity of Some Egyptian Spice Essential Oils," *J. Food Protect.* 52 (9): 665–667, 1989.

21. Akgul, A., Kivanc, M., and Bayrak, A., "Chemical Composition and Antimicrobial Effect of Turkish Laurel Leaf Oil," *J. Ess. Oil Res.* 1:277–280, 1989.

22. Aktug, S.E. and Karapinar, M., "Sensitivity of some common food-poisoning bacteria to thyme, mint and bay leaves," *Int. J. Food Micro.* 3:349–354, 1986.

23. Shelef, L.A., Naglik, O.A., and Bogen, D.W., "Sensitivity of some common food-borne bacteria to the spices sage, rosemary and allspice," *J. Food Sci.* 45:1042–1044, 1980.

24. Zaika, L.L., Kissinger, J.C., and Wasserman, A.E., "Inhibition of lactic acid bacteria by herbs," *J. Food Sci.* 48:1455–1459, 1983.

25. Azzouz, M.A. and Bullerman, L.B., "Comparative antimycotic effects of selected herbs, spices, plant components and commercial antifungal agents," *J. Food Protect.* 45:1298, 1982.

26. Conner, D.E. and Beuchat, L.R., "Effects of essential oils from plants on growth of food spoilage yeasts," *J. Food Sci.* 49:429, 1984.

27. Ueda, S., Yamashita, H., Nakajima, M., and Kawabara, Y., "Inhibition of microorganisms by spice extracts and flavoring compounds," *J. Jpn. Soc. Food Sci. Technol.* 29:111, 1982.

28. Hall, M.A. and Maurer, A.J., "Spice Extracts, Lauricidin, and Propylene Glycol as Inhibitors of *Clostridium botulinum* in Turkey Frankfurter Slurries," *Poult. Sci.* 65 (6): 1167–1171, 1986.

29. Ismaiel, A. and Pierson, M.D., "Inhibition of Growth and Germination of *C. Botulinum* 33A, 40B, and 1623E by Essential Oil of Spices," *J. Food Sci.* 55 (6): 1676–1678, 1990.

30. Bahk, J., Yousef, A.E., and Marth, E.H., "Behavior of *Listeria monocytogenes* in the Presence of Selected Spices," *Lebensm. Wiss. Technol.*, 23:66–69, 1990.

31. Deibel, K.E. and Banwart, G.J., "Effect of spices on *Campylobacter jejuni* at three temperatures," *J. Food Safety* 6:241–251, 1984.

32. Beuchat, L.R., "Sensitivity of *Vibrio parahaemolyticus* to spices and organic acids," *J. Food Sci.* 41:899–902, 1976.

33. Akgul, A. and Kivanc, M., "Inhibitory effects of selected Turkish spices and oregano components on some foodborne fungi," *Int. J. Food Micro.* 6:263–268, 1988.

34. Farag, R.S., Daw, Z.Y., and Abo-Raya, S.H., "Influence of Some Spice Essential Oils on *Aspergillus parasiticus* Growth and Production of Aflatoxins in a Synthetic Medium," *J. Food Sci.* 54 (1): 74–76, 1989.

35. Benjilali, B., Tantaoui-Elaraki, A., Ayadi, A., and Ihlal, M., "Method to Study Antimicrobial Effects of Essential Oils: Application to the Antifungal Activity of Six Moroccan Essences," *J. Food Protect.* 47 (10): 748–752, 1984.

36. Karapinar, M. and Aktug, S.E., "Inhibition of foodborne pathogens by thymol, eugenol, menthol, and anethole," *Int. J. Food Micro.* 4:161–166, 1987.

37. Al-Khayat, M.A. and Blank, G., "Phenolic Spice Components Sporostatic to *Bacillus subtilis*," *J. Food Sci.* 50:971–974, 1985.

38. Blank, G., Al-Khayat, M., and Ismond, M.A., "Germination and heat resistance of *Bacillus subtilis* spores produced on clove and eugenol based media," *Food Micro.* 4:35–42, 1987.

39. Collins, M.A. and Charles, H.P., "Antimicrobial activity of Carnosol and Ursolic acid: Two antioxidant constituents of *Rosmarinus officinalis* L," *Food Micro.* 4:311–315, 1987.

7

Simple Seasoning Blends

7.1 Introduction

This chapter will overview some of the simple seasoning blends available to the food industry. Simple blends mean that they are either simple formulations of a few ingredients, or simple in that they are commonly used blends. These blends are often used as ingredients without the user realizing that they are blends and not spices. A good example is chili powder. Chili *powder* is a blend of spices and other ingredients. Chili *pepper* is a spice which is the major ingredient in chili powder. The simple blends discussed in this chapter are ones which are available in the retail and foodservice trade, except for soluble seasonings which are available only in the processed foods industry.

7.2 Soluble Seasonings

Soluble seasonings are spice extractives on salt or dextrose carriers. An essential oil or oleoresin is plated on, or mixed with, the carrier. Salt is used most often since the size of the crystals provide a good mixing action which disperses the oil or oleoresin evenly. Dextrose is utilized when a high salt level cannot be tolerated in a specific food item. When using soluble seasonings on a salt carrier, care must be taken to reduce the salt level in the finished food item. Soluble seasonings are often used in the processed foods industry for many of the same reasons the extractives themselves are used. The advantage of soluble seasonings, however, is the ease of use.

They are dry, free-flowing powders compared to a liquid essential oil or oleoresin. A prime example is soluble black pepper versus the oleoresin black pepper. The latter is a thick, green, viscous liquid which separates on standing, is difficult to mix, and is hard to pour. It is also difficult to measure when used in small amounts. There are many advantages in using soluble black pepper. First is that it is a free-flowing powder, and thus is easy to weigh and add to a production batch. Second, the soluble seasoning is added in a larger volume than the oleoresins so it can be weighed more accurately. Finally, a soluble seasoning provides less waste to the food processor. Oleoresin black pepper is a very expensive ingredient, costing upwards of $12.00 a pound when bought in small amounts. Often this product is spilled or cannot be removed from the pail or gallon container, thus wasting product. The supplier providing the soluble black pepper absorbs these losses, which are a lesser percent, since a large amount is mixed at a time.

By evenly distributing the oil or oleoresin on the carriers, they disperse quite readily in most food systems. These soluble spices can be easily made in a simple ribbon or paddle blender. Although the oils mix in quite easily, the oleoresins may be slightly more difficult since they may bead up and no amount of additional mixing will break up the lumps. This can be solved by adding a small amount of propylene glycol or vegetable oil to the oleoresin to help reduce its viscosity. Another trick is to start with a high liquid to solids level in the blender and slowly add additional carrier while the blender is mixing. These two tricks can help produce smooth lump-free soluble spices.

Soluble seasonings cannot be bought on price alone. Many manufacturers claim some sort of equivalence to the ground spice, however, it varies by manufacturer. A difference in a half of a percent of the extractive can cause a large difference in price of the soluble seasoning. Soluble black peppers are available anywhere from 2% to 5% oleoresin black pepper. If investigating alternative suppliers, it is imperative to evaluate the flavor strength of the soluble seasoning and not just price alone.

Commonly available soluble seasonings include celery, black pepper, sage, garlic, and onion, although the last two are not true soluble spices but rather vegetable extractives. Many other soluble seasonings are available. They can be purchased for just about any spice.

Tables 7.1 and 7.2 give typical extractive levels for soluble celery and soluble black pepper.

Table 7.1 Typical Soluble Black Pepper Formulation.

Ingredient	Typical Range (%)
Oleoresin black pepper	2–5
Anticaking agent	up to 2
Salt or dextrose	to 100

Table 7.2 Typical Soluble Celery Formulation.

Ingredient	Typical Range (%)
Oleoresin celery	2–3.5
Anticaking agent	up to 2
Salt or dextrose	to 100

7.3 Celery Salt

Celery salt is a blend of ground celery seed with salt. It is used primarily in the retail and foodservice trades, although it is also used to some extent in the food industry. Typical levels of celery are 10%–25%, although some blends with the celery level as low as 5% are available. The remainder is salt and an anticaking agent. Once again, the price of celery salt must be based on strength of the celery flavor.

7.4 Garlic Salt and Onion Salt

Generally garlic and onion salts are made with granulated garlic and onion rather than the powdered products. Typical levels of onion and garlic range from 10% to 25% with the onion salt usually containing a higher level than the garlic salt. Anticaking agents are also added to these blends. The use of these products in the food industry is limited. Most industrial users will add garlic and onion separately from the salt.

7.5 Chili Powder

There are vast differences in chili powders in both flavor and appearance. As stated previously, chili *pepper* is the spice and chili *powder* is a blend of spices and other ingredients. Chili pepper has quite a bit of variation within itself. It can be a bright red to a dark brown and will have varying levels of roasted flavor notes as well as differences in pungency. Other ingredients which may be present in chili powder are red pepper, paprika, onion, garlic, cumin, Mexican oregano, coriander, and salt. In very inexpensive chili powder, extenders such as corn flour may be present. Table 7.3 gives typical ranges of these ingredients in a chili powder. Table 7.4 is the Federal Military Specification EE-S-631J for chili powder blend.

Chili powders are included as a simple blend since they are used by a large number of food manufacturers. Generally each food processor uses one chili powder for a variety of items and adds additional cumin, garlic, or other ingredients to individualize the flavor of each product.

One trap many manufacturers fall into is that chili powder is bought as a commodity like a spice. Chili powder is a seasoning blend with a large variation in

Table 7.3   Typical Chili Powder Formulation.

Ingredient	Typical Range (%)
Chili pepper	75–95
Salt	0–10
Cumin, ground	1–10
Mexican oregano, ground	1–10
Red pepper, ground	0–5
Garlic powder	0–5
Onion powder	0–5
Coriander, ground	0–2

Table 7.4   Chili Powder—Federal Specification EE-S-631J. Note: Chili powder with added salt shall not be treated with ethylene or propylene oxide gas.

Ingredient	Limit
Ground chili pepper[1]	77%–82%
Salt	not > than 8%
Cumin	not < than 8%
Oregano	not < than 4%
Garlic powder[2]	not < than 1%
Anticaking agent[3]	2% max
Antioxidant[4]	100 ppm max

[1] The ground chili pepper shall be a blend of Anaheim and Ancho variety of *Capsicum annum*, which will meet the ASTA color requirements of not less than 60.
[2] Spray-dried encapsulated natural garlic oil in a dextrose carrier may be substituted for garlic powder on an equivalent basis.
[3] Anticaking compound normally used is silicon dioxide. Silicon dioxide when used shall comply with the Food Chemicals Codex.
[4] Antioxidant normally used is ethoxyquin.

flavor. If requiring an alternative source of chili powder, it is necessary to have the vendor duplicate the flavor of the product currently being purchased.

7.6 Curry Powder

There are hundreds of variations of curry powder. This seasoning is very individualized in Indian cuisine. The Indians have hundreds of variations of curry and generally roast and mix each spice fresh specifically for each dish. In the United States, curry is not as popular or as differentiated; however, there are still many variations available. The main components of curry powder are turmeric for color, coriander, and cumin. Other spices present, often in significant levels, are fenugreek, ginger, celery, and black pepper. Spices present in smaller amounts can be

Table 7.5 Typical Curry Powder Formulation.

Ingredient	Typical Range (%)
Ground coriander	10–50
Ground cumin	5–20
Ground turmeric	10–35
Ground fenugreek	5–20
Ground ginger	5–20
Ground celery	0–15
Ground black pepper	0–10
Ground red pepper	0–10
Ground cinnamon	0–5
Ground nutmeg	0–5
Ground cloves	0–5
Ground caraway	0–5
Ground fennel	0–5
Ground cardamom	0–5
Salt	0–10

Table 7.6 Curry Powder—Federal Specification EE-S-631J.

Ingredient	Limit (%)
Turmeric	37.0–39.0
Coriander	31.0–33.0
Fenugreek	9.0–11.0
Cinnamon	Not < than 7.0
Cumin	Not < than 5.0
Pepper, black	Not < than 3.0
Ginger	Not < than 3.0
Cardamom	Not < than 32.0

red pepper, cinnamon, nutmeg, clove, caraway, and fennel. Salt is sometimes present. Table 7.5 gives a range of these spices in a curry powder formulation. Table 7.6 is the Federal Military Specification EE-S-631J for curry powder blend.

Curry powder is not a commodity and the flavor must be matched before any alternative vendors are approved. The variety of curry powder blends are endless. Most food manufacturers in the United States do purchase curry powder as a blend for formulating food items.

7.7 Pickling Spice

Pickling spices are used for a variety of products. Pickle making and the pickling of meat are two main uses. The variety of pickling spices is limitless with the majority

Table 7.7 Typical Pickling Spice Formulation.

Ingredient	Typical Range
Whole coriander	10–40
Whole mustard	10–40
Cracked bay leaves	10–20
Whole or crushed red pepper	5–10
Whole allspice	5–10
Whole dillseed	5–10
Whole celery seed	5–10
Whole black pepper	0–10
Whole cloves	0–10
Cracked cinnamon	0–10
Cracked ginger	0–5

containing whole and cracked spices. Pickling spices may also be soluble blends containing the essential oils and oleoresins plated on a dextrose carrier. This type of pickling spice is used only in the processed foods industry.

The major components of pickling spices are coriander, mustard seed and bay leaves. Many other spices are also present. Table 7.7 lists a summary of those items.

7.8 Poultry Seasoning

Poultry seasoning is a staple in many kitchens. It is a basic ground herb blend which goes well with poultry flavored foods and is a good flavor addition to stuffing mixes and chicken breadings. Spices usually present are thyme, sage, marjoram, and rosemary, in descending order. Other herbs can also be present but the above are the most common ones. This seasoning blend is used in the retail and food service trades as well as in the processed foods industry to some extent. Table 7.8 describes the Federal Military Specification EE-S-631J for poultry seasoning.

7.9 Pumpkin Pie Spice

Pumpkin pie spice is a common blend sold in the retail and food service trades. It also has some industrial applications in the bakery industry. Pumpkin pie spice

Table 7.8 Poultry Seasoning—Federal Specification EE-S-631J.

Ingredient	Limit (%)
Sage	72–78
Thyme	18–22
Pepper, black	4.5–5.5

Table 7.9 Typical Pumpkin Pie Spice Formulation.

Ingredient	Typical Range (%)
Ground cinnamon	40–80
Ground nutmeg	10–20
Ground ginger	10–20
Ground cloves	10–20
Ground black pepper	0–5

generally contains cinnamon, nutmeg, ginger, and cloves. Table 7.9 lists typical ranges for these spices. In addition, some pumpkin pie spice blends do contain a small amount of black pepper. Recipes from around the turn of the century generally contained the pepper. It is felt by some that the pepper enhances the other spice notes. It is no longer common practice to include black pepper in pumpkin pie spice.

7.10 Apple Pie Spice

Apple pie spice is not as common as pumpkin pie spice, however, it is available. The main flavor component in this blend is cinnamon. Other spices routinely included are nutmeg or mace and allspice. Occasionally, anise or fennel is included in low amounts. Table 7.10 lists those spices included in an apple pie spice blend.

7.11 Oriental Five Spice Blend

Five spice blend is common in oriental cooking. The five spices present are black pepper, cinnamon, anise, fennel, and clove. Traditionally, szechwan peppercorns and star anise are used in this product. Generally, black pepper and regular anise are utilized in these blends in the food industry. A typical five spice blend is located in Table 7.11.

Table 7.10 Typical Apple Pie Spice Formulation.

Ingredient	Typical Range (%)
Ground cinnamon	60–95
Ground nutmeg or mace	2–15
Ground allspice	2–15
Ground anise or fennel	0–10

Table 7.11 Typical Oriental Five Spice Blend.

Ingredient	Typical Range (%)
Ground cinnamon	25–50
Ground anise or star anise	10–25
Ground fennel	10–25
Ground black pepper	10–25
Ground cloves	10–25

8

Meat Seasonings

8.1 Overview of the Industry

This chapter will deal with meat seasonings. It is not meant to inform how to formulate sausage or other meat items, but merely tries to give information necessary to formulate seasonings for the meat industry. Levels of restricted ingredients, USDA labeling regulations as they apply to seasoning blends, and a few sample formulas are included. The technical aspects of formulating meat items are best left to the technical experts in the meat industry.

Meat seasonings are usually low margin items. Often companies will switch suppliers for a few cents difference in cost per pound. If formulating sausage seasonings, it is essential to have an economical source of ground mustard seeds. Often sausage seasonings contain a high level of mustard and unless grinding your own, it is hard to be competitive.

Certain seasoning companies are known in the industry to be primarily meat seasoning suppliers. This is usually due to two main reasons, the first being that many of the smaller seasoning firms were initially formed by large meat companies to provide seasonings to their processing plants and then were either expanded to sell seasonings outside the company, allowed to operate independently, or were sold. The second reason is that some seasoning houses were initially involved in meat seasonings due to their technical expertise. Many small meat companies have relied in the past on technical support from the seasoning company to formulate their meat items and teach them how to produce the product. Some of these seasoning companies provided the seasoning, the smoke flavors, the sausage casings, miscellaneous ingredients, and the technical support to produce processed meat items like summer sausage and wieners. Even fairly large companies in the past utilized the seasoning company as a technical reference much more than they do today. Now, most processed meat manufacturers have their own laboratory and research personnel.

Items that seasoning companies usually provide seasonings for in the red meat industry are fresh, cured, smoked, and dried sausages, nonspecific items such as meat loaves and luncheon loaves, ham brines, corned beef pickles, roast beef rubs, and products like chili and taco meat. Seasonings for poultry items include pumps and basting blends, sausage seasonings such as turkey bologna, ham and breakfast sausage, and marinades and glazes.

There are hundreds, or even thousands of possible flavor combinations for each type of product. The flavor of the product itself varies by region in the U.S. For example, chorizo bought in different geographic areas will be vastly different. It can be dry, semidry, fresh, cooked, cured, hot, or mild, fine or coarse grind, or red to pale orange. In addition, there are an infinite number of variations of flavor available.

8.2 Overview of Formulating

To formulate seasonings for the meat industry, it is essential to have a basic knowledge of USDA labeling regulations, including the flavoring regulations which became effective in March, 1991, the level of restricted ingredients in various products, and a basic knowledge of how meat items are produced. Ideally, a first time formulator should have the opportunity to apprentice with someone more knowledgeable in this area. In addition, the opportunity to duplicate meat seasonings gives the formulator a background as to which flavors are present in which products. Chapter 12 will detail the duplication of seasoning blends more fully. This chapter will attempt to provide some basic information to start formulating meat seasonings.

8.2.1 Meat Block

This is the amount of meat used in a formula. Seasonings and other ingredients are added on the basis of the meat block, typically in 100 pound increments. For example, the directions on a seasoning label would read: Use 6.5 pounds seasoning per 100 pound meat block. A meat processor makes his items in these 100 lb increments, either 500 pounds, 1000 pounds or 700 pounds, whatever his equipment will allow. Any other ingredients, including water, are added based on the 100 lb of meat. Many times manufacturers provide the seasonings in batch size bags for whatever amount of product the meat processor is making. In the example above, if it is a 500 lb meat block, then the seasoning would be packed in a 32.5 lb bag. Restricted ingredients are usually based on the amount per 100 lb meat block.

8.2.2 Cure

A cure is the product used to treat meat for a longer shelf life and give it a characteristic pink color and cured flavor. Bacon, ham, corned beef, bologna, and wieners are all cured. Curing meat products increases shelf life and stops the growth of *Clostridium botulinum,* which would be able to grow and form its deadly toxin in vacuum packed meat items. Cures contain salt, sodium nitrite and, less commonly, sodium nitrate (limited to some extent since the nitrate is associated with increased formation of nitrosamines during cooking, which have been found to be carcinogenic), and an anticaking agent. Sugar is also sometimes present. Some cures are colored with FD&C Red Dye #3, giving the product a pink color. This is done so meat manufacturers will not confuse the cure with salt in their plant. Sodium nitrite is restricted in sausage items to 156 ppm. Most cures contain 6.25% sodium nitrite and the usage level is 0.25 lb (4 oz) to 100 lb meat block. Other cures can contain 12.5% sodium nitrite. Other levels of nitrite cures for specific products are available, however the two types described above are the most common. Cures are never included with the seasoning because many seasoning components such as hydrolyzed vegetable proteins, contain amines and thus may combine with nitrites and nitrates to form nitrosamines which are carcinogens (21CFR 170.60). See Chapter 6 for a more complete discussion.

Cures are either sold separately in drums or packed in batch size amounts. In the 500 lb meat block example, 1.25 lb of cure would be packed in its own separate bag and placed inside or attached to the outside of the seasoning bag (cure twinpack or piggyback). The operator would then only have to add one bag of each product to his meat formula with no extra weighing of his seasoning ingredients. Some meat processors purchase all their seasonings in these batch size increments, others buy the seasonings in bulk.

Since sodium nitrite levels are regulated, seasoning manufacturers must analyze each lot of cure to confirm that it contains the proper amount of nitrite.

8.2.3 Curing Accelerator

The curing accelerator most often used in the meat industry is sodium erythorbate. A second, less used product is sodium ascorbate. Sodium erythorbate is the mirror image isomer of ascorbic acid (Vitamin C) although it has no vitamin activity. Cure accelerators help increase the pink color of a cured product and must be used in combination with a curing agent. They are limited to 550 ppm ($7/8$ of an ounce to 100 lb of meat). Sodium erythorbate is commonly added to the seasoning blend.

8.2.4 Brine

A brine is a water soluble solution of seasonings, salt, sugar, sodium erythorbate, phosphates, and cure which is pumped or injected into a meat item such as ham or corned beef. All flavoring materials should be water soluble although small amounts of garlic powder are possible due to its small particle size. Often oleoresins are used in this application with polysorbate 80 or other emulsifier present. The brine is formulated so that if the product is pumped 20%, the level of restricted ingredients is at the proper amounts. Pumping 20% means that if 100 lb of meat is pumped with this solution, then 120 lb of finished product results. See Table 8.1 for an example of a pump calculation.

Table 8.1 Pump (or Pickle) Calculation.

1. Start with percent pump desired. This is the pounds of pickle to 100# meat block.

2. Decide on amount of nonmeat ingredients to be delivered to the 100# meat block.

Example: 20% pump	
2.00#	Salt
0.75	Sugar
0.30	Phosphate
0.25	6.25% nitrite cure
0.055	Sodium erythorbate
0.25	Soluble spices on a dextrose carrier
3.605#	Total nonmeat ingredients

3. If the pump is 20%, then

20.0#	Is the total pickle weight
− 3.605	Total nonmeat ingredients
16.395#	Water required to make 20# of pickle

$$\frac{16.395\#}{8.34\#/gal \text{ (density of water)}} = 1.97 \text{ gallons of water}$$

4. To make up the pump with 200 gallons of water:

$$\frac{200 \text{ gal}}{1.97 \text{ gal}} = 101.52 \text{ twenty pound units of pickle}$$

5. The amount of nonmeat ingredients needed to prepare 200 gallons of a 20% pump is

2.00 × 101.52 =	203.04	Salt
0.75 × 101.52 =	76.14#	Sugar
0.30 × 101.52 =	30.46#	Phosphate
0.25 × 101.52 =	25.38#	6.25% cure
0.055 × 101.52 =	5.58#	Sodium erythorbate
0.25 × 101.52 =	25.38#	Spice extractives on a dextrose carrier
	365.98	Total dry weight
200 gal × 8.34#/gal =	1668.0#	Water
	2033.98#	Total pickle weight

6. To change to other pump percentages while keeping the dry ingredients the same per 100# of meat, one only has to change the amount of water in step 3.
    Example: for a 15% pump:
    15# − 3.605# = 11.395# water

Note: 1 pound = 454 g
     1 gallon = 3.78 l

8.2.5 Pickup

This term is utilized primarily in the poultry industry. If a 15% pickup is desired, then the poultry is marinated, vacuum tumbled, or injected so that 100 lb of chicken weighs 115 lb. This is important to know when formulating seasoning for the above types of items so the strength of the flavor, salt, and phosphate are kept at the proper level. Injected seasonings must be water soluble. Vacuum tumbled or marinated products can use some nonsoluble particulate ingredients.

8.3 Formulations

When formulating for meats, it is much more practical to formulate based on the weight of an ingredient needed for a stated amount of meat block, rather than working in percentages. To produce a product such as a wiener seasoning, it is important to work in weight of seasoning per 100 pounds of meat. When the formula is designed this way, it can be converted to percentages and the seasoning formula can be produced. If the formulator wants to reduce one item, such as dextrose, he can convert back to weight per 100 pounds, reduce the weight of the item, and calculate back to percentages. The usage per 100 pounds will decrease, and the percentages of ingredients will change, but the weight of the ingredients added per 100 pounds of meat will stay the same. See Table 8.2 for an example.

The 3.806 lb and the 3.556 lb are the amounts of seasoning added to a 100 lb meat block. The formula change reflects a 0.25 lb (4 oz) reduction in dextrose and thus a 0.25 lb reduction in usage per 100 lb of meat. This causes the formula percentages to increase, but not the amount of other ingredients which are added to the meat. To double check this, take 1.52/100 (percent of S/E in second formula) × 3.556 lb (seasoning usage) = 0.054 lb. This is the amount of sodium erythorbate added to 100 lb of meat in either formula. Calculating formulas in this way allows tighter control on the level of restricted ingredients. It also ensures that the other ingredients will stay the same while manipulating the formula.

These types of calculations, based on usages, are used most often in the meat industry. They can also be helpful when formulating products such as sauces and gravies. If blends are formulated in usages, increasing or decreasing various flavor ingredients while keeping salt and starch levels the same per cup or gallon of gravy mix, is very simple.

Table 8.2   Smoked Sausage Seasoning.

Item	# Per 100# Meat Block	% in Formula	New Formula # Per 100# Meat Block	% in Formula
Salt	2.25	59.13	2.25	63.26
Dextrose	1.00	26.27	0.75	21.09
Garlic powder	.125	3.28	.125	3.52
Black pepper, ground	.250	6.57	.250	7.03
Sodium erythorbate	.054	1.42	.054	1.52
MSG	.125	3.28	.125	3.52
Oil of coriander	.001	.025	.001	.03
Oil of pimento	.001	.025	.001	.03
Totals	3.806#	100.00%	3.556#	100.00%

8.3.1 Restricted Ingredients

Common restricted ingredients in cooked sausages and other cured meat items are as follows as of the publication date of this book.

8.3.1.1 Corn Syrup Solids

2% maximum of the finished product.

8.3.1.2 Sodium Erythorbate

Not greater than 550 ppm in a meat item. Usually referred to as $^7/_8$ oz per 100 lb of meat. If calculating sodium erythorbate—$^7/_8$ oz = .0547 lb/100 lb of meat = .000547, which is 547 ppm.

8.3.1.3 Sodium Nitrite

120–156 ppm, depending on the meat item. In sausages, 156 ppm is the limit. (4 oz of a 6.25% cure per 100 lb of meat is 156 ppm.)

8.3.1.4 Antioxidant

Includes BHA, BHT, and propyl gallate.

Dry sausage (pepperoni, summer sausage, etc.)—limited to .003% of the meat singly or .006% in combination. 100 lb of pepperoni could contain up to .006 pounds of BHA or .003 lb of BHA and .003 lb of BHT (100 lb × .003/100 = .003 lb).

Fresh sausage (pork sausage, italian sausage, etc.)—limited to 0.01% of the fat content singly and 0.02% of the fat content in combination. 100 lb of pork sausage containing 30% fat could contain up to .006 pounds of BHA or .003 lb of BHA and .003 lb of BHT (30 lb × .01/100 = .003 lb).

8.3.1.5 Sodium Phosphates

0.5% of finished product in meat and poultry products. Can be sodium tri-polyphosphate (STPP), sodium hexametaphosphate (SHMP), sodium acid py-rophosphate (SAPP), or a combination of these and other approved phosphates. When phosphates are used in brines, it is important to dissolve the phosphate in the water first and then add the salt. The water used in brines is very cold, often part ice, and if the phosphate is added to a salt brine it may not dissolve. Some of the newer phosphate blends are formulated to dissolve more readily in cold water.

8.3.1.6 Mustard

Up until the new flavoring regulations took effect in March 1991, mustard was limited to 1% in cooked sausages. Now, it is not limited as such, but only 1% nonmeat protein from all sources can be used in sausage. Since mustard is about

30% protein, it could be used at levels as high as 3% in cooked sausages, assuming no other nonmeat protein was used in the product. A practical limit of about $1^1/2\%$– 2.0% applies due to off flavor development and poor texture.

The legal regulations for meat and poultry can be found in the following government publications.

1. Meat and Poultry Regulations 9CFR, Part 200 to end.
2. Standards and Labeling Policy Book—January 1986 with revisions available. Food Safety and Inspection Service (FSIS).
3. Standard and Labeling Policy Memos.

An additional reference which is an excellent summary of the above is *Encyclopedia of Labeling Meat & Poultry Products, 9th Edition,* Jan F. deHoll. Meat Plant Magazine, 9701 Gravois Avenue, St. Louis, MO 63123. 1989. Every seasoning manufacturer should have this loose-leaf notebook available. It summarizes all pertinent regulations in the meat and poultry industry.

8.3.2 Natural Flavoring Regulations

The above discussion of mustard is a good lead-in to flavoring regulations as they apply to seasoning manufacturers. As discussed previously, in March 1991, a new flavoring regulation issued by the FSIS went into effect. This regulation defined "flavoring," "natural flavoring," and "natural flavor" as the following:

> Essential oils, oleoresins, essences, extractives, distillates or any product of roasting or heating which contains the flavoring constituents derived from any spice, fruit or fruit juice, vegetable or vegetable juice, edible yeast, herb, bud, root, bark, leaf or other edible portion of a plant. Spices, onion powder, garlic powder and celery powder, oleoresin black pepper, ginger, and garlic oil are examples (FSIS NOTICE, USDA, U.S. Government Printing Office: 1990-262-858:20312/FSIS). Any other item which is not listed above must:
>
> 1. Be listed by common or usual name or
> 2. Common or usual name with a sublisting of ingredients or
> 3. Subject to USDA approval for acceptable labeling.
>
> All proteinaceous materials are not flavoring, and must be listed by their common and usual name including *source,* such as hydrolysates and autolysates of animal, plant, dairy and yeast sources.

The result of this new legislation is that most ingredients must now be broken down to their component ingredients, which the FSIS decides upon. For example, a flavor blend to replace MSG may have been labeled as natural flavor in the past. It now has to be labeled with all its components, which may be: "maltodextrin, salt, autolyzed yeast extract, hydrolyzed vegetable protein, citric acid and natural flavor." This regulation has complicated labeling tremendously.

Reaction flavors are another problem. Generally reaction flavors are produced by the treatment of amino acids or other proteins along with sugar under heat to produce meat flavors.

8.3.3 Seasoning Formulas

Sample formulas are included in this section. One example from each category of common meat seasonings is given. Generalizations as well as specific regulations are included for each product discussed. This section is not meant to be all encompassing and does not include every regulation. Ingredients are presented in ranges and are based on amount per 100 lb meat block and not as formula percentages.

8.3.3.1 Fresh Sausage

Fresh sausages are primarily Italian, pork, bratwurst, and breakfast sausage. Many others are also available. The two examples included in this section are Italian and pork sausage since they are the two most common products of this category. Mustard is not used in fresh sausage since the enzyme present acts on the meat protein and produces a putrid-like flavor and odor. If mustard has been heat treated to destroy the enzyme prior to adding to the meat, then it can be used in the fresh sausage. This is called deactivated mustard. Paprika is not allowed in fresh sausage except for Italian, Chorizo, and Longaniza. Salt is added to fresh sausage at about 2–2.5 lb per 100 lb meat block. Dextrose can be present, usually at the 0.5%–1% level.

Italian sausage: Italian sausage has some special limitations in that it must contain pepper, fennel and/or anise to be called Italian. A sample formula is included in Table 8.3.

Pork sausage: paprika is not allowed in this type of sausage. Antioxidants are often added. See Table 8.4 for a sample formula. The granulation of the spices used can vary tremendously. Sage can be whole, rubbed, or ground. Red pepper can vary, either ground or crushed, and black pepper can be very fine to a cracked size. Sometimes pork sausage seasonings can be all soluble. Essential oils and oleoresins are plated on salt or dextrose so that no spice particles are visible. Typical levels of oils and oleoresins can be calculated from the extractive equivalency chart in Chapter 5.

8.3.3.2 Cooked Sausage

Bologna and wieners are typical cooked sausages. The flavor of these two items are usually the same, the difference being the diameter of the sausage. Cooked sausages

Table 8.3 Typical Italian Sausage Seasoning Formulation. Note: 1 oz = 28.4 Grams.

Ingredient	Typical Range
Anise, whole, cracked, or ground	1–4 oz
Fennel, whole, cracked, or ground	1–4 oz
Paprika	0–16 oz
Black pepper, ground	2–6 oz
Red pepper, ground or crushed	0–4 oz
Salt	32–40 oz

Table 8.4 Typical Pork Sausage Seasoning Formulation. Note: 1 oz = 28.4 Grams.

Ingredient	Typical Ranges	
Sage, ground, chopped, or rubbed	2–6	oz
Black pepper, ground	1–4	oz
Red pepper, ground or crushed	1–4	oz
Nutmeg, ground	0–0.5	oz
Salt	32–40	oz
Antioxidants if desired. Amount based on Fat content.		

are cured and may or may not be smoked. Binders are allowed to 3.5% and isolated soy protein up to 2% in certain sausages. Usually these items are not included in the seasoning blend due to the high percent used in the meat, but also because they are not often used since the name of the product must be qualified (beef frankfurter with soy flour added). Hydrolyzed vegetable proteins and smoke flavors are permitted. Sodium erythorbate is often included in the seasoning. Salt is used at the 2%–2.5% level. Dextrose at a level of 1% is usually provided by the seasoning. Bologna and wieners can be seasoned with ground spices or extractives. Extractives are the most common in these types of products because no spice particles are visible. If extractives are used, then the seasoning is simply spice extractives on a dextrose carrier, mustard, and sodium erythorbate. See Table 8.5 for a typical bologna or wiener formulation including restricted ingredients and salt.

Table 8.5 Typical Bologna or Wiener Seasoning Formulation. Note: 1 oz = 28.4 Grams.

Ingredient			Typical Ranges	
Spice extractives on a dextrose carrier			8–16	oz
including	1.0%–3.0%	oil pimento		
	1.0%–5.0%	oil nutmeg		
	0.5%–2%	oleoresin black pepper		
	0.25%–1.0%	oil clove leaf or stem		
	0%–0.5%	oleoresin capsicum 500,000 SHU		
	0%–0.5%	oleoresin paprika		
	0.5%–2.0%	oil coriander or rosewood		
	0%–0.5%	oil cassia		
Mustard, ground			16	oz
Onion powder			0.5–2.0	oz
Garlic powder			0.25–0.5	oz
Sodium erythorbate			0.875	oz
Salt			32–40	oz
Smoke flavor			0–1.0	oz
HVP			0–4	oz
6.25% Sodium nitrite cure (not to be blended into the seasoning, but added separately)			4	oz

8.3.3.3 Rubs

Rubs are commonly used on the outside of a large piece of meat to flavor and color the product. These items are generally used on corned beef, pastrami, and roast beef. The corned beef and pastrami rubs are usually a mixture of ground or cracked coriander with paprika, caramel color, a small amount of other spices, garlic, and onion for flavor. Coriander can be as high as 90%. Roast beef rubs are different in the fact that they generally do not contain as high a level of coriander. This type of rub contains a large percent of caramel color, dextrose, salt with some spice, onion, and garlic. It is used on the meat to create a dark brown to black coating on the exterior of the roast. Table 8.6 gives ranges for typical roast beef and corned beef rubs.

8.3.3.4 Dry and Semidry Sausages

This category of sausage includes pepperoni, salami, and summer sausage. These types of products are cured and contain a lactic acid starter culture which gives these products a characteristic "tang."

Pepperoni: Pepperoni contains the most seasoning of any semi-dry sausage. Most pepperoni is very orange in color due to the high amount of paprika and oleoresin paprika in the formula. Other characteristic flavors include anise and fennel, garlic, black pepper and red pepper. Since it is a cured product, the seasoning usually contains sodium erythorbate. Table 8.7 shows a typical pepperoni seasoning.

8.3.3.5 Brines

There are many products in which brines are used to impart flavor as well as to cure the product. The two most often made products in the United States are ham and corned beef. Ham is generally cured and flavored with a soluble brine because it is

Table 8.6 Typical Roast Beef and Corned Beef Rub Formulations.

Ingredient	Roast Beef Rub Typical Ranges (%)	Corned Beef Rub Typical Ranges (%)
Coriander, ground or cracked	0–10	60–90
Dextrose	20–75	0–20
Salt	0–20	usually 0
Caramel color	2–20	0–10
Onion powder	1–10	0–5
Garlic powder	1–10	0–5
Celery, ground	0–5	usually 0
Oregano, ground	0–5	usually 0
Basil, ground	0–5	usually 0
Black pepper, fine	0–5	usually 0
Black pepper, cracked	usually 0	5–25
Paprika	usually 0	2–40

Table 8.7 Typical Pepperoni Seasoning Formulation. Note: 1 oz = 28.4 Grams.

Ingredient	Typical Ranges	
Dextrose	16	oz
Salt	32–40	oz
Extractive of paprika, 100,000 CU	0.5–2	oz
Anise, whole	1–4	oz
Fennel, whole	1–4	oz
Fennel, ground	1–4	oz
Black pepper, ground	1–4	oz
Red pepper, crushed 40,000 SHU	1–4	oz
Sodium erythorbate	7/8	oz
Garlic powder	1–4	oz
6.25% nitrite cure (not to be blended in the seasoning, but added separately)	4	oz

injected or pumped to produce an evenly cured product. Ham seasonings usually contain spice extractives on a sugar or dextrose carrier, garlic and sodium erythorbate. Table 8.8 gives an example of a typical ham seasoning. Corned beef is soaked in a pickle seasoning which may or may not be soluble. Often a whole pickling spice is used.

Table 8.8 Typical Ham Seasoning. Note: 1 oz = 28.4 Grams.

Ingredient		Typical Ranges
Spice extractives on a dextrose or sugar carrier		8–16 oz
including	1%–5% oil cassia	
	1%–3% oil clove stem or leaf	
	1%–3% oil pimento	
	0.05%–0.5% oleoresin capsicum	
	0%–0.25% oleoresin celery	
	0.05%–0.25 oil bay	
	0.5%–2.0% Polysorbate 80	
	0%–0.5 oil soluble garlic (diluted oil of garlic)	
Sodium erythorbate		7/8 oz
Garlic powder		0–2 oz

9

Snack Seasonings

9.1 Overview of the Industry

Savory snacks are a huge industry. Sales in 1991 were $13.4 billion, or 4.92 billion pounds.[1] This chapter will discuss a variety of salty snack seasonings. The products included in this chapter are potato chips, tortilla and corn chips, extruded snacks, popcorn, nuts, and rice cakes. A breakdown of the volume of these snacks can be found in Table 9.1.

Flavored chips are a value-added item. The seasoning can make or break a product and sufficient sensory and market testing is necessary to produce an acceptable flavor. The seasoning also adds quite a bit of cost to the product. A seasoning of $1.50 a pound will add $0.18 to an 8 oz bag of potato chips. These figures are based on an application rate of 8%. This is a high figure compared to other products where the seasoning usage rate is often in the range of 1%–2%. Often the retail price of the flavored chip is not any higher than the plain chip, thus it is essential to get the most flavor for the money. It is important, however, to purchase a seasoning that tastes good rather than on price alone since it is so important to the sensory attributes of the final product.

Potato chips sold in the U.S. in 1991 were 1.57 billion pounds. Unflavored chips are still the biggest seller, having 69.7% of the market. BBQ is by far the most popular flavored chip, holding 12.7% of the market. Sour Cream & Onion is the next favorite, with 8.8% of the market. Cheese flavored chips are 3.5%. Other flavors including Cajun, Salt & Vinegar, Hot & Spicy, Jalapeno, and Onion hold 9.7% of the market. The remainder is unsalted and low salt potato chips. Total flavored chips are 30.3% or almost 475 million pounds a year.[1] If a seasoning is

Table 9.1 Snack Volumes by Type for 1991. [State of the Industry Report, *Snack Food World* 49 (6), SW-3–SW-51. 1992.]

Snack	#(in Millions)	% of Total Snacks
Potato chips	1,567	31.8
Tortilla chips	1,033	21.0
Snack nuts	389	7.9
Extruded snacks	274	5.6
Corn chips	244	5.0
RTE popcorn	134	2.7
Pork rinds	41	0.8

applied at 6%, the amount of seasoning supplied to the potato chip industry is 28.5 million pounds a year! These figures do not even take into account the seasonings for tortilla chips and other salty snacks.

There are many regional preferences in snack flavors. Salt and vinegar is an important potato chip flavor in the Northeast. It is almost nonexistent in other parts of the country. Hot and spicy products are popular and much hotter in flavor in the southwest and in certain urban areas. BBQ chips can come in many variations such as BBQ Mesquite, Grill BBQ, Hot & Spicy BBQ, and Hickory BBQ.

Common tortilla chip flavors are nacho cheese and ranch. New flavors are being added all the time, the hottest usually marketed in the southwest. It is often the regional manufacturers which do the most experimenting and have the most unique flavors. Generally, when a snack manufacturer introduces their version of an existing flavor, the major national branded items are the target product. If the same seasoning is applied to two different types of potato chips (wavy and plain or dark and light) or tortilla chips (corn or white corn), the seasoning will usually taste completely different on the two products.

The salty snack food industry is primarily a market of regional manufacturers. Each manufacturer produces products which their market desires. Kettle style chips are most popular in New England, where fabricated chips are most popular in the south.

There are four major national marketers of salty snacks: Frito Lay and Borden, which hold 38.7% and 9.0% of the market share, respectively. Borden markets under a variety of regional brand names. Eagle Snacks and Keebler, the dominant player of the fabricated chips, have 5.2% and 5.1% market share.[2]

Some of the current trends in the snack food market are as follows.

9.1.1 All Natural/No MSG

This trend is a niche market in which nontraditional snacks such as high fiber extruded products and other healthy "good-for-you" snacks are utilized. This trend is most often seen in smaller, innovative manufacturers. Rice cakes and croutons have also been marketed in this way. The mainstream snackers do not usually follow this trend. They may feel the market is not large enough since the people concerned with these issues are not big snack consumers. In addition, flavor preference wins out with the large snack manufacturers.

9.1.2 Low Calorie Snacks

This type of product is marketed similarly to the product described above. Low calorie snacks are often extruded from a variety of base products including rice, potato, wheat, and corn in many different shapes and sizes. Extruded snacks have a low fat content and if the seasoning is applied with a minimum amount of oil, they are low in fat and calories. Some manufacturers are using a gum or tack solution to cause the seasoning to stick to the snack without added oil. The snack may then have to undergo an additional drying step to reduce the moisture to a low enough level to maintain crispness.

In addition, Frito Lay has come out with a line of tortilla chips with $1/3$ less oil. This shows that the national manufacturers are also addressing the low calorie trend.

9.1.3 Unique Flavors

Currently, the snack food market is introducing a wide variety of new flavors, the more unique the better. The mainstream snackers have introduced a variety of new flavors, especially on tortilla chips in the last few years, but the regional manufacturers are often where the most innovation comes from. In addition, products such as rice cakes have come out with a variety of new flavors. Rice cakes are unique in that the traditional salty snack flavors such as BBQ, Sour Cream & Onion, and Cheese are used on the same base product as sweet flavors such as Honey Nut, Honey Cinnamon, and Apple Cinnamon.

9.1.4 Multigrain Chips

The big snack manufacturers are fighting for market share for the multigrain chip sales. Frito Lay began with Sun Chips and Keebler has introduced Quangles. This is a new trend in the snack market. Borden is supposed to be coming out with a multigrain chip in 1992.[1] This market is growing tremendously.

9.2 Overview of Formulating

Snack food seasonings are unique because they are topically applied. This causes the formulator to consider different important attributes than if the seasoning is added inside the product, as is the case of meats or sauces. Snack seasonings contain a large amount of extenders or bulking agents. This is due to two major factors, the first being that most snack manufacturers have an upper limit to the cost of the seasoning so extenders are added to ensure the cost is not prohibitive. Secondly, due to the importance of coverage, the snack manufacturer cannot decrease usage to decrease cost like a meat or sauce manufacturer can. For instance, a certain appearance, based on a seasoning applied at the 8% level, is expected. If a stronger seasoning is used at only 5%, the snack does not look as if it has enough seasoning on it and therefore is undesirable. On the other hand, in meat products, the seasoning is in the meat emulsion and therefore if it is made stronger, less seasoning can be used without any visual impact and the cost per unit is decreased.

One important factor which must be considered in applying seasonings to snack foods is whether the seasoning is to carry all the salt or the seasoning is to be applied to an already salted chip. Some chip and tortilla manufacturers, due to their process, salt the chips first and then add a low salt or no salt seasoning to the product. In this case, the seasoning can be applied at a lower level and still get the same coverage and flavor. It must be realized that if the salt is already on the chip, then a seasoning applied at 8% should add more flavor to a product than if the seasoning contains all the salt and it is applied at 8%. In the latter case, the characteristic flavor is actually only being applied at about a 6.5% level to the chip. The other 1.5% is salt. Snack manufacturers must realize that the seasoning purchased may also be more expensive if it is unsalted or contains a low level of salt since the salt is a very inexpensive ingredient at about 6–7 cents per pound.

Extenders often used in snack seasonings include dextrose, maltodextrin, wheat flour, torula yeast, corn flour, and whey. Seasoning companies will use small amounts of each to produce a product with a desirable ingredient statement. For example, in a sour cream and onion seasoning, sour cream solids, buttermilk solids, and onion powder are the most desirable ingredients to be at the top of the ingredient statement, but there is often only 8%–12% of each in the seasoning due to the high cost of these products. By formulating a product with the following percents, the ingredient statement can be made desirable and the cost minimized.

Buttermilk solids	15
Whey	15
Onion powder	12
Sour cream solids	9
Dextrose	9
Wheat flour	9
Balance of ingredients	31

The above example shows that 69% of the formula can be realized with a low cost while still retaining the following desirable ingredient statement: "Buttermilk solids, whey, onion powder, sour cream solids, dextrose, wheat flour. . . ." The balance of the ingredients would include salt, sugar, acids, parsley, etc. In dairy seasonings, it usually is acceptable to list whey first on the ingredient statement, thus allowing it to be used at upwards of 30% of the formula.

Snacks with topically applied seasonings require seasonings with a very small particle size. Salt should be flour or powdered salt with 20% or less retained on a U.S.S. #100 screen and the sugar should be a bakers special fine type or powdered sugar. Other ingredients used in snack seasonings must have a very fine or powdery consistency. The small particle size allows the seasoning to adhere to the snack. If the seasoning is applied in an oil slurry, a small particle size also allows it to pass through the spray nozzles.

Snack seasonings often utilize higher levels of flavors—both natural and artificial—than other seasoning blends due to the immediate and strong flavor desired when eating a snack chip.

Flowability of the seasoning is a very important factor for chip manufacturers since the seasoning must uniformly fall through small holes or flow easily through a tumbler to sprinkle on the chip. If small lumps are present or the seasoning does not flow evenly, it may miss some chips or clog the applicator. To help increase flowability, anticaking agents up to a 2% level can be added. These products will not only retard caking due to humidity, but will also cause the seasoning to flow much easier. Different types of anticaking agents and different brands of the same type of anticaking agents will affect the flowability of the seasoning in different amounts. On the other hand, it is not advantageous to use too much flow agent so the resultant seasoning is very dusty. This will make production conditions intolerable and will waste product. Usually a compromise must be made between flowability and dustiness since they are competing factors. A small amount of soybean oil can help to reduce dustiness in a seasoning. Another option to increase flowability of the seasoning is to adjust the particle size. If using a slightly larger granulation of some of the ingredients, it may help to reduce caking and increase flowability. Many times seasonings must be adjusted for flowability, dustiness and anticaking after a large production batch has been made.

There are many different ways to test flowability; however, the following methods seem to work well.

Angle of repose: In this method, a seasoning is allowed to flow unrestricted through a suspended funnel. The seasoning will form a cone shaped pile to varying degrees. By measuring the angle of repose (inverse tangent of the height of the pile/radius of the pile), a value can describe the flowability. To simplify the measurement, it is possible to let the seasoning flow into a cylinder of a known diameter and simply measure the height of the pile. Sometimes a vibrator is used so the seasoning can flow through the funnel. The steeper the cone, the less flowable the seasoning. The less steep the cone, the more flowable the seasoning.

Flow time: This is a fairly simple test. The most important factor is the type of funnels to use. Ideally, they should be stainless steel with a completely round discharge orifice. The funnels should have varying discharge diameters, from about 2 to 20 mm. Five different funnels in this range is desirable. The seasoning is placed in the suspended funnels and allowed to flow out. The funnel in which the seasoning flows at the slowest rate should be used. The flow time is the time in seconds in which a set amount of seasoning flows from the funnel. This method is most advantageous in comparing different samples of the same formula to optimize the best flow agent and level.

When formulating snack seasonings, it is essential to ask the snack manufacturers various questions which will determine which type of seasoning to present to the customer. For example, many sour cream and onion seasonings are similar;

however, there are differences in the salt level, the cost, the flavor, and various other factors. These questions are outlined below.

9.2.1 Will the Seasoning be Topically Applied or Applied in an Oil Slurry?

This will determine the strength and the characteristic of the flavor. If a seasoning is applied in an oil slurry, the flavor may be masked. The oil coats the tongue and thus may not allow all the flavors to come through. An example is a BBQ seasoning. A basic taste such as sour does not come through as sharply in an oil slurry as if the seasoning were topically applied and the acid allowed to dissolve directly on the tongue. On the other hand, if it is a cheese seasoning the oil slurry can actually enhance the flavor since the fatty texture complements the cheese. When cheese seasonings are not applied in an oil slurry, often powdered or beaded shortening is added to give a fatty background to the snack.

9.2.2 What is the Base Product the Seasoning will be Used On?

This is an essential question. A ranch seasoning for a potato chip may not be the same as for a tortilla chip. Corn based products are stronger in flavor which make them more difficult to season. An extruded corn or wheat product may take a different seasoning than a potato based extruded snack, which can have a cooked off-flavor present. In addition, the ideal salt level is different for different types of products. The lower the density of the snack, the higher percent of salt and seasoning is required to adequately flavor the snack. In other words, the higher the surface area to volume ratio, the higher the amount of seasoning required to flavor the product and to give the proper level of seasoning coverage. For example, a typical potato chip seasoning when the chip is unsalted, should have about 19%–25% salt and be applied at 8%. This translates to about 1.5%–2.0% salt on the chip. A popcorn seasoning, however, often has upwards of 25%–30% salt due to the higher surface area. Usually salt levels on popcorn are in the 2%–2.5% range. Applying the seasoning at 10% would translate to 2.5% salt on the snack. If a higher percent of seasoning is used, then the salt percent in the seasoning should be decreased. A popcorn seasoning applied at a level of 25% would only contain about 10% salt, thus adding the same 2.5% salt to the finished product.

If the seasoning is going to be applied to a new generation extruded snack or something unfamiliar, ask for a sample of the unflavored product. This way, a seasoning can be formulated specifically for the base product and inappropriate seasonings need not be presented. This will save the snack manufacturer and the seasoning company time and energy.

9.2.3 Is the Base Product Salted?

This is a critical question that most seasoning manufacturers forget to ask. For example, as described above, a seasoning for an unsalted potato chip should have between 19% and 25% salt in the seasoning if applied at the 8% range. Many chip manufacturers, however, apply the seasoning in the production process after the salt is already applied to the chip. In this case, the salt level should be 0%–8% in the seasoning. Depending on the product and how much salt is on the unseasoned chip, it is often desirable to add a small amount of salt in the seasoning.

If this essential question is not asked, the seasoning may be disregarded by the customer prematurely. The chip may taste much too salty if a high salt product for application to their salted chip is presented. On the other hand, the chip may not have enough flavor if a low salt seasoning is presented to a chip producer who applies the seasoning to unsalted chips.

9.2.4 What is the Target and Maximum Cost for this Seasoning?

This question will save a lot of time if the snack manufacturer has a very tight price restriction. It will also help determine if they are looking for a very inexpensive product or a high-quality seasoning. Determining price restrictions prior to formulation is desirable.

9.3 Formulations

9.3.1 Potato Chips

The seasoning can be applied by either drum tumbling or sprinkling on the chip while it is on a conveyor. The latter method results in a chip which is only coated on one side. As discussed previously, the seasoning may be applied to a salted or an unsalted chip. The seasoning is applied directly after frying, although usually it is allowed to cool slightly. If the seasoning is applied while the oil is too hot, the seasoning, especially one with high amounts of dairy products, may burn slightly and cause an off-flavor note. If the chip is completely cooled, however, the seasoning may not stick as well as it should. The application rate of the seasoning is approximately 6%–8%. See Table 9.2 for a sample barbecue formula.

9.3.2 Extruded Snacks

There are many extruded snacks in today's market. Extruded products are made by producing a dough of the base material, water, and a small amount of oil. This dough is subjected to a high level of heat, pressure, and shear in a cylindrical extruder. When it comes to the end of the cylinder, the dough is forced through a die. The change in temperature and pressure to ambient conditions causes the product to expand, or puff, thus producing an extruded snack. Different die shapes determine the shape of the snack, from balls, to cylindrical puffs, to wagon wheels and numerous other shapes.

The first products to be marketed were the "cheese puffs." These are corn puffs, called collettes in the industry, seasoned with a cheese seasoning. Whey, cheese,

Table 9.2 Typical BBQ Seasoning for 8% Application to Unsalted Chips.

Ingredient	Typical Ranges (%)
Salt, fine flour	19–25
Dextrose	10–20
Sugar, bakers special	10–20
Torula yeast	6–15
MSG	3–8
Other extenders which may include:	10–20
Maltodextrin	
Cornstarch	
Wheat flour	
Tomato powder	0–5
Autolyzed yeasts	0–12
Onion powder	2–8
Garlic powder	0.5–4
Chili pepper	1–2
Paprika	1–5
Other Spices—one or more of the following:	0.05–0.5
Celery, cumin, cloves, allspice, cinnamon,	
black pepper, red pepper	
Citric acid	0.5–1
Smoke flavoring	0.5–2
Oleoresin paprika	
40,000–100,000 CU	0.1–0.8
Disodium inosinate and Disodium guanylate	0–0.2
Flow/anticaking agent	0–2

acid, colors, flavors, and various other ingredients are mixed together to produce the seasoning which is applied in an oil slurry at 30%–50% of the weight of the collettes. The percent of seasoning in the oil is between 20% and 40% and is applied by spraying it on the collettes while they are in a drum tumbler.

Collettes come in two types, fried and baked. The baked puff is the lighter density product. The fried corn puff is a heavier density product with a crunchier bite. Additional flavors of collettes are not common, although Chili Cheese, and a Vinegar Hot Sauce flavor are available.

When formulating a cheese collette or other cheese seasoning, two approaches can be taken. The first is for the seasoning company to purchase a blend of cheese, whey, maltodextrin, flavors, and color (FD&C Yellows #5 and #6) and then blend this item even further to produce a product with an acceptable price. There are a few drawbacks to this approach. First, the seasoning will be more expensive since the seasoning manufacturer is purchasing the product from a cheese manufacturer who is making a profit on the cheese blend. In addition, the ingredient statement of the finished seasoning becomes very complicated since the cheese blend has a complicated label and the seasoning company adds additional salt, whey, flavors, and even sometimes additional artificial colors. The advantage of this approach is that much of the formulation work has already been done and it is simple to produce a flavorful cheese seasoning. The cheese blends are often co-spray-dried, giving a creamier texture even if high levels of whey are present, which can be granular when dry blended. The problem is that it may not be competitive in price. The second approach is to purchase a commodity-type uncolored cheese product and add the extenders as well as any flavors, colors, acids, etc., thus eliminating the cost of two blending operations and providing a product with a simpler ingredient statement. See Table 9.3 for a sample formula using the commodity-type uncolored cheese solids.

Extrusion is becoming popular in the specialty snack market for low calorie or other healthy products. These products have been made with a wide variety of base products: corn, wheat, rice, and potato to name a few. These types of products usually have the most unique flavors applied, and can be either savory or sweet. It is essential to request a base product to formulate the seasoning since flavor, density, and coverage level can vary widely. Requesting the manufacturers' desired topical application rate usually helps in formulation. Applying the seasoning at a 4% level or an 8% level will determine how strong the flavor should be and how dark the seasoning color should be. Many times these types of products are marketed to be all natural, no MSG, or other specific restrictions. It is helpful to request this information at the initial stages of formulation. "No Monosodium Glutamate Added" for-

Table 9.3 Cheese Blend for Extruded Collettes—Oil Slurry Application.

Ingredient	Typical Ranges (%)
Whey solids	10–30
Cheese solids	8–16
Buttermilk solids	10–20
Other extenders which may include: Maltodextrin or Wheat Flour	10–20
Dextrose	8–16
MSG	2–8
Salt, fine flour	10–20
Torula yeast	0–5
Autolyzed yeast	0–5
Nonfat dry milk	0–5
Lactic acid	1–2
Citric acid	0.5–1.5
Natural and/or artificial flavors	0.5–2
Buffers which may include: Sodium citrate Disodium phosphate	0–1
Disodium inosinate and guanylate	0–0.2
FD&C yellow #5 lake	0.6–1.0[1]
FD&C yellow #6 lake	0.1–0.5[1]
Flow/anticaking agent	0–2

[1] Dependent on the percent dye in the lake—15% or 40% are most common.

mulations can be made by using low amounts of disodium inosinate and disodium guanylate blends, autolyzed yeast, and other specialty "natural MSG replacers" currently being marketed in the food industry, although new labeling laws which go into effect in May 1994 will require autolyzed yeasts to be labeled as such and not as natural flavors.

9.3.3 Tortilla and Corn Chips

These products have a unique flavor of their own. For this reason, they need strong seasonings to complement the corn flavor. The most common flavors available are Nacho Cheese and Ranch. Other flavors are available such as Barbecue for corn chips, and Taco, Chili and Lime, and Salsa for tortilla chips. Tortilla chips are currently very popular products. Salt content on tortilla chips is usually about 1.5%–1.8%. The seasoning is applied in a manner similar to potato chips, to either salted or unsalted chips at the 6%–8% range. The chip application temperature is similarly important. Tortilla chip seasonings should have more visual impact than potato chip seasonings since the corn and tortilla chips are darker in color than a potato chip. The seasoning is more visually apparent on a potato chip due to the light color of the chip. Usually a brighter orange color for cheese base flavors or more red and green specks for a ranch flavor are used. Granulation requirements are similar to potato chip seasonings. See Table 9.4 for a sample Ranch Tortilla Chip Seasoning.

9.3.4 Popcorn

Popcorn usually requires a high seasoning application rate due to its low density. The seasoning must have a very fine granulation, both when applied topically or in an oil slurry. Application rates are similar to extruded corn puffs and are usually done with an oil slurry, especially in the case of cheese flavored popcorn. Sometimes the seasoning is applied topically. In this case, it must be sprayed with a fine mist of oil to make the seasoning stick. Popcorn and extruded cheese puffs are products in which the color of the product is extremely important. Butter flavored popcorn is typically yellow in color. Likewise cheese flavored popcorn is very orange in color with cheese and butter the dominant flavor notes. In addition to these two flavors, White Cheddar flavor has become very popular. This type of seasoning is a very high-quality cheese product, topically applied with an oil spray.

Some specialty shops have a wide variety of flavors for popcorn, from bubble gum to chocolate. These products are produced from flavors, colors, and shortening blends and are typically not supplied by the seasoning industry, but specialty suppliers to the retail shop trade.

9.3.5 Nuts

Seasoned nuts are becoming very popular. There are basically two types of seasoned nuts, those which are topically applied to oil roasted nuts, and those which are

Table 9.4 Ranch Tortilla Chip Seasoning—for Application to Unsalted Chips—8% Application.

Ingredient	Typical Ranges (%)
Salt, fine flour	19–25
Whey solids	8–15
Buttermilk solids	12–18
Other extenders which may include:	8–20
Wheat flour	
Maltodextrin	
Cornstarch	
Shortening powder	0–8
Dextrose	0–10
Tomato powder	1–5
Cheese solids	0–3
MSG	3–8
Onion powder	2–6
Garlic powder	0.5–3
Natural and/or artificial flavors	0.5–1
Lactic acid	0.5–2
Citric acid	0.5–1.25
Buffers including one or more of the following:	0–1
Sodium citrate, Disodium phosphate, Sodium acetate[1]	
Parsley granules or Imitation Parsley	0–3
Imitation paprika	0–1
Flow/anticaking agent	0–2

[1] Also imparts a vinegar flavor to the seasoning blend.

added to dry roasted nuts in two steps. Savory flavors for oil roasted nuts are applied with the oil they were roasted in to make the seasoning stick. Due to the dense nature of nuts, especially peanuts, a low application rate in the range of 3%–5% is used. Typical flavors include BBQ, Hickory, Chili Cheese, and Hot & Spicy. See Table 9.5 for a Hot & Spicy Nut sample formula.

Dry roasted nuts and products like honey roasted nuts have the seasoning applied with a tack solution. This is a dry product, mixed with water and containing maltodextrin or gums in which the nuts are tumbled. This tack solution causes the nuts to be sticky so the dry roast or honey roast seasoning can be applied without oil. The nuts are then roasted to produce the flavored nut. In the case of honey-roast nuts, a topical mixture of salt and sugar is sometimes applied at the end of the process while the nuts are still hot and tacky.

9.3.6 Rice Cakes

These are the newest products to be seasoned and are currently very much in demand. Savory flavors and sweet flavors are both applied to rice cakes. Savory flavors are usually applied in a 60% oil to 40% seasoning (or 50/50 blend) slurry at

Table 9.5 Hot and Spicy Nut Seasoning for Application to an Unsalted Nut at the 5% Level.

Ingredient	Typical Ranges (%)
Salt, fine flour	25–35
Extenders which may include:	10–20
Dextrose	
Maltodextrin	
Corn flour	
Chili pepper	5–15
Red pepper (40,000 SHU)	5–20
Black pepper, fine	0–5
Onion powder	4–8
Garlic powder	0.5–3
MSG	0–8
Oleoresin paprika, 100,000 CU	0.2–0.5
Oleoresin capsicum 500,000 SHU	0–0.8
Flow/anticaking agent	0–2

the 30%–40% level to the rice cakes. This translates to 12%–16% seasoning. The salt level of the savory flavors applied in the above manner should be about 6%–10%. Once again, the product has a very light density and has a large surface area so the seasoning level must be high. Sweet flavors have little or no salt, but 1%–5% salt in the dry seasoning can sometimes enhance the flavor. Sweet flavors can be applied in a glaze. See Table 9.6 for a Honey Nut rice cake seasoning.

9.3.7 Pork Skins

Pork skins are purchased from meat packers and processed into pellets which are then fried. Pork skin production is dominated by a few manufacturers. This is because the production of pork skins requires USDA inspection. Often a regional

Table 9.6 Honey Nut Rice Cake Seasoning 40/60% Oil Slurry Application at 30%.

Ingredient	Typical Ranges (%)
Sugar, bakers fine	65–90
Honey solids	5–10
Natural honey flavor	0.5–2
Natural nut flavor	0.5–2
Salt, fine flour	0–4
Extenders which may include:	10–20
Wheat flour	
Dextrose	
Flow/anticaking agent	0–2

pork skin manufacturer contract packs for other snack manufacturers to their specifications.

Pork skins have a strong meaty flavor which requires a strong seasoning to cover it. Often seasonings for this product are very hot and spicy since the target market desires hot seasonings. The seasonings are topically applied to a hot, fried pork skin. Temperature requirements are the same as those for potato chips.

Chapter References

1. Rickard, A., Werthner, J., and Levy, B., "State of the Industry Report," *Snack World* 49 (6), SW-3–SW-51 1992.

2. Kuhn, M.E., "Keebler: 1991 Marketer of the Year," *Food Business* 5:24–30, 1992.

CHAPTER

10

Sauces and Gravies

10.1 Overview of the Industry

In contrast to the seasonings discussed in the previous chapters, sauces and gravies are unique in the seasoning industry in that they are complete food items. Snack seasonings, meat seasonings, and even simple blends are used on or in other food products. Sauces and gravy mixes are mixed with water or other liquid such as milk or tomato sauce to produce a finished food item. Snack seasonings must be applied to a snack item, meat seasonings must be blended with beef, pork, or chicken, and simple blends are usually used as an ingredient in another food item.

Gravy and sauce mixes are sold in the retail market, usually packed in foil packets to produce 1 cup of a sauce or gravy. They are also sold in the foodservice market, often in 1 pound containers or batch sized bags to produce 1 or 5 gallons of product. Gravy and sauce mixes are also sold in bulk to the food industry, generally specifically formulated to produce a proprietary product, either for retorted or frozen food items.

The variety of sauces and gravies are tremendous. Gravies can be simple ones which are mixed with water, heated, and served in the home, such as beef, chicken, pork, turkey, or mushroom. Sauce mixes can be tomato based (spaghetti, pizza, creole, enchilada), cream based (alfredo, cheese, white sauce, butter) or unique items (lemon dill, tarragon butter, wine, dijon mustard). In addition, gravies and sauces can be made to withstand refrigerated storage, extended steam table holding, freeze-thaw cycles, high pH levels, retort, high-temperature short-time (HTST) processing, and microwave cooking. Products are formulated with either a cookup or pregelatinized starch. These types of starches can also be used in combination.

The liquid added to produce the product can be water, tomato sauce, milk, or a variety of other liquids such as orange juice or even vegetable oil. Water can be used to make a tomato based sauce if tomato solids are added to the dry mix and water can be used for a cream based sauce if dairy ingredients are utilized to imitate the creaminess and flavor of milk. It is essential when formulating the above products to know what the customer desires, whether it be a retail consumer, a restaurant chain, or an industrial account. These products must be custom formulated to perform correctly in the desired application.

10.2 Overview of Formulating

When formulating sauces and gravies to perform in a specific application, it is essential to know what type of starch to use. Starches for freeze-thaw stability, microwave application, stovetop cookup, and retorted products are different. It is essential to talk to the starch supplier when choosing a starch. Each company can offer starch products for the above applications by chemically modifying various starches of different sources. It is interesting to know what type of modifications are possible to produce specific functionalities (cross-linking, substitution, etc.), as are learned in the classroom; however, the starches used in the food industry are proprietary products. When choosing a starch it is more important to discuss with the supplier the functional characteristics desired rather than the type and degree of chemical modification. Specific starch recommendations will not be made in this book since specific brand names of items would have to be given. It is better to request a starch with a specific functionality. For example, if making a tomato sauce for frozen application, it is important to request a freeze-thaw stable starch that performs well in low pH applications. Describing the physical properties desired, such as opaque, nongelling, and short texture also helps. The starch vendor can then supply an appropriate product. Many starch suppliers have items which can be used in a wide range of products for many different applications. Other available starches can have pulpy characteristics, either in instant or cookup applications, or will mimic a fatty texture. For microwave applications, it is often desirable to use a combination of a cookup and an instant or pregelatinized starch. During the initial heating stage, the instant starch will suspend the cookup starch while it is approaching its gelatinization temperature, thus eliminating or decreasing the amount of stirring required.

10.3 Formulations

10.3.1 Gravies

A suggested method for formulating gravies is to calculate and work with ingredients on a usage basis as discussed in Chapter 8. In this way, each ingredient can be varied as required without affecting the amount of other ingredients in the formula. It is also easier to formulate a specific usage level by adding maltodextrin or other filler to make an even usage amount (for example, 1.25 oz gravy mix to 1 cup of water). A range of dry ingredients to liquid in a gravy is 0.75–1.0 oz per cup of water. A suggested starch level, dependent on type of starch, for gravies is 0.4–0.6 oz per cup of water or 0.4–0.6 pound per gallon of water. The proportions of an ounce of dry ingredients per cup is the same as the proportion of a pound of dry ingredients per gallon.

Most gravy mixes for the retail consumer contain a modified food starch along with wheat flour. Generally the modified food starches have a "short," clear texture, similar to cornstarch and gives the gravy stability. The wheat flour gives a more opaque or homemade appearance and not as "short" a texture.

Salt levels in a gravy will also vary, but a suggested starting usage is 0.06–0.10 oz per cup of water or 1–1.5 oz per gallon. The salt content seems to be decreasing in recent years due to the concern of salt in the diet. It must also be noted that hydrolyzed vegetable protein (HVP) and autolyzed yeasts, as well as some meat flavors also contain a significant amount of salt, up to 50%. The salt levels described above are in addition to normal levels of HVPs and autolyzed yeasts found in a gravy. When evaluating a gravy, it should be tasted on mashed potatoes or a meat item since the salt level should be appropriate for the finished food item. A gravy may taste salty when evaluated by itself, but when used on mashed potatoes, it may not since it must flavor and salt the total amount of potatoes.

By using the suggested amount of starch and salt as described above, the amounts of meat flavors, HVPs, onion, garlic, color, sweeteners, spices, and fillers can then be added to produce a high-quality gravy item.

Chicken and beef or brown are the two most common types of gravies. Typical chicken and beef formulas are found in Tables 10.1 and 10.2. All formulas in this chapter are expressed in ounces of dry ingredient per cup of liquid. Both chicken and beef gravies typically contain HVPs, meat flavors, and meat stocks to give the meaty note. Generally, HVPs and autolyzed yeasts are used since the cost of these items are low and are the most cost efficient way of adding meat flavor.

Dehydrated chicken and beef can be used in condimental amounts without being produced in a USDA inspected facility. The regulations for poultry as condimental ingredients can be found in the Meat & Poultry regulations 9CFR, part 381.15.

In addition to the regulation limits, meat items are costly and are often added simply so they can be listed on the ingredient statement. Rendered beef and chicken fat can also be used in condimental amounts to give a richer beef or chicken flavor.

Spices and spice extractives are also used in gravies. Brown gravies contain celery, black pepper, and sometimes thyme and oregano at low levels. Spice extractives are used when dark specks are not desired. Chicken flavored gravies contain much higher levels of celery than beef flavored products. In fact, it is possible to make a chicken flavored broth with salt, sugar, MSG, onion powder, oleoresin celery, oleoresin black pepper, and turmeric without any HVP or chicken flavor added at all. The turmeric gives the broth a yellow color and the celery, onion and pepper combination suggests chicken to the consumer. Sometimes sage and thyme are also added to chicken gravies.

Table 10.1 Typical Chicken Flavored Gravy Formulation for Retail Pack.
Note: 1 oz = 28.4 Grams.

Ingredient	Typical Ranges (oz)	
Modified food starch	0.10–0.20	
Wheat flour	0.30–0.50	
HVP, chicken flavors	0.05–0.15	
Whey, milk solids, other dairy ingredients	0–0.15	
Salt	0.06–0.10	
MSG	0.02–0.04	
Chicken fat	0–0.03	
Dehydrated chicken meat	0–0.02	
Turmeric, ground	.0005–0.0010	
Oleoresin celery	.003–.007	
Oleoresin black pepper	.003–.007	
Other ground spices	.001–.002	
Onion powder	0.08–0.015	
Garlic powder	0–0.005	
Sugar or dextrose	0–0.10	
Maltodextrin (add to even usage rate)	0–0.10	
Suggested usage:	0.85–1.15	ounces per cup of water

Table 10.2 Typical Beef Flavored or Brown Gravy Formulation for Foodservice
(Steam Table) Usage. Note: 1 oz = 28.4 Grams.

Ingredient	Typical Ranges (oz)	
Modified food starch	0.40–0.60	
HVP, beef flavors	0.04–0.08	
Beef stock or broth	0–0.04	
Salt	0.06–0.10	
MSG	0–0.04	
Sugar or dextrose	0.06–0.12	
Whey, milk solids or other dairy ingredients	0–0.15	
Caramel color	0.02–0.04	
Onion powder	0.03–0.04	
Spices	0–0.003	
Maltodextrin (add to even usage rate)	0–0.10	
Suggested usage:	0.85–1.15	ounces per cup of water

Onion and garlic are included in both chicken and beef flavored gravies. Sugar is added in small amounts. Whey and milk solids are sometimes included to simulate a creamier, richer flavor. Monosodium glutamate is usually included, although an acceptable product is possible without it.

Chicken flavored gravies use either turmeric or its oleoresin as a coloring agent. Beef flavored gravies use caramel color.

10.3.2 Sauces

Sauce mixes are formulated in a similar way as gravies. They are much more variable, however. The product is usually formulated to mix with water, milk, or tomato sauce but can also be mixed with a variety of other liquids. The usage level depends on what liquid media is being used. For example, a spaghetti seasoning that is added to a tomato sauce may use 0.5–0.75 oz per cup of sauce, dependent on amount of flavor and fillers added. If a cheese sauce to mix with water is formulated, the level of dry mix to liquid will be between 1.25 and 1.75 oz per cup of water. In this case, cheese solids and flavors must be added along with milk solids and other dry dairy ingredients to produce a creamy sauce. If this same cheese sauce is made to mix with milk, then the amount to add per cup of liquid would be decreased to about 1 oz per cup. Adding milk solids or tomato solids to the dry mix item can make the product more convenient to use, however the cost is higher and can sometimes make the product uneconomical. This is especially true in the case of tomato products. It is much cheaper for an industrial user to buy tomato paste and dilute it with water than to purchase a sauce mix containing all the tomato solids. Basically the processor would be purchasing a product in which he is paying for the tomato solids to be processed twice.

The starch level in sauces will vary much more than gravies, depending on the thickness desired. A suggested usage for a cream based sauce mix is about 0.5 oz per cup of water. Other thickeners such as gums are sometimes used to increase the viscosity. In an inexpensive spaghetti sauce mix, 0.15–0.25 oz starch is closer to the proper level. It is common for sauces to be formulated with instant starches so cooking is not required. However, the quality of the sauce texture and the stability of the product can be lower.

Salt levels also vary more in sauce mixes than in gravies, from about 0.05 to 0.10 oz per cup. The salt levels of other ingredients must also be considered.

10.3.2.1 Tomato Based Sauces

When formulating a tomato based item, it must be noted that some canned tomato sauces contain high levels of salt. If using tomato paste and diluting it down, the level of salt in the resultant tomato sauce is much lower than a prepared tomato sauce. Food manufacturers usually purchase paste since they do not wish to pay for shipping water. Consumers may use tomato sauce, which not only contains higher levels of salt, but other ingredients such as onion powder are usually present. When formulating items with these types of ingredients, it is essential to know what products the end user will use when preparing the sauce.

A rule of thumb for formulating with tomato paste is as follows:

Tomato paste/water 1:1 ratio ≈ Puree
Tomato paste/water 1:2 ratio ≈ Sauce
Tomato paste/water 1:3 ratio ≈ Juice

These figures do not imply the legal levels of tomato solids for selling these items, but are just for laboratory estimates. The actual legal levels for tomato puree and paste can be found in 21CFR 155.191 and for juice in 21CFR 156.145.

Tomato based sauces can be a variety of products including Italian (spaghetti, marinara, pizza), Mexican (enchilada, chili, salsa), Louisiana style (creole or jambalaya sauces), or a variety of others. Most of these items have some starch present, often dependent on the quality of the sauce. If it is a high-quality spaghetti or marinara sauce, for example, some of the viscosity will most likely come from a higher level of tomato solids than if the item is of a lower quality. Starch is less expensive than tomato. If a starch is used, an acid stable variety is necessary due to the low pH of the tomato base. Once again, the type of starch is also dependent on the further processing involved, whether it be retorting, microwaving, or freezing. In addition to starches, hydrocolloids such as xanthan or a variety of other gums may be used to increase the viscosity of the sauce. Gums are usually stable over a wide pH range.

Varying levels of sugar are present in tomato based sauces. A spaghetti sauce generally has a higher level of sugar than a pizza sauce. Usually a combination of acid and sugar are balanced until the desired sweetness level is achieved.

The spices are based on the type of sauce. An Italian sauce will contain garlic, onion, oregano, basil, fennel, marjoram, black pepper, red pepper if heat is desired, and possibly thyme. The different levels of these flavors and their balance produces different types of products. In addition, the spices can be added in ground or whole form, depending on what appearance of the finished sauce is desired. Italian tomato based sauces may also contain parmesan or romano cheese. Table 10.3 is a formulation for a simple but high-quality marinara sauce that is not thickened, but uses tomato solids to keep the viscosity high.

The flavor of a Mexican tomato based sauce is due to chili pepper, ground Mexican oregano, ground cumin, onion, garlic, black pepper, red pepper, and coriander. Cinnamon, cloves and allspice may also be present in low levels. If it is a picante or salsa, then cilantro, onion, garlic, and red pepper are used with very low levels of Mexican oregano and cumin. Vinegar is also a major flavor component in this type of product. Creole sauces, as well as many other cajun style sauces, contain oregano, garlic, onion, red pepper, white pepper, black pepper, thyme, and possibly sassafras.

10.3.2.2 Cream Based Sauces

Cream based sauces are another common type of product. These items can either be prepared with water or milk, but the formula must be adjusted. Generally, the cream

Table 10.3 Typical Marinara Type Tomato Sauce. Note: 1 oz = 28.4 Grams.

Ingredient	Typical Ranges (grams)
Sugar	3.75–6.25
Salt	0.63–1.88
Garlic powder	0.25–1.25
Onion powder	0.12–0.50
Oregano, ground Mediterranean	0.12–0.63
Basil, ground Egyptian	0.12–0.63
Garlic, minced	0–0.63
Basil, leaf Egyptian	0–1.25
Oregano, leaf Mediterranean	0–1.25
Parsley flakes	0–1.25

Usage: 7.5–12.5 grams per cup of tomato puree (paste/water ratio 1 : 1)

based sauces contain a more flour-like texture when thickened rather than a corn starch-type texture. If the product is not prepared with milk then the formulation must contain whey, milk solids, and other dry dairy ingredients to simulate the texture and flavor of milk. In addition, cream based sauces can be made with shortening beads, shortening powder, or nondairy creamer to increase the richness of the sauce. Shortening powders and beads generally do a better job of imitating richness than the nondairy creamers, which often impart an undesirable off flavor. Some of the flavors present in various sauces are described below.

White sauce: This type of sauce is formulated with wheat flour, modified starch, salt, shortening powder, milk powder, whey solids, buttermilk solids, butter, and cream or milk flavors. Spices may include white pepper, nutmeg and paprika.

Alfredo sauce: This sauce has a very high fat level that makes the product have a creamy texture. Powdered or beaded shortening at a much higher level than the white sauce will add this fatty texture. Parmesan and romano cheese powders (not grated, as this will make the product gritty) in addition to butter flavors will make a good alfredo sauce.

Country gravy: Country gravy is included under the sauce section since it is typically more similar to a white sauce than other types of gravies. It is also a very high fat sauce containing powdered or beaded shortening. Some manufacturers use nondairy creamers for the creaminess and flavor. Large pieces of black pepper, about 14 mesh, are typical for a country gravy. Sausage flavors and/or sage are often present.

Cheese sauce: Cheese sauces are similar to a high fat cream sauce with cheese powders, cheese flavors, and artificial colors present. Once again, the best quality sauce utilizes starches which mimic the wheat flour texture when possible. An opaque appearance is desirable. Autolyzed yeasts and yeast extracts can help to boost the cheese flavors. A small amount of blue cheese will also help increase the cheddar flavor. Using powdered shortening can improve the texture of the sauce, as will picking the right starch. Table 10.4 is a typical cheese sauce formula for a frozen application.

Table 10.4   Typical Cheese Sauce Mix for Water Addition. Note: 1 oz = 28.4 Grams.

Ingredient	Typical Ranges (oz)	
Modified food starch, freeze-thaw stable	0.50–0.75	
Nonfat dry milk	0.50–0.75	
Cheddar cheese solids	0.15–0.25	
Blue cheese solids	0–0.05	
Buttermilk solids	0–0.05	
Xanthan gum	0–0.005	
Cheese flavor	0–0.005	
Torula yeast	0–0.025	
Monosodium glutamate	0–0.025	
Artificial color alum lake yellow #5	0.00200	
Artificial color alum lake yellow #6	0.00075	
Disodium inosinate and disodium guanylate	0–0.002	
	1.25–1.50	ounce per cup of water. Heat to boiling, stirring constantly.

11

Ethnic Seasonings

11.1 Introduction

Ethnic seasonings are used in all types of products in the food industry. Ethnic spices and seasoning blends can be incorporated into sauce mixes, snack foods, frozen entrees, and even processed meats. Ethnic seasonings sold as simple blends are common also, such as Italian seasoning or Cajun seasoning. If formulating an authentic food item, it is best to consult numerous cookbooks to prepare the food item with a recipe to know what the product should look and taste like. For example, if a food manufacturer wants to introduce an authentic line of Greek style frozen entrees, the food technologist should, after determining the specific products, make them up using a variety of Greek cookbooks. If pastisio is one of the chosen dishes, then a recipe should be made up and evaluated. Formulating a product is easier when a target flavor has been defined.

Often food items are not authentic products simply because they are either formulated for the average American consumer or because the flavors are applied to a different food item than the product was originally designed for. The snack industry is a typical example of the latter, where the "typical" flavors of an ethnic cuisine are combined to produce a snack seasoning. An example of a cajun seasoning where the typical flavors associated with this regional American cuisine are blended along with other ingredients to produce a cajun snack seasoning. A second example is an Italian snack food seasoning. Not only are the characteristic spices used, but also tomato powder and parmesan or romano cheese solids can be incorporated to give a characteristic Italian flavor.

This chapter will list various ethnic categories and discuss the flavors associated with them. By incorporating these characteristic flavors into different base product formulations, a variety of products can be made. For example, an Indian curry blend can be used to produce a sauce, whether it be cream or yogurt based, a snack food, a chicken entree, or a rice dish. By knowing which spices and other flavors characterize a specific cuisine, a wide variety of ethnically inspired food items can be formulated.

11.2 Cajun and Creole

This southern Louisiana cuisine has received much attention in the last few years. Interest has decreased recently, although some items are here to stay. After every ethnic food fad slows down, generally some products become mainstream in the United States. Historically, Cajun cooking is the "down home" cooking of the bayous whereas Creole is the city or aristocratic cuisine. Both are characterized by tomato based sauces and roux (burned butter and flour) based white sauces. Common foods in this type of cooking are Jambalaya, Gumbo, Creole Sauces, Red Beans and Rice, and Blackened products. Typical spices for this type of cooking include the following: black, white, and red pepper, paprika, oregano, and thyme. Sassafras, or gumbo filé, is also typically included in cajun seasonings. This is the ground leaves of sassafras, which has a characteristic flavor as well as a gumming or thickening action, usually described as slimy. Sassafras stems, but apparently not the leaves, contain safrole, a known carcinogen (see Chapter 5). Other flavors typical of cajun cooking include onion, garlic and green pepper.

Cajun as a type of seasoning has gotten the reputation for being very hot. Generally, a simple cajun seasoning will be red in color from paprika, hot from all types of pepper and have a green note from the oregano or thyme. Onion and garlic also provide typical flavor notes.

11.3 Italian

Italian foods are probably the most common ethnic food we see in the United States today. Many sauces are tomato based, but white sauces are also common. Italian sausage was discussed in Chapter 8. Typical spices present in Italian products include oregano, marjoram, basil, thyme, rosemary, fennel, anise, black pepper, and red pepper. Garlic and onion are major flavor components along with tomato and hard grating cheeses such as parmesan and romano. Generally pizza sauces and pizza meat toppings have high levels of fennel. The major flavor components of red pasta sauces are oregano, marjoram, basil, and garlic.

11.4 Mexican

Mexican flavored products are also common in the United States. Taco meat, chili, and enchilada sauces are common. Chili powder is discussed in Chapter 7. Chili pepper and powder are the basis for many Mexican flavored products. Other spices used are cumin, Mexican oregano, red and black pepper, coriander, paprika, and small amounts of cinnamon and clove. Onion and garlic are also primary flavor constituents. Cilantro is increasing in usage lately and is used mainly in salsas and picante sauces with onion, garlic, and red pepper without the high levels of chili, cumin, and Mexican oregano present in most other Mexican products. Corn flour is used as a thickener in taco meat and chili but also provides flavor. Garlic and onion are also major flavor contributors. Many enchilada and taco sauces are tomato based, whereas the taco meat seasonings are not.

11.5 Caribbean

Caribbean seasonings are becoming more popular. There is really no clear-cut typical product since the Caribbean islands are made up of a large variety of cultures with many other ethnic influences such as French, Indian, and Spanish. Many of the products native to the islands influence the cuisine. Caribbean flavors can be tomato based, and often fruit based or include other sweet sauces. Fish, seafood, and unique items like conch meat are utilized. Bananas, plantains, black beans and rice, pineapple, and coconut are common ingredients. Tamarinds, a major flavor component in worcestershire sauce, are native to the islands and thus are often included in the cuisine. Jamaican jerk seasoning contains high levels of allspice, thyme, red pepper, garlic, and onion. Jamaican jerks are rubbed onto meats like a BBQ seasoning. Additional spices used in the Caribbean islands are bay, black pepper, cilantro, cinnamon, cumin, oregano, ginger, and saffron. Onions, especially scallions, and garlic are used extensively. Red peppers are often used, which is understandable since red peppers are native to this part of the world. Curry powders are also used in Caribbean cuisine.

Producing a Caribbean seasoning for a sauce or snack food item is difficult due to the variations in flavors utilized in the Caribbean. A sweet, hot product with garlic, onion, allspice, worcestershire, ginger, and thyme with some fruit flavor present is a good starting point for a "Caribbean seasoning." These are the types of flavors currently associated with these products in the food industry.

11.6 Indian

Indian cuisine is most commonly associated with curry. There are literally hundreds of curry combinations available. In India, curries are not generally sold preblended, but each dish is created individually with its own blend of spices. Coriander and other spices can be roasted to give a characteristic flavor. Spices almost always found in curry include the following: coriander, cumin, fenugreek, and turmeric. The coriander is generally at the highest percent, about 30%. Cumin is usually present at about 10% and gives the curry the distinctive bitter harsh flavor. Fenugreek can be present from 5% to 10% and gives a rounded background note to the curry. Turmeric provides a yellow color and musty flavor, present at levels between 10% and 25%. Other spices usually include the following: red and black pepper, cardamom, cloves, fennel, and ginger. Less common spices include mace or nutmeg, mustard, white pepper, cinnamon, and allspice.

Indian cooking is often hot. Yogurt dishes provide a contrast to the heat. Bean and legume dishes are common. Onion and garlic are used frequently as well as cilantro. Indian cuisine uses many of the spices native to the country such as cumin, coriander, black pepper, and turmeric. See Tables 7.5 and 7.6 for typical curry formulations.

11.7 Chinese

Chinese cuisine is characterized by a few distinct flavors, including soy sauce, sherry wine, vinegar, and sesame. Spices utilized in this cuisine are ginger, red pepper, black pepper, and a five spice combination (anise, fennel, clove, cinnamon, and black pepper) in certain dishes. Garlic and onions are also an integral flavor of the cuisine. Red pepper is usually used whole in dishes. Sesame is used whole or as an oil.

11.8 Others

Eastern European countries such as Hungary and Germany also use some distinctive spices. Dillseed, dillweed, and caraway are used in many foods. The carvone flavor component present in the essential oils of both dill and caraway is distinctive in the cuisine of these countries. Paprika in a sour cream base is the major component in many recipes from this region.

Scandinavian countries are known for their use of dillweed. Many fish recipes, like marinated herring, include dill. Sweet spices such as cinnamon, allspice, cardamom, and cloves are also typical.

Greek cuisine uses oregano and marjoram frequently. Mint and high levels of garlic are also used. Greek cooking is known for its use of lamb, feta cheese, and olive oil.

CHAPTER

12

Seasoning Blend Duplication and Tricks of the Trade

This chapter will address two goals. The first is to explain the steps involved in the duplication of a seasoning blend. The second is to give background information and "tricks of the trade" that can help in seasoning formulation.

12.1 Duplication

12.1.1 Introduction

Seasoning blends are duplicated for a variety of reasons. The first is to match a competitive blend at a cheaper cost for a specific customer. Most seasoning blends sold in the industrial market are unique to each customer. For example, Frito Lay has their unique ranch seasoning which only they purchase. Oscar Mayer has their own bologna seasoning. Matching a seasoning is desirable for the seasoning company since it not only gains new business, but more importantly, gets a foot in the door and allows a potential customer to see what the seasoning company has to offer. Sometimes the chance of success is better with duplications. It can be quicker to get business since the customer is already buying the product. Often once one blend is approved, the customer is more apt to consider your company when formulating new products. You become one of the approved seasoning vendors.

"New" formulation work versus matching existing blends is the most desirable since it gives your company a proprietary product other suppliers have to match. If the item is at a fair price and the service is good, the customer may not wish to look for alternative vendors. "New" formulations usually get a higher profit margin than duplications since the latter are sold on the basis of providing a cost savings to the customer. "New" formulations also take a lot longer to sell since the product must be approved and often has to go through market and consumer testing. The chance of success is also lower since there is a low success rate on new products in the marketplace.

Some industries seek out alternative vendors more often than others. The meat industry is a good example. These seasonings are often duplicated and the customer will switch for savings of only a penny or two. Meat seasonings are probably one of the easiest products to duplicate once a food technologist has some experience. They contain expected ingredients and list many ingredients by percentages due to USDA regulations, such as mustard, monosodium glutamate, hydrolyzed vegetable protein, and sodium erythorbate. The flavorings are also used at low levels in the meat products so it may be difficult to determine flavor differences.

Snack seasonings are harder to duplicate. The seasoning itself is more complex than other types of seasonings. Twenty-five or more ingredients are common. In addition, small flavor differences are easier to detect since the seasoning is used at a much higher level and it is applied topically rather than in a food item. In addition, artificial flavors are common. These have a unique flavor specific to the item. Therefore it is sometimes difficult to find a specific flavor with the same profile as the flavor used in the seasoning being duplicated.

Sometimes a customer will ask a seasoning company to duplicate the flavor of a competitor's product. This means that the product being duplicated is not a seasoning blend but rather a finished food item. This is very difficult. First, the seasoning is not isolated and second, other ingredient differences can come into play. If matching a competitive barbecue sauce, the amount of tomato solids and the type and amount of vinegar can affect the flavor tremendously. Even if the customer is provided the exact same seasoning, the food item may not match due to differences in processing methods and raw materials. Two potato chips that are different in thickness, brownness, or even fried in different types of oils, will taste very different even with the same seasoning on them.

12.1.2 Duplication Steps

When a seasoning is received for duplication, the ingredient statement should be listed out. It is essential to receive the ingredient statement on the *seasoning,* rather than the customers' finished product. The labels are often different due to the marketing department requirements and what the legal counsel decides is correct. It is best to list the ingredient statement out in full in an easily accessible place so it can be followed when formulating the product.

If salt is one of the ingredients, a salt test is the first step. A variety of methods can be used. Titration with silver nitrite is one method. This is very exact; however, it does get complicated when red colored items such as paprika or chili peppers are present. In this case, it may be difficult to determine an endpoint. There are also numerous analytical machines to use. Most methods determine chloride content. A standard is usually run first before the test product. Other ingredients such as hydrolyzed vegetable proteins (HVPs) and autolyzed yeasts contain up to 60% salt. Check the specification sheets for salt content for these products if they are in a blend. These amounts must be estimated into the salt percent. For example, a seasoning for duplication analyzes at 33% salt. The HVP can be estimated from the ingredient statement to be about 12%. If 50% of the HVP can be estimated to be salt, then 6% salt must be subtracted from the salt percentage, leaving about 27% salt added to the seasoning blend. Once the salt is known, an estimate can be made as to where the levels of other ingredients lie.

If dextrose is present, a test for reducing sugars is possible. This method will also measure for other reducing sugars present in the blend. In addition, since this is a titration method, if the seasoning has a high level of paprika or other color present, the endpoint may also be difficult to determine. Actual dextrose and sugar can be analyzed, however these test methods are expensive. A spectrophotometer and a purchased test kit can be used; this method relys on the glucose oxidase reaction.

Organoleptically, dextrose is not as sweet as sugar. It does give a cooling sensation on the tongue when tasted in a dry product.

Some simple physical tests may also be done. If there are large pieces of minced onion or parsley present, a sifting should be done to separate out the pieces. If, for instance, minced onion is present in a taco seasoning, then passing 100 grams through a #20 screen would be appropriate to determine the percent of minced onion. All other ingredients (including chili pepper) should pass through the screen leaving the minced onion on top of the #20 screen. The minced onion can then be weighed to determine the percent present. This is only a starting point, however, since large pieces will stratify in the test seasoning, making it impossible to get a representative sample. Secondly, the rest of the seasoning, when sitting for extended lengths of time, will tend to stick to the onion, especially when there is HVP or soybean oil present in the seasoning. This will give a falsely high percent.

The granulation of the salt, sugar, and spices should be determined by visual methods. Sometimes just noting if it is granulated or fine flour salt or a granulated or bakers special sugar is needed. If there are coarse pieces, it is helpful to know that coarse salts are usually opaque and coarse sugar particles are usually clear. If the pieces are large enough, picking them out with a tweezers and tasting them will determine if salt, sugar, or even citric acid is present. Spice granulation can be determined by a visual comparison to what is available as an ingredient. For example, if coarse pepper is present, it is helpful to separate the pepper and determine if it is a 10, 14, or 16 mesh by comparison to a known standard.

To determine which spices are present, it is helpful to put the seasoning in water at 1%–2% and observe. This makes it easier to identify the spices. By diluting the seasoning in water, the soluble ingredients will dissolve, leaving the insoluble ones floating or sinking in the water and therefore easier to see. Filtering the seasoning blend can also help determine how much of the item is soluble. Soluble ingredients would be salt, sugar, maltodextrin, etc. Items not dissolving could be spices. Small green specks should be ground herb and brown specks could be allspice, nutmeg, or clove. Paprika and chili pepper are red and brown in color, with chili pepper being quite coarse. Garlic and onion can be granulated or powdered, giving a cloudy solution.

Sometimes it is helpful to go a step further and filter the solution and look at the spice under about 10× magnification. By comparing to a known standard, it may help determine which spice is present. Taste is obviously the most important, but sometimes this technique is helpful when in doubt or when other avenues have been exhausted.

The amount of monosodium glutamate is difficult to determine by flavor unless it is at very high levels. At high levels it has a metallic-like flavor with almost a numbing sensation on the tongue. Evaluating the seasoning in the finished product helps to determine the amount. Usually if the flavor seems more rounded and stronger, more MSG is present. MSG has a unique appearance. It is shaped like small crystal rods. An estimate of percent MSG can be determined by observing the dry seasoning with the naked eye or under about 10× magnification compared to the control blend.

A pH test can be helpful to determine the amount of acid present. This analysis is usually done further into the duplication process. It is easiest to compare a control to the test sample at a 5% or 10% solution. This test may be deceiving since buffers may affect the test results. Buffers are often found in snack seasonings. Examples of buffers in snack food seasonings are disodium phosphate, sodium citrate, and sodium acetate, although the latter, in presence of an acid, gives a vinegar-like flavor. It is difficult to determine the amount of acid present by taste alone since sweetness from sugar and dextrose modifies the acid impact, making it difficult to determine the correct amount. It is best to determine the acid percent by flavor and then go back and adjust if the pH is not correct.

If the seasoning being matched is a product such as a pickling spice which contains a large amount of whole and cracked spice, it is sometimes easiest to take a representative sample of about 25–50 grams and physically separate the spices with tweezers into separate weighing dishes. Once the seasoning is separated, each spice can be weighed to determine percent. When using this method, mix up the calculated mixture in a large batch (about 500 grams) and observe it compared to the control. Sometimes adjustments have to be made if the sample taken was not representative.

12.1.3 Tasting

When first getting started duplicating seasoning blends, it is helpful to taste about a 1% solution of the spices to learn how to recognize the flavors. For example, assume a bologna seasoning with an ingredient statement as follows is the seasoning being duplicated: Dextrose, mustard (40.0%), sodium erythorbate (2.18%), spice extractives, and not more than 2% tricalcium phosphate added as an anticaking agent. Usage is 2.5 lb seasoning to 100 lb meat.

From the ingredient statement, the following estimation of the formula can be made:

Dextrose	55.82%
Mustard, ground	40.00%
Sodium erythorbate	2.18%
Spice extractives	1.00%
Tricalcium phosphate	1.00%

The mustard and sodium erythorbate percents are given. These are restricted ingredients as required by the USDA. Spice extractives are very concentrated and would not be more than 1%. Tricalcium phosphate should stop caking at about 1%. The dextrose amount is determined by difference. At this point, compare the flavor of the spice extractives listed in Table 8.5—Bologna Seasoning. To taste, plate 3% of the extractive on dextrose with 0.5% Polysorbate 80 as an emulsifier. Dilute 1% of this blend in water and taste. Compare this solution to the control bologna seasoning sample in Table 8.5 and see if that particular flavor can be picked out. By working back and forth one begins to learn what the spices and extractives taste like. Although typical extractives are listed in Table 8.5, a food technologist must be aware that often the developer adds additional oleoresins at low levels to make it difficult to duplicate and to give the customer a unique flavor to their brand. These flavors are not at levels such that it no longer tastes like a bologna seasoning, but they are high enough to taste as a background note.

Finally, it must be noted that when duplicating a seasoning blend, the product must be tasted in the finished food item at the suggested usage level. First, if any seasoning is added to a food product at a low enough level, it will taste the same. For example, if a seasoning is to be used at 8% on a chip and it is tested at 4%, it may taste identical, even though it is not really the same. The same can be said for meat seasonings. If it is to be used at 2.5% of the meat block and it is tested at 1% of the meat block, it may taste the same. However, when the customer makes a batch and uses it at 2.5%, the flavor probably will not match.

Other flavors present in the finished product can alter the seasoning impact and balance tremendously. The examples below illustrate this:

1. *Italian spice blend:* When duplicating a ground Italian spice blend containing oregano, basil, garlic, onion, salt, and black pepper, it was found that tasting in a water solution versus a tomato sauce had a large impact on flavor. The blend was to be used in a tomato based sauce. The customer listed a tasting method on their specification sheet of adding the blend to boiling water, letting it steep, filter, and then tasting it. The item being formulated was tasted in tomato juice in the lab. The customer was tasting the product in the hot, filtered water as described on the specification sheet and felt the balance of basil to oregano was off. When this test difference was noted, the customer tasted the product in tomato juice and felt it was the same. Tasting in the hot water did not show the seasonings to be the same. As a result, the customer changed their specification to include a tasting method in a tomato based solution.

2. *Taco meat seasoning:* A second example is the duplication of a taco meat seasoning. When duplicating the blend, it was being tasted in water to get a close approximation. The cumin and oregano were increased a number of times

to match the flavor of the control. After the products seemed close in flavor, they were evaluated in ground beef with dramatic results. The cumin and oregano were much too high and had to be decreased by about 33%. In this case, the meat and fat altered the flavor of the blend tremendously.

3. *Snack food seasoning:* Finally, the same situation occurred in the duplication of a snack seasoning. In this example, the seasoning was meant to go on an extruded potato snack. The base product was not available to work with so the seasoning was duplicated by tasting it topically on potato chips. When the customer received the sample and put it on the extruded snack with a very minimum amount of oil, it was found that the flavor was much less intense in the test sample versus the control sample. When the product was tasted on the chips during formulation, the strength of the seasoning had to be decreased since the product seemed much too strong.

If the seasoning is added to a snack in an oil slurry, the flavor impact may be much less compared to a seasoning which is added topically. In the latter method, the flavor impact, especially of the acids, is much higher. The oil slurry tends to mask flavors and hide the bite from ingredients such as acids.

Duplication of seasoning blends is an art and cannot be learned from a book, only from experience. This guide is meant as a suggested starting point. Seasoning blend duplication all comes down to taste. The food technologist must practice and learn to identify the spices and other flavors. The best way to learn this is to experiment. By tasting seasonings and identifying flavors, the technologist can learn how to duplicate them. It is best to start with a simple blend and work up to the harder ones. Sausage seasonings, especially simple ones like pork sausage or Italian sausage, are the best to start with. Simple blends like garlic salt, soluble spices, chili powder, and pumpkin pie spices are also easy places to start.

12.2 Tricks of the Trade

12.2.1 Introduction

The second part of this chapter deals with "tricks of the trade." This miscellaneous information on seasoning blends may help to duplicate seasonings or simply help to formulate seasoning blends. All the issues could never be addressed since each product and project is unique. It may, once again, help you get started and it may help as a reference when you get stuck. The Code of Federal Regulations (21CFR) sections are included to investigate the regulations on your own. Copies can be obtained from the U.S. Government Printing Office, Superintendent of Documents, Washington, D.C. 20402.

12.2.2 Colors

Two basic types of color are used in seasoning blends. The first are the "natural" colors—paprika, turmeric, caramel, annatto, beet powder, and carmine among others. The first four are the most common products, and come in dry or liquid form.

According to the FDA there is no "natural color" unless it is beet powder to color beet products. The regulations are in 21CFR Part 73. The CFR states that these "natural colors" must either be listed as artificial colors, since they are added to artificially color an item, or by their common name (i.e., paprika, turmeric, or extractive of paprika). For example, if a BBQ seasoning is colored with paprika, it can be listed as either "artificial" color on the label or as paprika. Most companies use the common name for these types of ingredients for a positive label impact. This has become standard practice in the food industry. In addition, the new labeling laws which go into effect in May 1994 also require noncertified or 'natural' colors to be labeled as 'added color.'

The second group of colors are the FD&C certified colors which consist of two types, the dyes and the lakes. The dyes are water soluble and very little color is apparent until the product is added to water. The lakes are the aluminum salts of the water soluble dye, formed by precipitate absorption on to a substrate of alumina and are used much more extensively in seasonings than the dyes. The lakes are insoluble pigments and are used primarily for surface color. An example would be a cheese snack seasoning which would use FD&C Yellows #5 & #6 to give a typical orange color. Dyes are often used in flavored drink or gelatin mixes and sometimes in seasonings for sauces and dips. They are mixed with seasonings but the color does not become apparent until dissolved in water. The new labeling laws which go into effect in May 1994 require all certified colors to be listed individually. The aluminum lakes must also include the term 'lake' after the name of the color.

Paprika, turmeric, and annatto all have disadvantages compared to the lakes. The main disadvantage is their inherent instability. These colors will fade when exposed to light and heat. The aluminum lakes will not fade. The natural color fading may be retarded by the use of a chelating agent in combination with an antioxidant as described in a patent held by Stange in 1963 (U.S. Patent #3,095,306). Basically, this patent states that the use of a weak chelating agent solution such as EDTA, plated on the salt or other carrier, along with a 20% solution of an antioxidant, such as BHA and BHT in soybean oil, can be added before the paprika, thus retarding the color loss to some extent. This patent is based on chelating the metal ions and then retarding the oxidative loss of the paprika color by utilizing the antioxidants. It will not stop color loss, but will slow it down. All these additives must of course be labeled on the seasoning ingredient statement. This tends to curb the use of this technology. It should be mentioned, however, that while the EDTA and the antioxidant are active ingredients in a seasoning blend, they may be considered "incidental additives" in a finished food item. Legal counsel should be consulted when making any decisions of this nature.

While color is being discussed, it must be noted that the surface color of a seasoning is not always related to the extractable color. Many factors affect the surface color. If using ground paprika for color, the longer the mix time, the darker the surface color of the seasoning. This is due to the heat developed from friction during the mixing process. The color is extracted from the paprika due to this heat and results in a darker surface color. For this reason, when matching seasonings, it is essential to evaluate the color of the blend in a water or oil solution and not simply as a surface phenomena.

Secondly, anticaking agents or the amount of oil in a seasoning blend can affect surface color development. Some silicon dioxides will lighten up the color of the dry mix extensively. On the other hand, the amount of oil present can also influence the amount of surface color. The higher the amount of oil, the darker the surface color of the seasoning, up to a point. If two seasonings with 0.25% and 1.0% oil are compared visually, the seasoning with 1.0% oil will appear much more orange in color when paprika is present due to the extraction of the pigments from the paprika and into the rest of the seasoning. When the seasoning is added to water and let sit for a few minutes, the orange color should be the same intensity.

Paprika, turmeric, and all types of oleoresins and essential oils should be plated on a granular product in the blend. Salt, sugar, dextrose, and maltodextrin are the ingredients of choice in that order. If the oleoresins are added to very powdery materials such as garlic or onion powder, they will lump up and not mix in. The powder will stick to the outside of the oleoresin and not allow it to mix in.

12.2.3 Anticaking Agents

Anticaking agents are chemicals used to stop a dry seasoning from caking from humidity, pressure, or too much liquid in a formula. They are also called flow agents and in this function do just that—they cause the seasoning to flow better. There are not only different chemicals, but also many different brands and types of each particular chemical which perform differently. The most commonly used anticaking agents are sodium silicoaluminate, silicon dioxide (also called silica gel), calcium silicate, calcium stearate, and tricalcium phosphate. These products can be used at levels of less than 2% of the seasoning. The regulations on these products are listed in the 21CFR in the following parts: sodium silicoaluminate (182.2727), silicon dioxide (172.480), calcium silicate (172.410). There are a few rules of thumb when using anticaking agents but in most cases, an individual study of what type of caking is occurring and the ingredients in the formula must be evaluated. Since there are an infinite variety of seasoning formulas with many ingredients involved, each must be evaluated individually for which anticaking agent is most appropriate. Looking at different conditioning agents at various humidity levels can help determine which one, either singly or in combination, will work the best. In addition, looking at the flowability of a seasoning and which anticaking agent is best suited to it is also a good idea. Flowability is discussed more thoroughly in Chapter 9. One point to note, however, is that more anticaking is not always better. If too much anticaking agent is used, the resultant dry seasoning becomes very dusty. Blending the seasoning can then be a problem. In addition, a dusty blend can cause problems in a food plant by making production conditions intolerable due to dust in the air. Product can also be lost into the air and on production equipment instead of on the product, thus causing the customer a monetary loss. This is especially noticeable in a topical application of a snack since the seasoning is applied dry rather than mixed with liquid ingredients. An additional problem results when oleoresin capsicum is in the seasoning blend. If this type of seasoning is very dusty, the resultant powder in the air is extremely irritating to the lungs and nasal passages.

There are basically three functions of a conditioning agent:

1. *Parting:* The conditioner actually coats the surfaces of the larger particles of the seasoning and gets between the particles. This is due to its very small particle size, causing a physical parting of the particles and thus induces flow and prevents caking.
2. *Moisture adsorption:* The conditioner is hydrophilic and therefore attracts moisture to a greater degree than the other ingredients, thus retarding moisture caking of the seasoning.
3. *Oil absorption:* The conditioning agent absorbs high levels of oil. If a seasoning has a high level of oleoresin paprika or other oil, it will absorb these oils and still provide a free flowing powder with less of a chance of caking.

There are several different anticaking agents that may be used in a variety of situations. *Tricalcium phosphate* is best suited for meat seasonings in which mustard is a high percent. This agent is used primarily to retard caking due to pressure of the weight of many multiwall bags stacked on top of each other. *Silicon dioxide* attracts and soaks up moisture before the other ingredients in a seasoning blend. After the silicon dioxide has reached its moisture limit, it will no longer retard moisture caking of the seasoning. In this sense, silicon dioxide simply extends the useful period of the seasoning. *Calcium silicate* is a good flow agent. It has a large amount of surface area and will soak up quite a bit of moisture. *Calcium stearate* is hydrophobic. It actually coats a product and will help keep water away from other ingredients in the seasoning. Because of this factor, it seems to help retard some of the more hydrophilic ingredients from attracting moisture.

In moisture sensitive items, it can be helpful to use some anhydrous products. Dextrose normally has some crystalline water present. The anhydrous version is a recrystallized version without water molecules present and therefore may not lose water into the rest of the seasoning.

12.2.4 Labeling

Labeling will be discussed in the context of formulating and duplicating seasoning blends and what is commonly done in the food industry. Any suggestions made here should be checked with the specific CFR regulations and should be cleared with an attorney.

As discussed before, paprika, turmeric, and annatto are colors and not spices. The extractives mut be listed separately from the ground spice. The "natural" colors may be listed by their common name or as an artificial color. For example, paprika may be labeled as paprika color or artificial color.

Spices and herbs may be listed separately or can be combined and listed as spices. Onion powder, garlic powder, and other granulations of these items must be listed as onion or garlic since they are considered vegetables and not spices. The same holds true for red and green bell peppers, tomato powder, dehydrated celery, and parsley.

When duplicating blends, it sometimes happens that these simple rules are not followed by the competitive seasoning companies. An example would be when paprika is present but the competing seasoning manufacturer does not list it on the ingredient statement but includes it under "spices." There comes a point when further duplication cannot be done while still meeting the ingredient statement on the competing product. The best way to handle such a situation is to inform the customer of the problem and tell them that the product is not labeled correctly. More often than not, the customer will ask for correct labeling. This type of problem is not always clear cut. In the case of chili pepper, paprika, and red pepper, there is sometimes a close distinction in what these items are since many products are from the same botanical species: *C. annum* and *C. frutescens*. For example, what is the difference between a low heat red pepper and a low color paprika? Between a bright red chili pepper and paprika? ASTA is currently addressing this issue and suggests that the labeling of chili pepper, paprika, and red pepper be always listed separately from the other spices.

Another labeling problem results in the different strengths of oleoresin paprika, turmeric, and capsicum. These products are produced as extremely concentrated versions and then diluted down to make the product easier to work with. For example, oleoresin paprika is produced as a 100,000 color unit product which is "standardized" with soybean oil by slightly diluting the concentrated oleoresin to make sure the product is always 100,000 color units. The paprika extractive is then diluted again to produce 40,000 and 80,000 color unit oleoresin paprika. These strengths are much more commonly utilized in the food industry. The question becomes, if one is using 40,000 color unit oleoresin paprika, must the product actually be labeled "soybean oil, extractive of paprika"? In other words, should the addition of the soybean oil determine the place of the paprika on the ingredient statement? Ideally, it should, but usually it is not since these items are sold and marketed as "oleoresin paprika." It is actually just a dilutant. In the case of the capsicums, there is even a larger shady area. The strongest oleoresin capsicum available is 1,000,000 SHU. This is often diluted to 500,000 and 200,000 SHU with oleoresin paprika. Ideally, the capsicum extractive and paprika extractives should be labeled separately. But where is that dividing line between capsicum and paprika? All are from the same species, but if not labeling the paprika, then the seasoning is actually misbranded because the product is artificially colored.

When formulating seasoning blends, often a proprietary compound product is used containing 3–10 separate ingredients. Examples would be worcestershire sauce powder and vinegar powder. These items must be listed as an ingredient with a parenthesis following that would list its component ingredients. It is possible to get a breakdown of ingredients from the vendor of the product, usually in ranges of ingredients which then can be incorporated into the listing of the other ingredients. Sometimes vendors are happy to provide this information for your internal confidential use. Sometimes they will not. Breaking down these compound products on the ingredient statement makes for a cleaner, less complicated label for your customer. It also makes it more difficult for competitors to duplicate the blend.

Finally, there is a law which states that if ingredients are present in less than 2% of the finished food item, they may be listed under the following statement: "contains less than 2% of the following ingredients: . . . ." This labeling method is underutilized in the food industry. It could save time and money if small adjustments have to be made in formulas from time to time. The ingredient statement would still be legal if small adjustments were made. In addition, the product would be more difficult to duplicate by competitors. Actually, the finished product may have the whole seasoning listed under this catch-all statement if used at less than 2% of the finished product.

12.2.5 Synergistic Ingredients

Some ingredients, when used together, can be synergistic in potentiating other flavors in seasoning blends. For example, there are many items which can boost a cheese flavor note. Cheese is an expensive ingredient and any way to increase that note in a seasoning blend is desirable. Malt and yeast (torula and autolyzed), onion and garlic in low levels, smoke flavor, and citric and lactic acids will all boost the cheese flavor in a seasoning to some extent. Small amounts of blue cheese to a cheddar blend—about 10% of the cheddar—helps to strengthen the cheddar note. Levels of 1%–2% of the malt, yeast, onion, and garlic are common. Less than 0.5% of the smoke flavor and acids is appropriate. The malt and yeast work best in a liquid system in contrast to the onion and garlic which seem to help most often in a snack seasoning or other dry topical applications.

A combination of red and black pepper also has a synergistic effect. Black pepper is usually described as having a front of the mouth or whole mouth heat while red pepper is a back of the throat heat. Using these two items in combination will produce a heat sensation that is hotter than the sum of the two products alone.

12.2.6 Flavors

Natural and artificial flavors are often added to seasoning blends. Examples would be a sour cream flavor in a sour cream and onion or ranch seasoning, a jalapeno flavor for a cheese sauce mix, or a tomato flavor in a salsa seasoning. Flavors must be used judiciously, since too much can cause off-flavor notes. When a vendor gives a suggested starting usage, it should be realized that the usage is usually based on the *finished product*. If making a cheese sauce mix, then the starting usage may be based on the finished cheese sauce with the liquid present, not just the dry mix.

Two types of flavors should be used in seasonings. The first is the spray dried or other powdered flavor. These items can be used at any level, limited only by cost and strength, in a dry seasoning blend. They are usually more expensive (or simply less concentrated) than their liquid counterparts since they are spray dried with a nonflavor carrier. Oil soluble flavors also work well in seasoning blends. The only drawback is the level of flavor which can be added to a dry seasoning, usually limited to about 4%. Higher amounts than this will cause the seasoning to be too wet. Adding anticaking agents will help to retard this. Oil soluble flavors should be added to the dry mix in the same manner as oleoresins and essential oils. Water soluble flavors are not recommended for dry seasoning blends. When used in small amounts, they will work, however if used in any amount above about 1.0% of the dry mix, they cause problems. Water soluble flavors tend to dissolve the salt, sugar, dextrose, or other dry ingredient they are being plated on and thus cause lumps of dissolved material to form. This phenomenon is not noticeable when mixing small seasoning amounts in a laboratory situation. It occurs to a much greater degree when making production size batches of a seasoning blend.

12.2.7 Microbiology

It is important to pay attention to the total plate count, yeast and mold count, E. coli, and coliform count in seasoning blends. It is essential to know what type of finished product the seasoning is going into. Some food products will tolerate higher counts than others. It is, however, unnecessary to pay a premium for low bacteriological counts when the food item does not require it. Spices, as discussed previously, can have very high microbiological counts. It is possible to reduce those counts with ethylene oxide or irradiation. But it costs money to do this and often it is not necessary to reduce counts that low. Regular onion powder may have counts up to 900,000 per gram. Onion powder with lot selection is available with total plate counts of less than 100,000, but at a premium cost.

To determine the maximum microbiological specification for a blend, it is necessary to determine what is the limit, or specification, for each ingredient in the blend and multiply that by the percent of that ingredient. Add these up to give the maximum total plate count possible for the seasoning. This information can be obtained from the supplier of each ingredient or from in-house testing if your company produces the products.

Once the maximum total place count is determined, it is necessary to discuss with the customer what the limit on the blend should be. The best example is chip seasonings versus dip seasonings. A potato chip seasoning is applied to the chip in the dry state and it stays in the dry state. This is not conducive to microbiological growth. A high maximum total plate and yeast and mold count specification will cause no problem for the finished food item or the consumer. On the other hand, a dip seasoning must have very low counts. If the seasoning is added to sour cream, it must withstand refrigerated storage in a liquid environment for an extended period of time. This is conducive to mold growth. The microbiological counts on this type of seasoning must be very low, ideally less than 10,000 total plate count with very low yeast and mold count.

12.3 Why Seasoning Blends?

Seasoning blends are purchased by industrial customers for a wide variety of reasons. It may be that they do not have an adequate research and development staff to produce new products and use the seasoning company to formulate products for them. It may be more cost efficient for them to purchase blends, or it may be that the seasoning company is better suited to produce a seasoning with a specific flavor profile. Either way, there are a number of factors a company should consider when determining if purchasing blends is cost efficient.

First, purchasing seasoning blends simplifies ordering and warehousing of ingredients. For example, compare purchasing a seasoning blend of 20 items versus buying and storing all those ingredients separately. The ease of ordering and warehousing one item versus 20 is obvious. In addition, the cost of the labor to weigh each ingredient is high. If each day, 20 different ingredients have to be batched for 15 different batches, that is 300 items each day which must be weighed and stored separately. If each ingredient is weighed into a separate bag, this equals 300 bags a day. In addition, each time an ingredient is weighed, there is some amount of spillage.

Consistency can be a problem for many food manufacturers. Weighing each ingredient individually and adding each separately to the batch gives another source of error. By purchasing seasoning blends in batch size bags, they can simply be poured in the batch at the proper time. The seasoning is blended in 2000 or 5000 pound batches, thus eliminating a source of inconsistency: each batch is the same and therefore eliminates a source of error in the finished product. Finally, it must be noted that most seasoning companies buy large amounts of items whereas the food company may only buy small amounts. Some examples are flavor enhancers, acids, and specific spices. Purchasing blends not only ensures that these ingredients are fresh, but also that the best possible ingredient cost is being utilized.

Appendix

The following is a list of spice, seasoning, and extractive suppliers the reader may want to contact for additional information.

S = Seasoning suppliers
P = Processed spice suppliers
O = Oil and oleoresin suppliers
B = Broker of spices or oils or oleoresins
I = Importer spices or oils or oleoresins
R = Reconditioner of spices

S   ABC Research Corp.
          3427 SW 24th Ave.
          Gainesville, FL 32607
          904-372-0436

B,O,S   Accurate Ingredients, Inc.
          160 Eileen Way
          Syosset, NY 11791
          516-496-2500

O   Adam, Joseph, Corp.
          5740 Grafton Road,
          P.O. Box 273
          Valley City, OH 44280
          216-225-9125

I,O   Adron, Inc.
          94 Fanny Road,
          P.O. Box 270
          Boonton, NJ 07005
          201-334-1600

S   Advanced Food Systems
          69 Veronica Ave.
          Somerset, NJ 08873
          908-828-7878

O   Agumm Inc.
          171 Lexington Ct.
          Red Bank, NJ 07701
          908-872-0701

S	Ajinomoto USA Inc. 500 Frank W. Burr Blvd. Teaneck, NJ 07666 201-488-1212	S	Armour Food Ingredients Co. Bardstown Rd. Springfield, KY 40069 606-336-5221
S,P,O	All American Seasonings, Inc. 1540 Wazee St. Denver, CO 80202 303-623-2320	P	Asmus Spice Co. 8750 Grinnell Detroit, MI 48213 313-923-6170
I	American Mercantile Corp. Kevin Wright Bld., 5690 Summer Ave. Memphis, TN 38124 901-373-6434	S,O	Assets, Inc. 422 Rt. 206, Ste. 175,081 Somerville, NJ 08876 908-874-8004
P	American Products Co. 2606 Brenner Dr. Dallas, TX 75220 214-357-3961	S	Baker Seasoning Labs 1813 Eagles Cove Friendswood, TX 77546 713-996-1729
P	American Roland Foods Corp. 71 West 23rd St. New York, NY 10010 212-741-8857	S	Bakon Yeast Inc. P.O. Box 651 Rhinelander, WI 54501 715-362-6533
S	AMPC, Inc. 2325 N. Loop Dr. Ames, IA 50010 515-296-7100	P,S	Baltimore Spice Co. P.O. Box 5858 Baltimore, MD 21208 410-363-1700
S	Anderson Clayton/Humko Products Inc. P.O. Box 398 Memphis, TN 38101 800-238-5765	S	Baromatic Corp. P.O. Box 7 Great Neck, NY 11022 516-482-1469
I	Arco Establishment USA 83 Cedar Lane Englewood, NJ 07631 201-569-8585	P	Basic American Foods P.O. Box 599 Vacaville, CA 95696 800-635-4708
S	Ariake USA Inc. 1977 W. 190th St. Torrance, CA 90504 310-768-8015	P,S	Bavaria Spice Co. 455 Douglas Ave. Altamonte Springs, FL 32714 407-774-8345
P	Armanino Farms, Inc. 4420 Enterprise St., P.O. Box 1887 Fremont, CA 94538 800-431-9344	P	Bayseng Spice Co. Nine Archer Circle Moraga, CA 94556 415-376-7550

S	Beatreme Foods Inc. 352 E. Grand Ave. Box 749 Beloit, WI 53511 608-365-5561	S	Bush Boake Allen 7 Mercedes Dr. Montvale, NJ 07645 201-391-9870
S	Bell Flavors & Fragrances Inc. 500 Academy Northbrook, IL 60062 708-291-8300	P,S	Cade-Grayson Co. 2445 Cades Way Vista, CA 92083 619-727-1000
S	Berje Inc. 5 Lawrence Street Bloomfield, NJ 07003 201-748-8980	P	Cain's Coffee Co. 13131 Broadway Extention Oklahoma City, OK 73125 405-751-7221
S	Bernard Food Industries Inc. P.O. Box 1497 Evanston, IL 60204 708-869-5222	P,S	Cajun Magic, Inc. P.O. Box 770034 New Orleans, LA 70177 504-947-6712
S,P,O	Bio-Botanica, Inc. 75 Commerce Dr. Hauppauge, NY 11788 516-231-5522	S	California Truffle Co. 1230 Churchill Downs Woodland, CA 95695 916-661-3505
S	Blend-Pak Div., Dacus Inc. P.O. Box Drawer 2067 Tupelo, MS 38803 601-842-6790	P,S	California Vegetable Concentrates P.O. Box 3659 Modesto, CA 95352 209-538-1071
S	BMB Specialty Company Box 2309 Decatur, AL 35602 205-350-0602	P,S	Cal-Compac Foods 4906 West First St. P.O. Box 265 Santa Ana, CA 95352 714-775-7757
P,S	Bolner's Fiesta Products, Inc. 426 Menchaca St. San Antonio, TX 78207 512-734-6404	P,S	Carmi Flavors & Fragrances 6330 Scottway City of Commerce, CA 90040 213-888-9240
P	Botanicals International 2550 El Presida St. Long Beach, CA 90810 310-637-9566	B	Central Indonesian Trading Co. Inc. 150 Broadway, Suite 811 New York, NY 10038 212-233-5310
B,O	Broch, Henry, & Co. 9933 Lawler Ave. Suite 340 Skokie, IL 60077 708-816-6225	S	Champlain Industries Inc. 25 Styertowne Rd. Clifton, NJ 07012 201-778-4900

B	Champon, L.A. & Co., Inc. 1404 Oak Tree Road Iselin, NJ 08830 201-283-2000	S,P	Custom Food Products 730 N. Albany Ave. Chicago, IL 60612 800-621-8827
O	Chart Corporation 787 E. 27th St. Paterson, NJ 07504 201-345-5554	P,S,O	C&K Ingredient Technology Corp. 110 Liberty Court Elyria, OH 44035 216-324-0509
S	Chef Paul Prudhomme's 824 Distributors Row Harahan, LA 70123 504-731-3590	I	Daarnhouwer Inc. P.O. Box 1928 Fort Lee, NJ 07024 201-585-0100
S	Continental Seasonings 1700 Palisades Ave. Teaneck, NJ 07666 800-631-1564	P	De Francesco & Sons, Inc. 47641 West Ness Firebaugh, CA 93622 209-364-6138
B	Cooper, L.J., Co. 116 John Street New York, NY 10038 212-406-3970	P	Deep South Blenders 3763 Derbigny St. Metairie, LA 70001 504-834-5817
B	Cordovi, V.A., Inc. Two Park Ave. Manhasset, NY 11030 516-627-6610	S	Dell Flavorings 352 E. Grand Ave. Beloit, WI 53511 608-365-5561
S	CPI Corp. 816 E. Funston Wichita, KS 67211 316-267-5533	S,O	Derived Aromatics 25 Donald Ave. Kendall Park, NJ 08824 601-297-8520
S	Creative Seasonings Inc. P.O. Box 8049 Salem, MA 01970 508-744-5655	P	Dilijan Products Inc. P.O. Box 145 Ringoes, NJ 08551 201-806-6048
S,P	Cresent Foods P.O. Box 3985 Seattle, WA 98124 206-461-1400	S,P	Dirigo Corp. P.O. Box E4 Boston, MA 02127 800-345-9540
P	Cresent Manufacturing Co. P.O. Box 3985 Seattle, WA 98124 206-461-1447	S,P	Diversitech Inc. 2411 N.W. 41 St. Gainesville, FL 32606 904-377-7073
B	CTC Spice Corp. 152 Madison Ave. Suite 300 New York, NY 10016 212-689-4330		

I   DMT New York, Inc.
        20 Exchange Place
        32nd Floor
        New York, NY 10005
        212-363-7410

P,S   Durke-French Foods, Inc.
        P.O. Box 942
        Wayne, NJ 07474
        201-633-6800

S   Eatem Foods Company
        1829 Gallagher Dr.
        Vineland, NJ 08360
        609-692-1663

S   Edlong Corp.
        225 Scott St.
        Elk Grove Village,
        IL 60007
        708-439-9230

P,S   Elite Spice Co.
        7151 Montevideo Rd.
        Jessup, MD 20794
        410-796-1900

B   Elton, John H. Inc.
        118-21 Queens Blvd.
        Forest Hills, NY 11375
        718-520-8900

S   Ettlinger Corp.
        2970 Maria Dr.
        Northbrook, IL 60062
        708-564-5020

S,P   Excalibur Seasoning Co. Ltd.
        1317 N. Fourth
        Pekin, IL 61554
        800-444-2169

S   F & C International
        890 Redna Terrace
        Cincinnati, OH 45215
        513-771-5904

P   Farmarco Ltd. Inc.
        1381 Air Rail Ave.
        Virginia Beach, VA 23455
        804-460-3573

S,P   Feinkost Ingredient Co. USA
        103 Billman Street
        Lodi, OH 44254
        216-948-3006

S   FIDCO Inc.
        4 Gannett Drive
        White Plains, NY 10604
        914-397-7600

S,P   First Spice Mixing Co.
        33-33 Greenpoint Ave.
        Long Island City,
        NY 11101
        800-221-1105

S   Flavor Dynamics, Inc.
        4001 Apgar Dr.
        Somerset, NJ 08873
        908-271-7773

S   Flavor Innovations Inc.
        177 Ryan St.
        South Plainfield, NJ 07080
        908-754-2020

P,O,S   Flavorite Labs, Inc.
        P.O. Box 1315
        Memphis, TN 38101
        601-393-3610

S,P   Flavotech
        100 Churchill Road
        West Point, MS 39773
        601-494-3741

S,P   Food Flavors Co., Inc.
        2959 S. Spruce
        Wichita, KS 67216
        316-522-0303

P,S   Foran Spice Co., Inc.
        7616 S. Sixth St.
        Oak Creek, WI 53154
        414-764-1220

I   Franklin Trading Co., Inc.
        990 Franklin Ave.
        Garden City, NJ 11530
        516-294-6524

P   Freeze-Dry Products
USA, Inc.
     5725 Paradise Dr. #850
     Corte Madera, CA 94925
     415-924-5211

O,S   Fritsche Dodge & Olcott
     76 Ninth Ave.
     New York, NY 10011
     212-929-4100

S,O   Gallard-Schlesinger
Industries, Inc.
     584 Mineola Ave.
     Carle Place, NY 11514
     516-333-5600

P   Gel Spice Co., Inc.
     48 Hook Road
     Bayonne, NJ 07002
     201-993-0700

P,O,S   General Spice, Inc.
     238 St. Nicholas Ave.
     South Plainfield, NJ 07080
     201-753-9100

S,P   Georgia Spice Co.
     3600 Atlanta Ind. Pkwy. NW
     Atlanta, GA 30331
     404-696-6200

S,P   Gilette Foods, Inc.
     751 Rahway Avenue
     Union, NJ 07083
     908-688-0500

P   Gilroy Foods, Inc.
     P.O. Box 1088
     Gilroy, CA 95021
     408-847-1414

O   Givaudan-Roure
     100 Delawanna Ave.
     Clifton, NJ 07015
     201-365-8000

S,P   Glencourt Inc.
     2800 Ygnacio Valley Rd.
     Walnut Creek, CA 94598
     415-944-4316

B   Glenn Industrial Sales
     509 Commerce St.
     Franklin Lakes, NJ 07417
     201-337-9360

S   Global Foods
     91 Sycamore Place
     Highland Park, IL 60035
     708-433-9434

S,O   Globe Extracts Co.
     10 Davids Drive
     Hauppauge, NY 11788
     516-273-6200

S   Golden Dipt Co.
     12813 Flushing Meadow Dr.
     St. Louis, MO 63131
     314-821-3113

I   Golombeck, Morris J., Inc.
     960 Franklin Ave.
     Brooklyn, NY 11225
     718-284-3505

S,P   Gourmet Club Corp.
     20 Potash Road
     Oakland, NJ 07436
     201-337-5882

P   Great Lakes Intl.
Trading, Inc.
     P.O. Box 432
     Traverse City, MI 49685
     616-947-2141

P,S   Griffith Laboratories USA
     1 Griffith Center
     Alsip, IL 60658
     708-371-0900

S   Hallams Inc.
     P.O. Box 700
     Nixa, MO 65714
     417-725-2601

P   Harris Freeman & Co., Inc.
     1380 N. McCan St.
     Anaheim, CA 92806
     714-630-8404

S	Hasegawa T., USA, Inc. 14017 E. 183rd St. Ceritos, CA 90701 714-522-1900
P	Hega Food Products 238 St. Micholas Ave. South Plainfield, NJ 07080 201-753-9100
P,O,S	Heller Seasonings & Ingredients, Inc. P.O. Box 128 Bedford Park, IL 60499 708-581-6800
I	Herbarium, Inc. 11016 152nd Ave. Kenosha, WI 53142 414-857-2373
P	Hershey Import Co., Inc. 700 E. Lincoln Ave. Rahway, NJ 07065 908-388-9000
I	Horn, E.T., International 16111 Canary Ave. La Mirada, CA 90638 714-523-8050
S	IDF, Inc. 2003 E. Sunshine, Suite E Springfield, MO 65804 417-881-7820
S	Illes Company 5527 Redfield Dallas, TX 75235 214-631-8350
S	Indian Harvest P.O. Box 428 Bemidji, MN 56601 218-751-8500
P	Integrated Ingredients 1420 Harbor Bay Pkwy. Suite 210 Alameda, CA 94501 415-748-6300

S	Intek International Food Products, Inc. 119D Shoreline Rd. Barrington, IL 60010 708-382-4997
B	International Brokers, Inc. 185 Ridgedale Ave. Cedar Knolls, NJ 07927 201-539-0707
P	Jeffords, Doug, Co. 504 Arlington Ave. Nashville, TN 37210 615-255-2592
S,O	J.E. Toll Co. 25 Donald Ave. Kandall Park, NJ 08824 201-297-8520
S,O	Kalsec, Inc. P.O. Box 511 Kalamazoo, MI 49005 616-349-9711
S	Kasco Corp. 1569 Tower Grove Rd. St. Louis, MO 63110 314-771-1550
I	Kazemi, A., & Co., Inc. 6335 E. Alta Hacienda Dr. Scottsdale, AZ 85251 602-945-1029
S	Kerry Ingredients, Dairyland Div. 5348 W. 125 St. Savage, MN 55378 612-890-5305
S,O	Kraus & Co., Inc. 21070 Coolidge Hwy. Oak Park, MI 48237 313-542-4737
P	Kroger Company P.O. Box 25469 Columbia, SC 29224 803-733-1610

I   K.H.L. Flavors, Inc.
     59-25 63rd Street
     Maspeth, NY 11378
     718-894-8200

O   LaMonde Ltd.
     500 S. Jefferson St.
     Placentia, CA 92670
     714-993-7700

S   Land O Lakes,
     Food Ingredient Div.
     P.O. Box 116
     Minneapolis, MN 55440
     612-481-2064

P   Lawry's Foods, Inc.
     570 West Avenue 26
     Los Angeles, CA 90065
     213-224-5875

S,P Lebermuth Co., Inc.
     Box 4103
     South Bend, IN 46624
     219-259-7000

S   Lee Kum Kee Inc.
     304 S. Date Ave.
     Alhambra, CA 91803
     818-282-0337

S   Legg, A.C., Packing Co., Inc.
     P.O. Box 10283
     Birmingham AL 35202
     205-324-3451

S   LeGout Foods
     9353 Belmont Ave.
     Franklin Park, IL 60131
     800-323-6490

S   LJ Minor Corp.
     30003 Bain Bridge Rd.
     Solon, OH 44139
     415-453-8555

I   Lombard World Trade
     116 John St.
     New York, NY 10038
     212-406-9770

I   MacAndrews & Forbes Co.
     Third Street &
     Jefferson Ave.
     Camden, NJ 08104
     609-964-8840

S   Major Products Co.
     66 Industrial Ave.
     Ferry, NJ 07643
     201-641-5555

I   Malagasy Agencies, Inc.
     20 Potash Road
     Oakland, NJ 07436
     201-337-9226

R   Manhattan Milling &
     Drying Co., Inc.
     38-56-62-85 Water Street
     Brooklyn, NY 11201
     718-624-7282

O,S Manheimer, J., Inc.
     47-22 Pearson Place
     Long Island City,
     NY 11101
     718-392-7800

P   Marinpak Corp.
     23 Pamaron Way
     Novato, CA 94949
     415-883-6511

B   Marmorek, Hebert, & Son
     P.O. Box 140036
     Brooklyn, NY 11214
     718-256-8080

S,O Marnap Industries
     225 French St.
     Buffalo, NY 14211
     716-897-1220

I,S Martin, Wm. E., & Sons,
     Co., Inc.
     P.O. Box 408
     Port Washington,
     NY 11050
     516-883-6626

P,S McClancy Seasoning Co.
     One Spice Road
     Ft. Mill, SC 29715
     803-548-2366

B   McClement Sales Co.
      1S280 Summit Ave.
      Oakbrook Terrace,
      IL 60181
      708-691-1800

B   McClintock, W.L., Co., Inc.
      19700 Mt. Ladden Drive
      Castro Valley, CA 94552
      415-889-6422

P,O,S McCormick & Company, Inc.
      11350 McCormick Road
      Hunt Valley, MD 21031
      301-771-7301

O   Medallion International, Inc.
      944 Belmont Ave.
      North Haledon, NJ 07508
      201-427-7781

O,S Meer Corporation
      P.O. Box 9006
      North Bergen, NJ 07047
      201-861-9500

S   Menu Magic Foods
      Box 22236
      Indianapolis, IN 46222
      317-635-9500

B   Mercantum (U.S.) Corp.
      225 Broadway
      New York, NY 10007
      212-233-0412

S   Mid American Dairymen, Inc.
      Box 1837
      Springfield, MO 65805
      417-865-9641

S   Mid-America Food Sales
      3701 Commercial Ave.
      Northbrook, IL 60062
      708-480-0720

S   Milani Foods
      2525 Armitage Ave.
      Melrose Park, IL 60160
      708-450-3189

P,S,O Milwaukee Seasonings, Inc.
      P.O. Box 339
      Germantown, WI 53022
      414-251-9230

I,P,S Mincing Trading Corporation
      528 Ferry Street
      Newark, NJ 07105
      201-465-0066

P   Minn-Dak Growers Ltd.
      18175 Red River Rd.
      Wahpeton, ND 58075
      701-642-3300

B   Mueller, Ludwig, Co., Inc.
      Two Park Ave.
      New York, NY 10016
      212-532-1050

P   Mutual Spice Company
      2125 83rd Street
      North Bergen, NJ 07047
      201-869-2330

S,O,P Natural Seasoning Co.
      P.O. Box 352
      Summit, IL 60501
      708-458-4118

S,P New England Spice Co.
      60 Clayton St.
      Dorchester, MA 02122
      617-825-7900

S   North American Lab
      1717 W. Tenth St.
      Indianapolis, IN 46222
      317-635-9500

O   Northville Laboratories, Inc.
      1 Vanilla Lane
      Northville, MI 48167
      313-349-1500

S,P Northwestern Foods, Inc.
      P.O. Box 14415
      St. Paul, MN 55114
      612-644-8060

S   Nu Products Seasoning
      Co., Inc.
      179 Railroad Ave.
      Ridgefield Park, NJ 07660
      201-440-0065

S   Nu-World Amaranth, Inc.
     P.O. Box 2202
     Naperville, IL 60567
     708-369-6819

S,O   Ogawa & Co., Ltd.
     1080 Essek St.
     Richmaon, CA 94801
     510-233-0633

S,O,P   OM Ingredients Co.
     P.O. Box 398
     Memphis, TN 38101
     608-241-6833

S   Ottens Flavors
     1234 Hamilton St.
     Philadelphia, PA 19123
     215-627-5030

I   Overseas Produce Corporation
     129 Halstead Ave.
     Mamaroneck, NY 10543
     914-698-2828

P   Pacific Foods
     21612 88th Ave. S.
     Kent, WA 98031
     206-852-7000

P   Pacific Spice Company, Inc.
     722 Stanford Ave.
     Los Angeles, CA 90021
     213-626-2302

O   Penta Manufacturing Co.
     P.O. Box 1448
     Fairfield, NJ 07007
     201-575-7475

S,P   Presco Food Seasonings, Inc.
     P.O. Box 152
     Flemington, NJ 08822
     201-782-4919

S   Private Brands Inc.
     707 N. Western Ave.
     Chicago, IL 60612
     312-342-7770

S   Quest International
     Ingredients
     1090 Pratt Boulevard
     Elk Grove Village,
     IL 60007
     708-593-8484

S   Ramsey Laboratories, Inc.
     2742 Grand Ave.
     Cleveland, OH 44104
     216-791-9200

I   Reliable Mercantile Co., Inc.
     401 Broadway
     New York, NY 10013
     212-925-8496

S,P   Robertet Flavors
     P.O. Box 247
     S. Plainfield, NJ 07080
     908-561-2181

P   Rogers Foods/Chili Products
     P.O. Drawer R
     Turlock, CA 95381
     209-667-2777

P   Rykoff/Sexton, Inc.
     761 Terminal Street
     Los Angeles, CA 90021
     213-622-4131

P   Safeway Stores, Inc.
     2800 Ygnacio Valley Road
     Walnut Creek, CA 94598
     415-944-4525

P   San Francisco Spice
     Company, Inc.
     P.O. Box 476
     Orinda, CA 94563
     415-254-1568

P   San Jacinto Spice Ranch
     P.O. Box 877
     San Jacinto, CA 92383
     714-654-4619

S   San-J International Inc.
     2880 Sprouse Dr.
     Richmond, VA 23231
     804-226-8333

S,O,P   Saratoga Specialties
        200 Wrightwood
        Elmhurst, IL 60126
        708-833-3810
P   Saroni Total Food Ingredients
        P.O. Box 1918
        Oakland, CA 94604
        415-895-5681
P   Sauer, C.F. Company
        2000 W. Broad St.
        Richmond, VA 23220
        804-359-5786
B   Sayia, A.A., & Co., Inc.
        One Newark Street
        Hoboken, NJ 07030
        201-659-4504
B   Schlichting, Harry
        90 Bryant Ave., 1d-Dorset
        White Plains, NY 10605
        914-948-3612
I,P,S   Schoenfeld & Sons, Inc.
        147 Prince Street
        Brooklyn, NY 11201
        718-858-8200
S,P   Schreiber, R.L., Inc.
        1741 N.W. 33rd St.
        Pompano Beach, FL 33064
        800-624-8777
B   Scott, E.L., & Co., Inc.
        One World Trade Center,
        Suite 1313
        New York, NY 10048
        212-432-0100
S   Seafla, Inc.
        11371 Williamson Rd.
        Cincinnati, OH 45241
        513-489-3331
S,P,O   Seasonings Etcetera
        433 W. State St.
        Columbus, OH 43215
        614-464-0857
I   Seven Brothers Trading, Inc.
        3400 San Fernando Road
        Los Angeles, CA 90065
        213-254-7000

P   Sinochem (USA), Inc.
        Two World Trade Center
        Suite 2222
        New York, NY 10048
        212-432-2100
S   Skidmore Sales &
        Distributing Co.
        10310 Julian Dr.
        Cincinnati, OH 45215
        800-468-7543
S   Sokol & Company
        5315 Dansher Road
        Countryside, IL 60525
        708-482-8250
P   South Texas Spice Co., Inc.
        P.O. Box 680086
        San Antonio, TX 78268
        512-684-6239
P   Specialty Seeds, Herbs &
        Spices
        12623 SW Green Drive
        Culver, OR 97734
        503-546-3019
P   Spice Islands
        P.O. Box 7004
        San Francisco, CA 94120
        415-981-7600
S,O,P   Spice King Ltd.
        6009 Washington Blvd.
        Culver City, CA 90232
        213-836-7770
P   Spice Products Company
        20333 South Normandie
        Ave.
        Torrance, CA 90509
        213-775-6541
S,P   Spicecraft
        4140 Fullerton
        Chicago, IL 60639
        312-489-7000
S,O,P   Spicetec, Ltd.
        185 Alexandria Way
        Carol Stream, IL 60188
        708-861-5078

S   Stancase Seasonings
      P.O. Box a-11 Bergen Sta.
      Jersey City, NJ 07304
      201-434-6300

S   Steibel Industries Corp.
      120 East State Street
      Oldsmar, FL 34677
      813-855-6601

S   Stewart, J. & Co.
      1440 Hicks Rd.
      Rolling Meadows,
      IL 60008
      708-259-9555

S   Takasago Corp. USA
      P.O. Box 1908
      Teterboro, NJ 07608
      201-288-1401

P   Tampico Spice Co., Inc.
      5941 S. Central Ave.
      Los Angeles, CA 90001
      213-235-3154

S,P,O   Technical Sales Associates
      361 Frontage Rd. #127
      Burr Ridge, IL 60521
      708-789-6220

S   Todd's Ltd.
      P.O. Box 4821
      Des Moines, IA 50306
      515-266-2276

S,P   Tone Brothers, Inc.
      P.O. Box AA
      Des Moines, IA 50301
      515-262-9721

I   Transit Trading Corporation
      196-198 West Broadway
      New York, NY 10013
      212-925-1020

S   Tri-State Specialties, Inc.
      4430 So. Tripp Ave.
      Chicago, IL 60632
      312-247-0160

P   Tropical Spices, Inc.
      13243 Rosecrans Ave.
      Santa Fe Springs,
      CA 90670
      213-921-0932

B   Uhe, George, Co., Inc.
      76 Minth Ave.
      New York, NY 10011
      212-929-0870

O   Ungerer & Co.
      P.O. Box U
      Lincoln Park, NJ 07035
      201-628-0600

I   Van de Vries Trading Corp.
      150 Varick Ave.
      Brooklyn, NY 11237
      718-497-5541

P   Van Drunen Farms
      300 W. 6th St.
      Momence, IL 60954
      815-472-3100

P,S   Whole Herb Company
      P.O. Box 1085
      Mill Valley, CA 94942
      415-383-6485

S   Williams Foods, Inc.
      13301 W. 99th Street
      Lenexa, KS 66215
      913-888-4343

S   Williams West & Witts
      Products Co.
      212 Cook Street
      Michigan City, IN 46360
      219-879-8236

S   Witt, F.W., & Co.
      1106 S. Bridge St.
      Yorkville, IL 60560
      800-942-0857

P,O,S   Wixon Industries, Inc.
      1390 E. Bolivar Avenue
      Milwaukee, WI 53207
      414-481-8900

I Woodhouse, Drake &
Carey, Inc.
 127 John Street
 New York, NY 10038
 212-820-1000

I World Commodity
Trading, Inc.
 98 Cutter Mill Road
 Suite 333N
 Great Neck, NY 11021
 516-829-4120

S World Flavors Inc.
 76 Louise Dr.
 Ivyland, PA 18974
 800-562-2946

I,P World Spice Inc.
 223-235 Highland Pkwy.
 Roselle, NJ 07203
 201-245-0600

I Xenia Food
Communications, Inc.
 P.O. Box 25919
 W. Los Angeles, CA 90025
 213-479-1221

S,P Zuellig Group NA, Inc.
 2550 El Presidio
 Long Beach, CA 90810
 310-637-9566

Index